30 O MINUTES **A DAY** TO A
Healthy Heart

ASSOCIATION MÉDICALE CANADIENNE · CANADIAN MEDICAL ASSOCIATION

30 MINUTES A DAY TO A
Healthy Heart

With Andrew Pipe, CM, MD

Reader's Digest

The Reader's Digest Association (Canada) Ltd.
· Montreal ·

30 Minutes a Day to a Healthy Heart

© 2006 The Reader's Digest Association, Inc.
© 2006 The Reader's Digest Association (Canada) Ltd.
© 2006 Reader's Digest (Australia) Pty Limited
© 2006 Reader's Digest Association Far East Ltd.
Philippine Copyright 2006 Reader's Digest Association
    Far East Ltd.

Library and Archives Canada Cataloguing in Publication

30 minutes a day to a healthy heart: one simple plan
to conquer all seven major threats to your heart / from the
editors of Reader's Digest and the medical professionals of
the Canadian Medical Association, with an introduction
of Andrew Pipe.—1st Canadian soft cover ed.

Includes index.
ISBN 0-88850-955-0

1. Heart—Diseases—Prevention—Popular works.
I. Reader's Digest Association (Canada) II. Canadian
Medical Association III. Title: Thirty minutes a day to a
healthy heart

| RC672.T53 2006 | 616.1′205 | C2006-900640-7 |

We are interested in receiving your comments on the
content of this book.
Write to: The Editor, Books and Home Entertainment,
Reader's Digest (Canada) Ltd.,
1100 René-Lévesque Blvd. West, Montreal, QC H3B 5H5

To order additional copies of *30 Minutes a Day to a
Healthy Heart* or to request a catalogue, please call our
24-hour Customer Service hotline at 1-800-465-0780.

For more Reader's Digest products and information, visit
our website at **www.rd.ca**

Printed in China

06 07 08 09 10 / 5 4 3 2 1

For Reader's Digest Canada

Senior Project Editor
Pamela Johnson

Contributing Writers
Frederic J. Vagnini, MD
Selene Yeager

Nutritionist
Fran Berkoff, RD

Senior Designer
Andrée Payette

Contributing Editor
Robert Ronald

Design Concept
Jane McKenna

Illustration
Andrew Baker

Copy Editor
Judy Yelon

Production Manager
Gordon Howlett

Reader's Digest
Association (Canada) Ltd.
Vice President,
Book Editorial
Robert Goyette

For Reader's Digest Association, Inc.

Editor-in-Chief
Neil Wertheimer

President and Chief
Executive Officer
Mary Berner

For CMA Media Inc.

Medical Editor
Catherine Younger-Lewis,
MD, MJ

Consulting Physician and
Contributing Author
Andrew Pipe, CM, MD

Consultants
Marketa Graham, BSc, RD, CDE
Carol E. Miller, PT (Dip),
    BA (Hon Eng), BAA (Journ)
Julie Pacaud Yeaman, BA, BEd
Susan Yungblut, BSc (PT), MBA

Director
Glenda Proctor

Program Manager,
Book Publishing
Christine Pollock

Assistant
Nunzia Parent

For the Canadian Medical Association

President
Ruth Collins-Nakai, MD, MBA,
    FRCPC, FACC

Secretary General and CEO
William G. Tholl

Note to readers

Foreword

Did you know that the majority of Canadians, including children, now have one or more risk factors for heart disease? Did you also know that most of the risk factors or problems that contribute to heart disease and stroke can be prevented?

Cardiovascular diseases, which include diseases of the heart and blood vessel system such as stroke and what is known as peripheral vascular disease or "poor circulation," are still the number one killer of both men and women in North America. Most Canadians think that breast cancer kills more women, but, in reality, all cancers together do not kill as many Canadians as heart diseases and stroke. So it is important that we all learn everything we can about this scourge and, once we have learned, take the next step and act.

This book helps us do just that. It gives us a simplified explanation of heart problems and what we should expect of ourselves and what we can expect of the health care system.

The Canadian Medical Association's vision is to have a healthy population and a vibrant medical profession. It is natural, then, that a large portion of CMA effort is directed to health promotion activities to teach, encourage and support Canadians and health care workers to become healthier and happier. Part of the CMA's mandate is to ensure that the public is informed on health issues and to help physicians across the country do their best to provide individual information to patients. A book such as this contributes accessible, reliable, understandable and current information so that all Canadians can benefit.

Enjoy your reading, then enjoy your life in a heart-healthy way!

Ruth Collins-Nakai, MD, MBA, FRCPC, FACC
President
Canadian Medical Association

Contents

1 What we know today about your heart

2 Welcome to the 30-Minutes-a-Day Plan

3 Heart-healthy eating

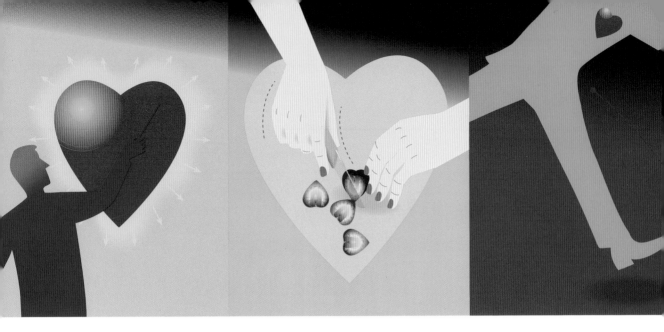

Introduction

"Whenever I meditate about a disease," observed Louis Pasteur, the great French scientist,
"I never think of finding a cure, but rather a means of its prevention." These are wise words from one
whose discoveries dramatically influenced the reduction of the food-borne infectious illnesses that
plagued the early years of the last century. They are also wise words today, when chronic diseases, often
of our society's own making, claim countless lives and contribute to an enormous burden of ill health.

Of all the chronic diseases that affect Canadians, coronary artery disease is the leading cause
of premature death and disability. This modern epidemic of heart disease is spawned to a significant
degree by tobacco addiction, increasing societal levels of obesity and inactivity, and the associated
disruptions in metabolism and elevations in blood pressure and levels of blood cholesterol that inevitably
follow—particularly in those with a family history of or genetic predisposition to heart disease. Those
changes contribute directly to the development of injury and inflammation in the walls of our arteries,
resulting in an accumulation of cholesterol and other debris that we call atherosclerosis.

Pasteur would be astonished to see that we have the capacity to prevent a considerable proportion
of the disease that results when our coronary arteries—the pencil-lead vessels that bring blood
and oxygen to our heart muscle—become obstructed or blocked by the buildup of atherosclerosis.
He would be perplexed that many people are still addicted to tobacco and, at a time when we have an
unprecedented availability of fresh fruits and vegetables, that large quantities of fat and salt predominate
in our diets. He would be chagrined to note that we are increasingly sedentary and progressively more
obese. He would be saddened that many of us find ourselves locked into lifestyles that are stress-laden
and time-pressured. He would be determined, no doubt, to focus on simple ways to address the
constellation of these risk factors—factors that, when present, enhance an individual's likelihood
of developing heart disease. And, I am confident, he would be a strong advocate of the approaches
to health promotion and disease prevention that are found in the pages ahead.

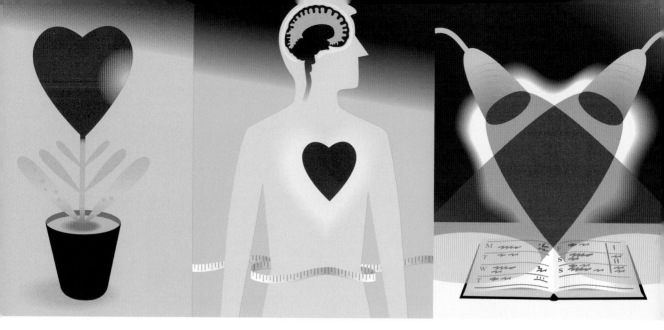

"Success," it has been said, "consists of doing ordinary things extraordinarily well." I am often struck in my clinical practice by the large number of individuals who are focused or preoccupied with "trendy" or complex considerations relating to heart health. Captivated by the latest diet craze or fascinated by some new exercise machine, many have lost sight of the reality that simple, sustained approaches to heart health are the most efficient, effective and ultimately enjoyable route to success.

30 Minutes a Day to a Healthy Heart provides a clear description of the factors that underlie the changes in coronary artery walls that ultimately result in atherosclerosis. Moreover, it provides careful, sensible guidance as to how simple lifestyle changes that anyone can easily adopt can dramatically lower risk while adding immeasurably to an overall sense of well-being.

In the chapters ahead you will develop an understanding of the processes that damage blood vessels. More importantly, you will learn how to minimize or avoid them. In this one volume you will find practical, meaningful and relevant advice as to how you can make simple—and enduring—changes that will benefit you and your family. Contemporary approaches to the prevention and management of heart disease are described in a way that will allow you to appreciate and acquire the benefits afforded by lifestyle change and, when needed, highly effective medical therapies. The approach is practical, the goals are realistic, and the advice is sensible and scientifically sound.

Successful health promotion ultimately consists of making healthy choices the easy choices. As you learn to take advantage of the insights and information found within these pages, you will discover how easy it can be to make healthy choices—and minimize your chances of developing heart disease.

Andrew Pipe, CM, MD
Director, Prevention and Rehabilitation Centre
University of Ottawa Heart Institute

Take good care of your heart and it could keep you fit, active and happy for a surprising number of years.

SMOKING

CHOLESTEROL

HIGH BLOOD PRESSURE

EXCESSIVE BODY FAT

METABOLIC SYNDROME

OXIDATIVE STRESS

CHRONIC INFLAMMATION

What we know today about your heart

The truth is, although we know more about the human heart than ever before, we treat our hearts with little respect.

Your heart's full potential

In a perfect world, coronary heart disease—which kills almost 75,000 Canadian men and women each year—would not claim lives prematurely at the age of 45, 55 or 65. Hearts would pump bravely and reliably on, overcoming what seem today like impossible odds, to help many of us survive past our 100th birthdays.

Clinical experiments, together with research into the health and lifestyle of the world's oldest living people, concur on one indisputable point: your heart wasn't built to fail in the prime of life. It was designed to last at least three score years and ten— though perhaps not until you've reached the very old age of 120, as some longevity experts suggest. But, all too often, this ingenious, fist-size pump—an amazing, non-stop machine made of muscle, nerves, blood vessels and electrical transmitters—is destroyed by everyday temptations, like tobacco, the triple cheeseburger, hours of TV viewing and a stressful world that rushes by faster than we ever thought possible.

Living testimony

If you want proof of your heart's untapped potential, consider the people of Okinawa, a Japanese island-state in the East China Sea. This island has the world's highest proportion of people over the age of 100. Okinawa has an incredible 35 centenarians for every 100,000 residents; Canada has 12.

A traditional lifestyle that values serenity and spirituality, daily exercise and a diet low in saturated fats and high in fruit, vegetables, soya protein and fish, has meant that Okinawa's death rates from coronary heart disease are 18 per 100,000; Canada's are 233. Carved into a stone slab facing the sea in one tiny fishing village in Okinawa is an ancient local saying. It reads: "At 70, you are still a child, at 80, a young man or woman. And if at 90, someone from Heaven invites you over, then say, 'Oh go away, and come back when I am 100.'"

Western journalists flocked to Okinawa once researchers had alerted the world to its incredibly heart-healthy lifestyle. They found fit, healthy people leading full lives without drugs, nursing homes or life-support systems. A 100-year-old villager outdrank a film crew half her age; a 96-year-old who practised martial arts beat a 30-something boxing champion on national television; a 105-year-old woman who killed a poisonous snake with a fly swatter became a local legend.

The key to longevity

Meanwhile, medical tests revealed how such feats were possible. The centenarians had remarkably healthy hearts, apparently youthful arteries, low cholesterol and little of the oxidative stress that triggers atherosclerosis, the dangerous plaque build-up that can cause heart-stopping blood clots.

Even more surprisingly, researchers who studied 600 of Okinawa's oldest residents concluded that a healthy lifestyle accounted for 80 per cent of the extraordinary health demonstrated by their hearts, while genetic disposition was responsible for just 20 per cent. The researchers believe that if we in the West lived more like the Okinawan people, many coronary care units could be permanently shut down.

Heart and stroke disease around the world

Death rates from cardiovascular disease—the clogged arteries that can cause heart attacks and brain-damaging strokes—vary widely from nation to nation, a reflection of global differences in diet and lifestyle. Here's the lowdown—this table shows the number of deaths in 2002 linked to coronary heart disease and stroke per 100,000 people. Canadians are doing better than some Europeans, but we have a long way to go.

Russia	828
Romania	505
Hungary	470
Finland	334
Germany	306
United Kingdom	304
Italy	282
Canada	233
United States	233
Switzerland	213
Australia	190
China	182
Japan	177
France	140

To achieve this, we'd have to learn the art of living Okinawa-style—including a slow, lower-calorie eating practice called *hara hachi bu*, which means eating until you're just 80 per cent full; a relaxed outlook on life known as *taygay*; and deep, meditative spirituality.

The past few decades have brought sad proof that Okinawan heart health is not the result of lucky genes; island residents under the age of 50 now have the highest heart disease rates in Japan, as a result of increasingly Western diets and lifestyles.

This example of how care and nutrition affect the human heart is echoed in findings from population studies around the world.

According to the Icelandic Longevity Institute, Greenland's native Inuit people have dramatically lower rates of heart disease than their Danish neighbours on the same icy continent, due to a diet of fish rich in heart-nurturing omega-3 fats.

A study published in *The Lancet* found that men who lived on the island of Crete, eating a diet rich in Mediterranean sun-ripened produce, beans, local olive oil, wine —and lots of fish—had a striking 50 to 70 per cent reduction in the risk of recurrent heart disease compared to men eating a healthy Western diet. This was despite the fact that cholesterol levels in subjects following both the Cretan and Western diets were almost identical. Medical researchers had first become interested in the "Cretan diet" after a 15-year study found men from Crete to be healthier than those in other countries— Finland, Yugoslavia, Japan, Greece, Italy, the Netherlands and the United States.

What was particularly significant was the fact that the men from Crete also had half the overall death rate of those in Italy, even though both groups ate a Mediterranean-style diet. The main difference was the high consumption of fish among the Cretans.

A happy, active life will nurture a healthy heart.

Heart disease in Canada

In today's world, our hearts are in constant danger, despite decades of advances in every aspect of cardiology (the science of heart health and disease). Each week, it seems, we are informed of new heart risk factors or remedies. Researchers have identified certain genes that may be linked to cases of heart attack in families with a strong history of heart disease, and others that may increase risk in certain populations or increase the risk of certain underlying tendencies.

Doctors also know more and more about which medications will lower your heart attack risk by keeping your cholesterol levels low and your blood pressure even. The ability of health professionals to help smokers address their tenacious addiction has never been greater.

Yet this year alone, more than 70,000 Canadians will have heart attacks. Sadly, more than a quarter of these heart attack victims will die. Cardiovascular disease remains the single largest cause of death in Canada. It is responsible for roughly one-third of all deaths each year.

The Heart and Stroke Foundation of Canada notes that while deaths from heart disease have decreased 51 per cent since 1979, it continues to kills 32 per cent of men and 34 per cent of women in Canada each year—more than three times the number of deaths caused by lung cancer and breast cancer combined.

A disturbing new trend in Canada is the number of young persons developing heart disease risk factors. Roughly 40 per cent of teenage girls are physically inactive, over 30 per cent of men and women in their twenties are overweight and Canadian men and women 15 to 29 years old make up the largest proportion of smokers.

The lifestyle connection

How could this be happening in 21st-century Canada? The truth is, despite our knowledge, we treat our hearts with little respect. A happy, active life will nurture a healthy heart. The way we live now poses unprecedented threats. Most people eat too much and exercise too little. Sadly, 20 per cent of Canadians remain addicted to nicotine.

Our food choices are often horribly unhealthy, flooding our bodies with the worst types of fats and carbohydrates while starving them of beneficial fats, fibre and antioxidants that are vital to health. And the stress that is so often a part of our lives compels our bodies to cope with abnormally high levels of damaging stress hormones and robs us of essential leisure time for relaxing.

That little pump and, most crucially, the arteries which transport blood around the body, weren't designed for the onslaughts of the 21st century. The heart muscle itself needs a constant supply of oxygen-rich blood, delivered via a network of coronary arteries. If a clot blocks an artery, or if the lining of any of these supply lines becomes diseased, causing plaque which constricts the artery, the heart faces an immediate oxygen deficit.

Oxygen-starved heart muscle hurts—which explains the short-lived chest pain called angina. Worse still, oxygen-deprived heart muscle can die quickly, leading to heart attack, heart failure and even death.

Women's hearts break, too

If you think that cardiovascular disease is strictly a man's problem, think again. Most Canadian women have at least one risk factor for heart disease and nearly 39,000 Canadian women die each year from cardiovascular disease. It claims more women's lives than cancer, accidents and diabetes combined.

Even more worrying is the fact that although heart disease kills seven times as many women as breast cancer, most women are far more aware of breast cancer. One recent poll showed that only 8 per cent of women identified heart disease and stroke as their greatest health concern. For many years, some doctors didn't even really believe that women developed heart disease. Some doctors continue to overlook uniquely female cardiovascular risks, sometimes even to the point of misdiagnosing or dismissing women's heart attacks while they're happening.

The men-only myths

Two widely believed myths persist: that only men have heart disease and that women are at risk only in old age. The truth is that by the age of 70, one Canadian women in five has already been told by a physician that she has or has had heart problems.

Other lifestyle and medical conditions play a part. Diabetes increases the risk of developing heart disease in women much more than in men. It is believed that the interaction of female hormones, blood sugar and insulin may be responsible.

Canadian women tend to be more inactive than Canadian men. An inactive woman doubles her chance of developing heart disease. And finally, women have been less successful than men in quitting smoking.

Here's what you need to know

■ Women play down their own risks. A Heart and Stroke Foundation of Canada survey found that upward of 60 per cent of women polled thought that breast cancer was the leading cause of death in women in Canada—while only 17 per cent correctly identified heart disease as the major cause of death in Canadian women.

■ The misconceptions are not unique to Canada. A recent British Heart Foundation report highlighted women's lack of knowledge about the main risk factors for developing heart disease. Only 8 per cent correctly named high blood cholesterol, 5 per cent high blood pressure and 12 per cent family

Is it a heart attack? Dial 911

If you think you or someone else may be having a heart attack, don't hesitate—dial 911 and let the experts decide. Most heart attack deaths happen in the first hour after an attack begins but people often wait hours before calling for help. Experiencing chest pain or any of the symptoms listed here for more than a few minutes, warrants calling an ambulance immediately. At the same time, a 325 mg ASA tablet (the standard-sized pain-relief tablet) should be taken, unless the individual is allergic. The tablet should be chewed to get it into the system more quickly.

CHEST DISCOMFORT Most heart attacks involve discomfort in the centre of the chest that lasts more than 30 minutes even when the sufferer is resting, or goes away and comes back. It may be described as a sort of uncomfortable pressure, squeezing, heaviness, congestion, fullness or pain.
DISCOMFORT IN OTHER AREAS OF THE UPPER BODY Symptoms can include pain or discomfort in one or both arms, the back, neck or jaw.
SHORTNESS OF BREATH This symptom may occur with or without chest discomfort.
OTHER SIGNS Other important features, which may be the only manifestations, are breaking out in a cold sweat and also lightheadedness or overwhelming fatigue or weakness.

history as factors that increase the likelihood of developing the disease.

■ Compared to 25 per cent of men, 38 per cent of women will die within one year of a first heart attack. Yet only 40 per cent of women with angina or who have had a heart attack are taking ASA and only 25 per cent are taking statins.

■ Menopause is a defining moment for women and heart disease. Before menopause, a woman's naturally high estrogen levels protect her heart. After the menopause, women have higher cholesterol levels, which may increase their risk of heart disease, especially if their level of triglycerides (another type of fat particle in the blood) is raised too. In general, women who have high levels of triglycerides (over 3.9 mmol/l) and low HDL "good" cholesterol (under 1.2 mmol/l) have greater risks for heart disease than do men with similar levels.

■ The causes of heart disease are different for women. Women who smoke are twice as likely to have heart attacks as male smokers. Depression is also a stronger heart risk factor for women than men.

Feel the beat

Your heart rate—the number of beats per minute—can help you and your doctor to assess your heart's fitness. A normal range is 60 to 80 beats per minute while you're resting. A faster beat may simply indicate that you've just run up the stairs so you wouldn't be late for your appointment (physical activity boosts heart rate). Fever; a short illness such as a cold, flu or a stomach bug; and anxiety can also cause a temporary elevation. But a consistently fast resting heartbeat can be a sign of trouble, such as anemia, thyroid problems or a cardiovascular defect.

To check your heart rate, make sure you have been resting for 5 to 10 minutes. Have a clock or watch with a second hand ready, then use the pads of your fingers to find your pulse—try your inner wrist or your neck. Count the beats for 15 seconds, then multiply by four.

■ Women have risk factors that men don't face. Taking contraceptive pills is one example: high blood pressure is two to three times more common in women who take oral contraceptives—especially in those who are overweight. Also, women whose blood pressure rises during pregnancy, then returns to normal after delivery, are more likely to have high blood pressure later in life.

■ Many women's heart attacks don't include classic chest pain. A recent study of more than 500 female heart attack survivors found that top symptoms were shortness of breath, feeling weak and/or fatigued, breaking into a cold sweat and dizziness—not the classic heart attack signs recognized by most emergency medical personnel. Forty-three per cent felt no chest pain at all.

What women should do

Until just a few years ago, doctors recommended HRT (hormone replacement therapy) to postmenopausal women as a heart protector. But in 2002, a U.S. study found that it didn't shield hearts at all and in fact raised the risk of blood clots in the first year or so. Another study showed that women who took a combination of estrogen and progestin—the most common form of HRT—had a 41 per cent increase in stroke over a five-year period compared with those who took a placebo.

Talk to your family doctor about your own heart risk. Then, stop smoking if you are a smoker, eat wisely, exercise—climbing stairs or walking instead of using the car counts as exercise—and try and reduce stress in your life, be aware of fluctuations in your weight, waist measurement, cholesterol levels and blood pressure—and discuss any worries with your doctor. This is good advice for men, too. So why do we all keep missing this simple truth?

Shift your focus

Your life depends on the health of your coronary arteries but these key blood vessels are no match for the fat you eat in a stuffed-crust pizza, the pollution in a pack of cigarettes, endless sitting in cars, behind desks or glued to the TV; the stress of over-long working weeks or a difficult daily commute. So often we could help but don't—consider, the redundant exercise-bike or the fitness video you keep meaning to use but never quite get around to. We'll also explain why good dental hygiene is absolutely vital.

Instead of living life for the benefit of our hearts, we tend to ignore it, perhaps hoping that the latest scientific breakthrough will rescue our hearts when they start to falter. Yet many of us could avoid medical intervention —just by giving our hearts the care they need.

What precisely causes heart attacks? Doctors can describe the process in medical detail. It's damage to your coronary arteries, the vital supply lines to the heart muscle. Coronary artery disease is significantly related to cigarette consumption and oxidized fat that gets into the lining of the arteries and causes plaque, which gradually narrows the artery and may eventually break down and erode causing a complete blockage of the artery.

And what damages arteries in the first place? Principally, smoking, hypertension and high cholesterol. Most cardiologists and other medical professionals agree that there is overwhelming statistical evidence to demonstrate that the combination of all three places people at very high risk. All are associated with the way we live.

The global evidence

In late 2004, a major study involving 30,000 people across the globe showed that 90 per

cent of heart attacks were caused by just nine risk factors. Five of these were purely lifestyle related: smoking, stress, sedentary living, eating too few fruits and vegetables and, perhaps most surprising, abstaining from alcohol.

The remaining four are more medical in nature, but don't be fooled—each one is closely and directly linked to lifestyle choices. The four are abnormal cholesterol levels and high blood pressure (mentioned above), plus diabetes and abdominal obesity. What is intriguing and important about this study is that it spanned 52 countries and involved men and women of all ages, races and socio-economic backgrounds. It revealed that whether you are a poor woman in Calgary or a rich man in Tokyo, exactly the same risk factors can cause heart attacks—in most

cases, smoking, sitting too much, eating poorly and encountering too much constant stress. So don't be one of those people who is waiting for science to protect their hearts. The truth is—and it's one of the most important truths in this book—that adopting a healthy lifestyle can begin working on all the medical causes of heart attacks at the same time.

It is useful to know what the various threats are, and we give you a concise, well-informed roundup of the seven major risk factors in the next chapter. But our real goal in this book is to show you how to combat all of them with one simple program that tackles their root cause—the sedentary, calorie-and-fat-laden, television-watching, anxiety-ridden modern lives that many of us lead.

The path to a healthy heart

This is the foundation of the 30-Minutes-a-Day Plan. Here are some of the most effective steps you can take—without adding more jobs to your to-do list or expenses to your monthly budget—to protect your heart in the way nature intended.

If you smoke you can in fact instantly make savings; smoking is widely recognized as the leading cause of vascular disease, damaging arteries and leading to both heart attacks and strokes. Quitting smoking can be tough, but heart-smart living can also be as simple as laughing at a difficult situation rather than just getting angry.

It means going for a stroll after your evening meal, and not always watching television. It means having an apple for dessert rather than apple crumble, or spending 15 minutes enjoying a cup of homemade cocoa (see the heart-healthy cocoa tip on page 107) curled up on the sofa, instead of watching the news while eating potato chips.

It's doing 5-minutes-a-day strength-training while the coffee brews in the morning or taking a 3-second meditative pause when the "you've got mail" alert sounds on your computer.

The message is quite simple: for a cost of no more than 30 minutes a day, you can take powerful, scientifically proven steps to overcome life's biggest heart threats, including smoking, high cholesterol levels, high blood pressure, stomach fat, insulin resistance, inflammation, free radicals and a host of other factors that researchers are still endeavouring to understand, such as homo-cysteine and a cholesterol particle called lp(a).

Here, then, is an outline of the plan that will enable you to take them all on and win.

♥ **Focus on small changes for big results** Fast, simple diet modifications can cut cholesterol by 30 per cent. A 5-minutes-a-day weight-training program can replace 10 years' worth of lost muscle tissue. This book is packed with time-saving lifestyle changes that get results, don't cost a fortune and are easy to stick with in the long run.

♥ **Conquer "sitting disease"** Canadians are leading increasingly sedentary lives with many of us getting less than 30 minutes of moderate exercise per week. Yet our bodies are built for daily activity. We'll show you how to build healthy movement into your life, no matter how jam-packed your days are.

♥ **Eat fresh foods** Fresh, whole foods don't have to cost more or take more time to prepare than the processed stuff. These wholesome, delicious foods—fresh fruits and vegetables, grains, fish, meats, dairy products and even soya—not only taste good, they also protect your heart by reducing blood fats, lowering elevated blood sugar, calming inflammation and fighting destructive free radicals. We'll show you the easiest way to start eating more healthy foods and fewer packaged products.

♥ **Get organized to quit smoking** Simple planning, appropriate preparation and the assistance of health professionals can dramatically improve your chances of being a successful quitter. We've got specific advice you'll find helpful.

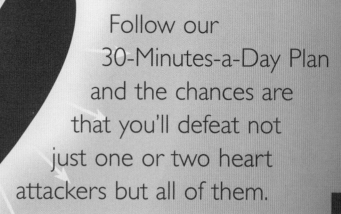

Follow our 30-Minutes-a-Day Plan and the chances are that you'll defeat not just one or two heart attackers but all of them.

♥ **Know your numbers** If you want to see tangible results then track your success by keeping tabs on certain essential numbers, including your weight and your waist measurement. All adult Canadians should know these "vital statistics" but virtually none of us do. For help sticking to the program, we'll also tell you which four things to monitor on a daily basis—a task that should take about 30 seconds each evening. It's very simple.

♥ **Avoid toxins** From tobacco to trans fats, sugar to environmental pollutants, the toxins we allow to enter our bodies seem to wreak havoc with our hearts first. Your body doesn't have to be a dumping ground for hazardous waste. We'll show you how to clean it up.

♥ **Find joy** A growing body of research links hostility, impatience and bearing grudges with poor heart health; in contrast, forgiveness, friends and optimism are linked with healthier hearts. Do you have a heart-threatening personality type? Find out—and learn how to live a more joyful life.

The heart attackers Doctors vigorously debate this list but, based on our best current knowledge, here are the primary medical and lifestyle conditions that affect the heart, along with the page number on which you'll find a full briefing.

THE **7** MAJOR ATTACKERS

1 SMOKING — page 24
2 CHOLESTEROL — page 26
3 HIGH BLOOD PRESSURE — page 30
4 EXCESS BODY FAT — page 34
5 METABOLIC SYNDROME — page 38
6 OXIDATIVE STRESS — page 41
7 CHRONIC INFLAMMATION — page 44

ADDITIONAL ATTACKERS

TRIGLYCERIDES — page 29
HOMOCYSTEINE — page 48
APO(a) AND APO(b) — page 48
Lp(a) — page 49
NITRIC OXIDE — page 49

The 7 deadly heart attackers

Each month, medical journals publish hundreds of studies about heart disease, covering everything from A (for artery-clearing angioplasty) to X (for xanthoma, a cholesterol deposit under the skin). The U.S. National Library of Medicine, which maintains the world's most comprehensive database of published health research, lists more than 500,000 research papers about heart disease alone. Despite all that knowledge, almost 75,000 people in Canada (and half a million Americans) die from coronary heart disease each year.

Criticism has been levelled at the nature of much medical research that focuses on very narrow questions, such as whether an increase in intake of a specific nutrient causes any change in a particular body chemical. It is suggested that too much fine detail stops us from seeing the wood for the trees: if the proverbial wood is the human heart, and each tree in the wood is one aspect of what affects the heart (cholesterol, vitamins, exercise and so forth), then perhaps too many medical studies focus on a single branch of a single tree. It could be argued that many studies focusing on small details reveal little about the big picture. On the other hand, doctors maintain that while there is a lot of research on minutiae, there's also a lot of epidemiology—population studies taking a broader view—which is why we know as much as we do about links between heart disease and associated risk factors, for example, in terms of lifestyle or environment.

The way such research is reported can affect our attitude. Journalists are often focused on single issues, such as high cholesterol or high blood pressure, when each is just one tree—albeit a major one—in the wood. The truth is, major heart risks are interwoven—they rarely occur singly—and the more you have, the greater your risk of heart disease.

Researchers and drug companies are taking note of this heart truth. The recent major British Heart Protection Study, reported in *The Lancet* in 2002, showed that patients at high risk of coronary heart disease benefit from drug treatment whatever their baseline cholesterol level. In other words, benefit depends on a patient's combination of risk factors. Doctors are now urged to use scoring systems based on several risk factors to assess overall risk of coronary disease.

Isn't it time you looked beyond the details, too? That's what the 30-Minutes-a-Day Plan is all about: showing you the big picture—plus giving you a plan that combats all the attackers at once. When you treat yourself as one integrated system—mind, body and spirit—achieving heart health is so much easier. An added bonus is that you'll also cut your risk of diabetes, cancer and other major health threats.

Lurking: the attackers

You may wonder why, if one plan can reduce all of the major risks to your heart, you should bother learning about each one. There are a few answers. First, the media talks a lot about these risks—it can be confusing. Learning the facts will give you the knowledge to help put the "news" in perspective and keep you focused on what matters. And knowing how the heart attackers interconnect, and how certain lifestyle choices can affect several at once, is very empowering. You'll be far more convinced of the power of the 30-Minutes-a-Day Plan when you understand its basis.

The heart's most powerful enemies

So this is what you need to know—a concise run-down on the seven most dangerous attackers that your heart faces. In the next little while, you will learn something about all the heart-related topics and issues that matter most.

You will find out how conventional wisdom about heart disease has evolved over the past 50 years—from a simplistic view of health to a more sophisticated modern approach. You will discover how each attacker develops in your body, trace the ways our 21st-century lifestyles fuel these menaces and learn how to assess your risk for each.

You will also become aware of the strong links between the seven major attackers—such as how abdominal fat fuels at least three other attackers, the killer role of tobacco and how "sitting disease"—a sedentary lifestyle and negligible exercise—triggers high blood pressure, oxidative stress and all the rest.

Major heart risks are interwoven—they rarely occur singly.

HEART ATTACK 1
Smoking

In the 1960s the dangers of tobacco addiction were first identified—and quickly overshadowed by advertising that portrayed smoking as glamorous, sophisticated and part of a gracious lifestyle.

More than 40 years later, tobacco's deadly toll continues, and heart disease is a common result of smoking. Most Canadians mistakenly believe that lung cancer is the most common consequence of smoking cigarettes. They're wrong. Dead wrong.

Each year tobacco claims thousands of lives because of its direct role in stimulating the buildup of plaque along blood vessel walls, interfering with the delivery of oxygen to the heart, raising blood pressure and increasing heart rate—all of which contribute to heart disease and heart attacks. The evidence is clear: if you're a smoker the most important thing you can do to enhance your heart health is to quit. As soon as possible. The "gold standard" of heart disease prevention activity is to help smokers stop smoking. It's not easy; unless you've been a smoker you won't understand how difficult it can be to break free from the claws of nicotine addiction. But as you'll read later (see pages 200 to 204), there's much more that can now be done to provide smokers with assistance, real assistance, in quitting.

Most smokers began as adolescents and were convinced of two things. They were never going to have health problems, and they could quit whenever they wanted. Wrong on both counts. Individuals exposed to as few as four or five cigarettes a day, for a few days in a row, rapidly become addicted to nicotine.

The cigarette is one of the most sophisticated and deadly drug-delivery devices in our community. Carefully designed to ensure the most rapid delivery of nicotine possible, modern cigarettes contain a bewildering variety of chemical products—nearly 5,000—many of which cause cancer while others conspire to affect a variety of other body systems and organs.

There's no quicker way to get a drug into the circulation than to inhale it. Heroin, when injected into a vein, takes 14 to 18 seconds to reach the addiction centres of the brain. Nicotine and its 5,000 fellow-travellers in inhaled cigarette smoke are transported through the lungs into the blood stream, and almost instantly to the heart. They are then immediately pumped into the arterial circulation. Remarkably, the nicotine arrives at the addiction centres in the brain in six to eight seconds! (The nicotine uptake is even more rapid if you smoke a "free-basing" cigarette—one in which ammonia is added to the cigarette tobacco to make the smoke more alkaline, which increases the speed with which nicotine is absorbed.)

The moment you light a cigarette you begin to produce carbon monoxide, a chemical that knocks oxygen from its perch on red blood cells and consequently limits its ability to carry oxygen. At the same time nicotine and other chemicals are increasing blood pressure, causing the heart's blood vessels to narrow, raising the heart rate, and making the blood "stickier" and more likely to clot. But that's not all. Other constituents of tobacco smoke damage the vessel walls making it more likely that deposits of cholesterol and other materials may start to accumulate. As those lesions grow they can fragment and trigger a blood clot. The resulting obstruction prevents blood flow to the heart muscle and a heart attack or myocardial infarction (MI) results.

And many of the same mechanisms operate even if you aren't a smoker but share the air with those who do. Exposure to second-hand smoke means that you inhale the same chemicals with much the same result—your heart rate rises while the oxygen levels in your blood decline. So do yourself a favour: stay away from second-hand smoke. If someone in your family is a smoker, have them smoke outside, never in the house or the car!

Ironically, a cigarette increases the heart's requirements for oxygen while actually reducing the available oxygen. It's like putting your foot to the floor while holding down on the power brakes—and we all know what happens in those circumstances!

Nicotine is also an irritant to the heart and can stimulate the development of rapid, irregular heartbeats that may quickly deteriorate into something called ventricular fibrillation—a totally ineffective quivering of the heart muscle that pumps no blood and is the most common cause of sudden death—which explains why smokers are particularly prone to "sudden cardiac death."

Most smokers know why they should quit and want to quit, but have problems withstanding the uncomfortable reality of nicotine withdrawal. Later in this book (see pages 200 to 204), you'll get valuable hints and specific advice that can dramatically enhance the likelihood of successful smoking cessation. The most powerful predictor of ultimate cessation is the number of times quit attempts have been made in the past.

In Canada, there has been a dramatic reduction in smoking over the past decades, but we can do better. And we will.

HEART ATTACK 2
Cholesterol

Cholesterol first made U.S. headlines in the 1950s; it took 20 years before the rest of the world began to accept this new element of the heart attack equation.

Too much saturated fat in the diet equals too much cholesterol in the bloodstream equals clogged arteries and heart attacks. Despite the fact that heart disease has been one of the leading causes of death in Canada for the last 100 years, nobody wanted to hear that the delicious things in life—butter, cheese, cakes and ice cream—just might spell doom.

The story centres on Dr. Ancel Keys, a researcher at the University of Minnesota. During World War II, Dr. Keys produced "K" rations—nutritious brown-boxed meals for the U.S. military. In the early 1950s, he noted that well-fed American businessmen had soaring rates of heart disease, while rates among people living through food shortages in post-war Europe declined.

After studying men in seven countries— Finland, Greece, Yugoslavia, Italy, the Netherlands, Japan and the United States— and comparing their blood cholesterol levels, intake of saturated fats and cardiovascular disease rates, Dr. Keys concluded that a "strong association" existed between saturated fats and heart health. Dr. Keys, who was featured on the cover of *Time* magazine, recommended cutting saturated fat and eating more polyunsaturated fats (such as sunflower oil) to lower total cholesterol levels. Less total cholesterol, he reasoned, would lead to fewer heart attack deaths. It was the basis for the 1950s heart-healthy "prudent diet," designed to improve cholesterol levels and ward off heart disease. But the cholesterol story wasn't that simple.

Fast-forward to the 21st century. Cholesterol isn't necessarily a villain. Your liver (and your intestines and even your skin) manufactures this soft, waxy stuff every day to help your body to build cell membranes and produce sex hormones, vitamin D and fat-digesting bile acids. The raw material for your body's cholesterol is dietary fat.

The real key to heart-healthy cholesterol levels, experts now say, is a balance between two basic types: "lousy" or "bad" low-density lipoproteins (LDLs) and "healthy" or "good" high-density lipoproteins (HDLs). The latest news is that heart experts are finding that the higher your HDLs and the lower your LDLs— essentially, the closer you can come to the "natural" cholesterol balance observed in hunter-gatherer societies—the lower your risk of blocked coronary arteries and heart attack.

LDLs: keep them low

Like delivery vans packed with fat droplets, LDLs are designed to navigate the bloodstream, feeding liquefied cholesterol directly to your cells. Problems arise when too many LDLs crowd the blood, then get laid down on artery walls and sucked by cells into the tissue-thin inner lining of coronary arteries, forming the foundation for heart-threatening plaques. Over time, these plaques—a mix of fat, cholesterol, calcium and other cellular sludge—can narrow coronary arteries so less blood flows to your heart muscle.

New research also suggests that one type of LDLs—small, dense LDLs—is especially lethal. These tightly packed particles are easily damaged by free radicals in the bloodstream (free radicals are highly active molecules that can proliferate and cause serious damage). The tiny LDL particles can then penetrate artery walls with ease, laying the foundation for the plaque buildup of atherosclerosis. (For more on these LDLs, read about oxidative stress on page 42.)

The bottom line is that high amounts of LDLs in your bloodstream increase your risk of atherosclerosis; low levels reduce it. What's the safety zone? All research indicates that the lower your LDL levels, the lower your risk of heart disease. In a provocative study published in March 2004 in the *Journal of the American Medical Association*,

researchers found that high doses of cholesterol-lowering medications (statins) that targeted LDLs halted the progression of heart disease and cut mortality rates by 28 per cent. But no drug is without side-effects, some people develop muscle pain and other problems when they take statins.

What's your risk? Cholesterol

One type of cholesterol—LDL—is bad for you, so you want to aim for a low reading, preferably under 3.5 mmol/l (millimoles per litre of blood). If you already have heart disease, your doctor will want to reduce LDL even further to less than 2.0 mmol/l. The other cholesterol—HDL—is good for you, and you want a reading above 1 mmol/l. Ideally, your total cholesterol—including LDL levels of 3.5 mmol/l or lower—should be below 5 mmol/l. If your levels are persistently higher, your doctor is likely to suggest measures to help to reduce it and may offer drug treatment too.

TOTAL CHOLESTEROL LEVEL ASSESSMENT

less than 5 mmol/l	ideal
5.2 mmol/l–6.4 mmol/l	moderately high
above 6.5 mmol/l	high

2 CHOLESTEROL
What you need to know

Cholesterol is a waxy substance, produced from the fats you eat, that your body uses as the building block for cell walls, hormones and a digestive fluid called bile acid. There are two main types: "bad" LDLs, which form the basis of artery-clogging plaque, and "good" HDLs, which carry LDLs to the liver for elimination.

HOW IT ACCUMULATES Central fat (around the stomach), a diet high in saturated fat and lack of activity can all prompt your liver to churn out more and more LDLs. A diet low in monounsaturated fat and a life devoid of exercise can deplete helpful HDLs, as can smoking and diabetes.

WHAT'S NEW

New targets Recent studies show that healthy LDL levels should be even lower than previously suspected, and healthy HDLs should be higher—especially for women, who have naturally high HDL levels prior to menopause.

Excess LDL cholesterol is sucked into arterial walls, forming the foundation for heart-threatening plaques that can narrow the artery and eventually break off.

Forget the "rusted pipe" theory of clogged arteries Deadly plaque doesn't grow on artery walls, it develops in the walls themselves. LDLs start the process by being sucked in through the inner lining of blood vessel walls. One type, small dense LDLs, is especially dangerous because it enters the walls easily.

Don't overlook triglycerides This blood fat is measured if your doctor takes a lipid profile, which measures all the blood fats. High triglycerides are linked to higher risk of heart attack, especially in women.

DETECTING IT There are no physical clues as to the levels of cholesterol in your bloodstream; only blood tests can reveal them. A standard test, performed by your doctor, measures total cholesterol, LDLs and HDLs, in millimoles per litre of blood (mmol/l).

STANDARD MEDICAL CARE More than a billion dollars is spent on cholesterol-lowering statin drugs in Canada every year, a number that is expected to grow as researchers advise prescribing these effective drugs to a wider audience. Evidence grows that statins, while lowering cholesterol, also act in additional ways to improve arterial health and reduce cardiac disease. The next goal is better HDL-raising drugs. Some doctors prescribe niacin supplements to bolster HDLs.

VIABILITY OF SELF-TREATMENT Very high for the majority of people. Most of us put ourselves at risk—by eating an unhealthy diet, by smoking, by being overweight or by failing to exercise sufficiently. However, some of us have inherited a metabolic tendency to have high cholesterol levels and medication is necessary to lower cholesterol levels.

Meanwhile, diet alone can lower cholesterol levels and, although no diet that targets LDLs alone has yet been devised, the 30-Minutes-a-Day Plan will help you to cut your LDLs. You'll eat less saturated fat, get more physically active and control a range of newly discovered heart risks—such as chronic inflammation, insulin resistance and oxidation—that magnify the deadly potential of LDL cholesterol.

HDLs: cholesterol goodies

High-density lipoproteins, or HDLs, race around your bloodstream grabbing LDLs and transporting them to the liver for disposal. HDLs actually fuse with LDLs and remove their cholesterol cargo. New evidence suggests that HDLs also act as antioxidants, blocking LDLs from causing plaque-promoting damage. (Antioxidants slow down or stop damage or destruction in the body caused by oxidation. They are found mainly in fresh fruits and vegetables, fish and seeds.)

HDLs are so potent that every 0.1 increase in HDL levels reduces heart attack risk by 3 to 4 per cent; a high HDL level offers such powerful protection that it can even reduce the threat posed by other heart risks, such as diabetes or being overweight. Low HDLs, in contrast, are dangerous because they leave your heart unprotected against LDLs and another damaging type of blood fat, known as triglycerides. (Your HDL level should ideally be 1.3 mmol/l or higher; below 1.1 mmol/l is considered "low.")

In 2004, the American Heart Association raised its recommended HDL levels for women by 25 per cent; the Heart and Stroke Foundation of Canada's advice is to aim for higher than 1.2 mmol/l for women and 1.0 mmol/l for men. Boosting HDLs can be helped by eating good fats found in foods such as oily fish, nuts and olive oil, and exercising regularly.

Triglycerides: push down the "other" blood fat

Triglycerides aren't a form of cholesterol, but because they act in a similar way and have similar effects, they are often grouped with cholesterol in any discussion of heart risks. Triglycerides are bits of fat in the bloodstream that collect excess calories from the food you eat and whisk them away to fat cells for long-term storage.

Triglycerides can also become the raw material for LDLs, making them another dangerous actor in the heart disease drama. Newer studies suggest that triglycerides alone can predict heart risk, as they encourage atherosclerosis, especially in women. Recent research even suggests that too many of them can form a blockage in your blood vessels so the appetite-curbing hormone leptin can't send the "stop eating" signal to your brain when you've had enough pasta. Abdominal fat, excess alcohol intake, uncontrolled diabetes and a lack of exercise increase your chances of having high triglycerides. Triglycerides are measured in the same way as cholesterol, in millimoles per litre. They rise after eating so a blood test is usually done after an overnight or 12-hour fast.

On the 30-Minutes-a-Day Plan, you'll probably see your levels fall. If lifestyle changes are not enough to reduce your triglycerides, your doctor may advise medication or a dietary supplement such as fish oil.

What's your risk?

LEVEL (mmol/l)	RISK
under 1.7	normal
over 2.0	high
over 4.5	very high

HEART ATTACK 3
High blood pressure

Imagine a peaceful river meandering between meadows and wheat fields. It rounds a bend and drops into a narrow, rock-walled canyon. Abruptly, the gentle flow becomes a fierce torrent.

Now imagine your arteries and their delicate, branching capillaries growing narrow and stiff—a consequence of inactivity, of stress, of being overweight, of the doughnut and coffee you have for breakfast. Inside, unseen and unfelt, your blood hurtles along like a river squeezed into a canyon, banging so forcefully against artery walls that it can injure and weaken them.

Ultimately, this pressure can rupture blood vessels in the brain (causing a stroke) or the abdomen (causing an abdominal aortic aneurysm). It can cause the heart muscle to enlarge and weaken, and is a powerful promoter of atherosclerosis in the coronary arteries, the precursor to heart attack.

High blood pressure (hypertension) is recognized as a leading cardiovascular risk factor and, because it is initially largely symptomless, has often been dubbed the "silent killer." A staggering 42 per cent of Canadians with high blood pressure are unaware of its presence. About 23 per cent of Canadians have been diagnosed with high blood pressure, but only 16 per cent of

those are both treated and controlled. High blood pressure is responsible for most of the 50,000 strokes suffered by Canadians each year. The odds are an astonishing 90 per cent that you'll develop high blood pressure sooner or later—whether you're a man or a woman. While men under 55 are more likely than women to have high blood pressure, once women reach 55 they tend to catch up with, and even overtake, the men. The condition is less common in younger adults but more common in people of Afro-Caribbean origin and from the Indian sub-continent.

In a gruesome experiment in 1733, Stephen Hales, a British vet and botanist, first demonstrated the force of blood pressure by attaching a thin brass tube to a horse's neck artery; he reported that blood shot nine feet up the tube.

In the intervening years, an Italian physician developed a non-invasive way to check human blood pressure—the sphygmo-manometer, a version of which is still used by doctors today. Insurance companies noticed that higher blood pressure was linked to

3 HIGH BLOOD PRESSURE
What you need to know

Hypertension occurs when arterioles—the small thin-walled branches of an artery—become stiff and inflexible, and cause hypertension by increasing resistance to the blood flow. High blood pressure in turn damages artery walls, making them more vulnerable to plaque buildup. It also weakens and enlarges the heart.

HOW IT HAPPENS Genetics may account for 30 per cent of cases of hypertension. For the rest of us, it's a combination of higher-than-normal fluid content in the bloodstream, often due to an excessively salty diet plus narrower, stiffer arteries—the result of atherosclerosis, inactivity, overweight, chronic stress and/or diabetes.

WHAT'S NEW

New guidelines Optimal blood pressure is below 120/80.

Damage and death risk rise sooner than expected Evidence from 61 blood pressure studies suggests that risks of fatal heart disease and stroke may begin when blood pressure is as low as 115/75. Risk doubles with each 20-point rise in the first number in a reading (systolic pressure) and each 10-point rise in the second number, diastolic pressure.

Excess fluid in the blood stream, coupled with narrowed or hardened arteries, can cause blood to flow with greater force, damaging arterial walls.

DETECTING IT Digital blood pressure monitors are gradually replacing the most widely used method of checking blood pressure, in which a doctor or nurse straps a black cuff to your arm, applies a stethoscope, pumps up the cuff until it cuts off blood flow, and measures the results as pressure is released. (Home blood pressure devices are fine for daily monitoring, but you should also have supplementary checks at your doctor's office, where the equipment is properly calibrated and the results recorded.) High blood pressure usually has no symptoms that you can feel or see.

STANDARD MEDICAL CARE About 7 million Canadians have been diagnosed with high blood pressure. Many take medications to improve it. The most popular are diuretics (or "water pills"), which reduce the amount of fluid in the bloodstream. There are several classes of artery-relaxing drugs that are also widely prescribed, including alpha and beta blockers, ACE inhibitors, angiotensin II receptor blockers and calcium channel blockers.

VIABILITY OF SELF-TREATMENT Very helpful for most people, dietary changes can act as a natural diuretic, lowering blood pressure as effectively as some medications. Meditation, exercise, losing weight and stopping smoking also help.

earlier death; the first low-salt diet—a menu of plain rice and fruit—became the first blood pressure-lowering health food diet in the mid-1940s. Drug companies devised the first successful class of hypertension drugs—diuretics—in the 1950s, and they are still first-line drugs on the market today.

The basics

Researchers are now beginning to understand precisely how modern life and genetics team up to cause high blood pressure.

■ **Your heart** The harder it has to work, for instance, when you're digging the garden, the happier it is and the healthier you will be. The transient rise in blood pressure when you exercise is quite normal and healthy, unless you already have high blood pressure

or atherosclerosis. But unrelenting stress—hourly, day in day out—puts constant pressure on your arteries and causes damage.

■ **Your arteries** Your arteries are lined with smooth muscle that can expand or contract as blood flows through. The more elastic your arteries, the less resistant they are to the flow of blood and the less the force that's exerted on their walls. But if your arteries are clogged with plaque, your blood pressure will rise as blood is forced through a narrower channel.

■ **Your kidneys** They control how much sodium your body contains and thus how much water stays in your blood (sodium retains water). More water means more fluid trying to get through the blood vessels—and higher blood pressure.

■ **Your hormones** So-called stress hormones make the heart beat faster and the arteries narrow, which raises blood pressure. Other

The harder your heart has to work, for instance, when you're digging the garden, the happier it is ...

What's your risk?
High blood pressure

Blood pressure measures the force of blood against artery walls while the heart is contracting at full force and while it's resting between beats. You can have your blood pressure checked regularly by a doctor or nurse. If you want to learn about measuring it at home, go to the Heart and Stroke Foundation of Canada's website at:
www.heartandstroke.ca/bloodpressure

BLOOD PRESSURE (mm Hg)	CLASSIFICATION
below 120/80	optimal
120–129/80–85	normal
130–139/85–89	high-normal
140–159/90–99	mild hypertension
160–179/100–109	moderate hypertension
160/110 and above	severe hypertension

Don't discount "accidental" high blood pressure

You gulped a coffee in the car, ran across the parking lot and only just made your doctor's appointment on time. Now you're in the office and the office nurse has just said your blood pressure is a little high. Should or shouldn't you worry, considering the past hour's intensity?

Answer Yes. You should take even this "circumstantial" hypertension seriously. New research suggests that even one high blood pressure reading, regardless of circumstances, presages future heart disease risk and should not be ignored by doctors or patients. Researchers looked at the medical records of 5,825 patients treated for high blood pressure, then looked to see who developed health problems over the next five years. Those with a 10-point increase in systolic pressure during a doctor's office appointment had a 9 per cent higher risk of heart disease, a 7 per cent higher risk of stroke, and a 6 per cent higher risk of experiencing a first stroke or heart attack.

hormones regulate blood pressure; drugs known as ACE inhibitors lower blood pressure by controlling these hormones.

Act now

While high blood pressure is a known killer—it plays a role in 75 per cent of all heart attacks and strokes—more than 4 out of 10 Canadians with hypertension don't know they have it. Others know they've got it but don't have it under control.

But doctors are not ignoring the potential risk of high blood pressure. Lower is better, say all doctors, who believe that it's time to get serious about high blood pressure. Ideally, blood pressure should be less than 120/80, though up to 129/85 is deemed normal. (The first number represents systolic pressure, the force of blood against artery walls during a heartbeat; the second number, or diastolic pressure, is the pressure when the heart is relaxed between beats.)

Damage to arteries actually begins at blood pressure levels that doctors have previously considered optimal. Evidence gathered from 61 studies suggests that for most adults, the risk of death from heart disease and stroke begins to rise when blood pressure is as low as 115/75, although many

doctors may view this as over cautious. The Heart and Stroke Foundation of Canada defines high blood pressure as a systolic blood pressure reading consistently above 140 mm Hg and/or a diastolic pressure over 90 mm Hg. The foundation notes, however, that exercising 30 to 45 minutes three times a week can reduce one's systolic pressure by 10.4 mm Hg and diastolic by 7.5 mm Hg.

Perhaps the least mysterious thing about blood pressure is this: self-help measures can work and may help you to avoid having to take diuretics or other BP lowering drugs. Even if you are taking medication, healthy lifestyle changes are worthwhile. From proven, practical steps (losing weight cuts blood pressure significantly, as does limiting salt) to mental relaxation techniques, meditation or practising your faith, there are many small daily changes that can lower blood pressure.

Losing just 10 per cent of your body weight could lower your high blood pressure down to a normal range, without drugs. So could a diet rich in fruit and vegetables. And try to avoid taking too many non-steroidal anti-inflammatory drugs (NSAIDs). Studies have shown that regular consumption of these painkillers may also raise hypertension risk.

WHAT WE KNOW TODAY ABOUT YOUR HEART

HEART ATTACK 4
Excess body fat

Once upon a time, fat was the ultimate status symbol—a sign of health and wealth, sex appeal and fertility, all rolled into one cuddly bundle.

Before the dawn of the 20th century, a lean frame indicated a personal history of sickness, meagre meals and little money. Even in life insurance circles, fat was seen as a cushion against disease.

That was then, this is now—the era of huge portions of french fries, tubs of popcorn, iced Danish pastries and sugary drinks, with deskbound days, then nights in front of the television or surfing the Internet. Excess body fat is now the norm: 43 per cent of men and 34 per cent of women are overweight. Another 22 per cent of men and 23 per cent of women—that's almost one in four of us—are clinically obese. Surveys show that the rates in Canada for obese and overweight people are amongst the highest in the world.

In fact, being overweight is the most common nutrition-related health problem in North America. Roughly 60 per cent of all adults are overweight. Of those 60 per cent, more than 20 per cent are obese and thus at increased risk for an early death. And it doesn't end with the adults. More than 25 per cent of all Canadian children and adolescents are considered overweight or obese—a trend that continues to grow.

How can love handles and a pot-belly be so deadly? A growing mountain of research reveals that killer fat is abdominal (or central) fat—the stuff packed around, and sometimes in, your internal organs. While hip, thigh and bottom fat are relatively benign, stomach fat increases your odds for high blood pressure, blood clots and high cholesterol.

Abdominal fat also starts a chain of biochemical events that leads to insulin resistance—a precursor of Type 2 diabetes, heart disease, stroke, breast and prostate cancer, and kidney failure.

The reason stomach fat is so dangerous is that, far from being held in reserve until your body needs extra energy, it is continually released into your bloodstream in the form of artery-clogging fatty acids that your liver converts into harmful LDL cholesterol.

Abdominal fat also releases other compounds—among them, appetite-regulating hormones and immune system chemicals—that open the door for three huge heart risks: atherosclerosis, metabolic syndrome and inflammation. Even if they're slim elsewhere, so-called "apples"—men and women who carry a large amount of

How can love handles
and a pot-belly be
so deadly?

4 BODY FAT
What you need to know

Your body naturally contains millions of fat cells. Each one is an expandable pouch filled with fat droplets, called lipids, that are made of fats, sugars and amino acids derived from the foods you eat. Under normal circumstances, your body uses fat tissue to cushion bones, to regulate temperature and as fuel when blood sugar runs low.

HOW IT ACCUMULATES When you eat more food than your body needs to function, fat cells expand until they fill to capacity. If there are plenty more calories to be stored, your body manufactures new fat cells. (Until recently, experts believed the human body stopped producing new fat cells after puberty. Now they know that overeating can trigger fat cell production in adults.)

WHAT'S NEW

Central fat Not all body fat is equally bad. The body's most dangerous fat collects in your abdominal cavity, packing around internal organs. This central fat releases hormones that upset body chemistry, significantly raising your risk of heart disease and other major conditions.

Abdominal fat continually releases fatty acids and chemicals into the bloodstream that can lead to atherosclerosis, chronic inflammation and metabolic syndrome.

The role of carbohydrates Research is confirming that eating an excessive amount of simple carbohydrates (that is, sugar, white flour, rice, potatoes) contributes to weight gain. But it is important to ensure that you eat plenty of complex carbohydrates, including fruit and vegetables, for their fibre and antioxidant benefits.

DETECTING IT That's easy: look in the mirror. Check your BMI. Step on the scales. Measure your waist. Being overweight is a health condition that is easy to measure and monitor.

STANDARD MEDICAL CARE Canadians spend billions of dollars each year on prescription diet drugs, weight-loss surgery, diet programs, over-the-counter weight-loss supplements, health clubs, diet drinks and artificial sweeteners. But buyer beware—most claims for over-the-counter weight-loss pills are exaggerated. Prescription drugs, which usually suppress appetite or block fat absorption, tend to produce only modest weight loss, while weight-loss surgery is sometimes risky.

Researchers are testing the potential of several hormones to curb appetite. They're also looking at ways to subdue ghrelin, the so-called hunger hormone, though there is, as yet, no commercially available weight-loss miracle drug.

VIABILITY OF SELF-TREATMENT High for many people. Healthy eating, combined with physical activity and improved stress management, will help to reduce body fat over time in many cases.

abdominal fat—often have almost identical waist and hip measurements. "Pears," on the other hand, carry weight on their hips and thighs and have a distinct difference between waist and hip measurements, which is a much healthier shape.

If you think you may have a risky waistline, wrap a tape measure snugly around the narrowest part of your naked waist. Generally, men with waists over 100 cm (40 in.) and women with waists over 90 cm (35 in.) are at higher risk. We consider central fat so serious that we have listed waist measurement as one of the six most important numbers to keep track of for your health (for more details, see "6 numbers that can save your life" on page 216).

How can you get rid of this fat? Don't rest your hopes on surgeons simply being able to remove it in years to come.

There are other, much healthier ways to begin trimming this dangerous stuff. On the 30-Minutes-a-Day-Plan, you'll eat less saturated fat and virtually no trans fats. Diets high in saturated fats—such as butter, fatty meats, ice cream and whole milk— make you pile on the central fat, as do trans fats, the fats that give many packaged cookies and snack foods their crunch.

You'll increase your fibre intake—proven to whittle abdominal fat. You'll relax and enjoy life more, because stress and high levels of the stress hormone cortisol are closely linked with central fat storage. And, you will find yourself more physically active and feeling better as a result.

What's your risk? Excess body fat

Is your weight in the danger zone? One of the most popular measurements today is BMI (body mass index), which takes into account both your weight and height. Many websites and health reference books have tables to help you find your number but, if you have a calculator, here's how to determine your precise BMI. It's a useful number to know, as most doctors, other health experts and even insurance companies use it to gauge the healthiness of your weight.

■ Your weight in kilograms (1 kg = 2.2 lb).
■ Your height in metres and square it (m^2).
■ Divide your weight by your height in m^2.

FOR EXAMPLE, if you weigh 70 kg and are 1.71 m tall, your BMI is 24:
■ 70 kg
■ 1.71 x 1.71 = 2.92 m^2
■ 70 ÷ 2.92 = 24 (23.97 to be exact!)

For adults aged 20 and older, BMI rankings fall into the following categories.

BMI	RANKING
20 to 25	Normal
25 to 30	Overweight
30 plus	Obese
40 plus	Extremely obese

HEART ATTACK 5
Metabolic syndrome

You can't see it or feel it. Metabolic syndrome—a cluster of risk factors indicating out-of-kilter body chemistry—may affect thousands of Canadians.

Metabolic syndrome has been referred to as a "public health time bomb" because it is a condition that may not be recognized—until it's too late. Metabolic syndrome is not a newly discovered disease—rather it is a cluster of conditions, including obesity, insulin resistance or Type 2 diabetes, hypertension, high triglycerides and low HDL cholesterol levels that, in combination, raise the risk of cardiovascular disease and diabetes. It is also linked to infertility and cancers of the breast, prostate and colon.

The main reasons for its current prevalence are simple—pot-bellies and too little exercise. The numbers are going up in direct proportion to Canada's epidemics of obesity and inactivity. Interestingly, researchers have found that insulin resistance seems also to be linked with poor fetal nutrition, especially in combination with rapid growth in childhood.

Thousands of Canadians are believed to have metabolic syndrome, and some experts estimate that the figure could be much higher, saying that every overweight and obese adult (60 per cent) and child (26 per cent) may have it.

The condition is a basic malfunction of the systems that keep your cells fuelled with blood sugar. Suppose you've just eaten a bowl of oatmeal. Normally, levels of the hormone insulin rise slightly after you eat a meal, persuading cells to absorb the blood sugar provided by your breakfast. In metabolic syndrome, the cells cannot obey insulin's signal. It appears that central fat—the abdominal fat you've already read about—releases some surprising chemicals into the bloodstream, including immune system messengers called cytokines.

Cytokines block signals from insulin to cells to let sugar in, so then your cells have no fuel and blood sugar is building up in the bloodstream. Your pancreas responds by producing more insulin until, eventually, insulin overcomes cytokines and cells get the blood sugar they need.

People with metabolic syndrome can have insulin levels two or three times higher than normal—levels that can stay elevated for decades. All that excess insulin is a recipe for heart disease. It boosts triglycerides in your bloodstream, lowers levels of "good" HDLs and allows higher than normal amounts of fat to end up in your bloodstream after a meal—and stay there longer. Insulin also converts "bad" LDLs into smaller, denser particles that can easily enter artery walls forming the foundation for plaque.

Additionally, it raises concentrations of fibrinogen in the bloodstream, allowing blood to clot more easily. It is hardly surprising that metabolic syndrome is so dangerous for your heart.

There's no simple test for it, though your doctor may use a two-hour glucose-tolerance test as an indicator. The only signs are a few slightly worrying symptoms that, individually, may not even bother you or your doctor.

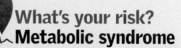

What's your risk?
Metabolic syndrome

If you have at least three of the following warning signs, you may already have metabolic syndrome; as a result, high insulin levels may threaten your heart more than you or your doctor realize.

■ Central obesity—having a waist measurement of more than 102 cm (40 in.) for men or 88 cm (35 in.) for women
■ Higher-than-normal blood pressure (140/90 or higher)
■ Higher-than-normal triglycerides (1.7 mmol/l or higher)
■ Below-normal HDL cholesterol: under 0.9 mmol/l for men or 1 mmol/l for women
■ Type 2 diabetes or impaired glucose tolerance, which produces a blood glucose level of 7.8 mmol/l or higher at 120 minutes on an oral glucose test

OTHER FACTORS THAT RAISE YOUR RISK
■ Overweight: a body mass index (BMI) higher than 30
■ A sedentary lifestyle
■ Protein in the urine (microalbuminuria) as a result of kidney disease—a classic marker for damage caused by diabetes
■ Being over the age of 40
■ South Asian, West African or Caribbean ethnicity
■ A family or personal history of Type 2 diabetes, high blood pressure or cardiovascular disease
■ Acanthosis nigricans: patches of thick, brownish, velvety skin at the neck, armpits, groin or, for women, under the breasts
■ Polycystic ovary syndrome, a female infertility problem
■ For women, a history of diabetes during pregnancy

5 METABOLIC SYNDROME
What you need to know

This little known but widespread condition is linked to various risk factors including sustained high levels of insulin in the bloodstream. People with this condition have a raised risk of heart disease and heart attack as well as stroke, Type 2 diabetes, cancer and infertility in women.

HOW IT HAPPENS This ultimate lifestyle disease is the direct result of too little exercise and too much central fat. The two conspire to make muscle and liver cells resist the messages from insulin, a hormone that persuades cells to absorb blood sugar. Your body responds by pumping out more insulin. In the end your cells do absorb blood sugar—but insulin levels may remain dangerously high for decades.

WHAT'S NEW

Metabolic syndrome suppresses "good" HDL cholesterol and raises triglycerides

•It keeps extra fat in circulation after a meal and turns ordinary "bad" LDLs into lethal small, dense LDLs. It also raises the risk of blood clots.

Abdominal fat releases a chemical that interferes with the absorption of blood sugar in your body. This causes a damaging buildup of insulin in the bloodstream.

Evidence of a link between stress and metabolic syndrome A European study in 2002 gave the first conclusive biological evidence of a link between stress and metabolic syndrome. Encouragingly, the study found that the harmful effects of stress were at least partly reversible through measures like losing weight or lowering blood pressure.

DETECTING IT There is a reasonably good standard medical test for measuring insulin levels as well as blood glucose levels during a glucose tolerance test. This is likely to be used increasingly as the importance of metabolic syndrome is realized. Even without a test, there is a likelihood that you have metabolic syndrome if you have at least three of the warning signs listed on the previous page.

STANDARD MEDICAL CARE Doctors advise patients to lose weight and increase levels of physical activity. They may also recommend drugs such as statins to deal with high levels of blood cholesterol and other drugs to manage high blood pressure.

VIABILITY OF SELF-TREATMENT Self-care is the best treatment for metabolic syndrome. Even a little exercise lowers insulin levels and boosts insulin sensitivity. Weight loss also makes your cells more sensitive to insulin, so your body doesn't have to pump out vast quantities anymore.

HEART ATTACK **6**
Oxidative stress

Scientists are now discovering a possible mechanism for the chemical changes that precede atherosclerosis, the underlying hidden pathway to heart disease.

This research involves linking various forms of environmental assault on the body—both factors you can control, such as your diet, any drugs you take or smoking, and those you can't—environmental pollution or radiation, for example. Interest is focused on oxidative stress—cell damage caused by roving molecular rogues called free radicals. Your body produces large amounts of potentially destructive free radical oxygen molecules through such round-the-clock processes as breathing and digestion.

At any given moment, your bloodstream is filled with free radicals, whose destructive power stems from each having a single, unpaired electron. The problem is that they require another electron to balance themselves out. So these unstable particles "steal" electrons from other molecules in the body. This damages genes, proteins and lipoproteins—and raises your risk of heart disease, cancer and other diseases.

Normally, your body's own defences—including antioxidants from the foods you eat—quickly mop up rampaging free radicals.

If, however, you smoke, are overweight, don't exercise enough, get too anxious, have metabolic syndrome or opt for fast food such as chips and cola too often, this cleanup doesn't happen. And it also doesn't happen if your cells are pumping out extra free radicals while neutralizing the effects of ultraviolet light, pollution, tobacco smoke, too much alcohol or even too many drugs—whether prescription, over-the-counter or illegal. When your body's natural antioxidant defences become overwhelmed, you've got oxidative stress.

Researchers now believe that oxidative stress is a key turning point for heart health; they think it's the condition that switches atherosclerosis from "off" to "on." The decisive moment seems to be when LDL particles are oxidized. It is then that their cargo of cholesterol becomes more deadly and more likely to end up clogging arterial walls.

To your immune system, oxidized LDLs, which researchers call LDL-ox, look like grotesque invaders. Immune cells known as macrophages trap them and in the process they become the fat-filled foam cells that form the foundation for plaque. LDL-ox also seems to make plaques grow larger and burst, leading to heart-stopping blood clots. High levels of LDL-ox can double your heart attack risk.

Japanese researchers have found that people with high levels of oxidized LDL are more likely to suffer from severe heart disease: patients who had a heart attack had levels of oxidized LDL four times higher than those in a healthy control group.

Many agree that the evidence suggests that oxidized cholesterol may accelerate the furring of the arteries that can lead to a heart attack. Oxidation may be prevented to a degree by eating a diet rich in fruit and vegetables as these are full of antioxidant nutrients.

HDLs shield LDLs from oxidative damage.
"Good" cholesterol doesn't simply ferry LDL cholesterol back to the liver for excretion. It also protects and repairs LDLs by safely siphoning off oxidized fats, which is another good reason to eat foods that increase HDL levels in your body.

If you have metabolic syndrome your LDLs are more vulnerable to oxidation. As a result, you're more susceptible to heart disease. Even if your LDL levels are in the normal range, having metabolic syndrome raises the odds of your LDLs being the small, dense type easily damaged by free radicals.

Sophisticated blood tests can tell you if you have these super-dangerous LDLs, but there's a simpler way to check. If blood test results show that you have low HDLs plus high triglycerides, you probably have small, dense LDLs as well. Even simpler: if you think you have metabolic syndrome, this is another reason to get more exercise, lose weight and eat fewer refined carbohydrates. Nurturing your natural antioxidant defence

What's your risk? Oxidative stress

The more of the following risks you have, the higher the odds that free radicals are damaging your cardiovascular system.

- Smoking
- Being overweight
- Metabolic syndrome or diabetes
- Too little exercise
- A diet that doesn't include at least five servings of fruit and vegetables daily
- Mental or emotional stress

system is one of the most enjoyable aspects of the 30-Minutes-a-Day Plan.

You'll get a rainbow of colourful, antioxidant-rich produce and juices at every meal, learn a time-saving secret that doubles the antioxidant value of vegetables, discover a crunchy salad topper that boosts your body's natural antioxidant system and become expert at shopping for the fruits and vegetables that are best for your heart.

You'll also learn the facts about the glut of antioxidant supplements on the market and why one of the longest recommended antioxidant capsules—vitamin E—may not help to cut LDL-oxidation and may even compromise heart health. And you'll discover soothing, 3-minute meditations and everyday yoga poses that let you build oxidation-busting calm into the busiest of days.

6 OXIDATIVE STRESS
What you need to know

Oxidative stress is the term for damage caused by destructive oxygen molecules called free radicals. Our bodies produce free radicals naturally when we breathe, digest food and neutralize alcoholic drinks and drugs of any type, and when cells convert fat and carbohydrates into energy. When free radicals attack LDL cholesterol, it converts into the form that promotes atherosclerosis.

HOW IT HAPPENS Free radicals are usually eradicated by the body's natural antioxidant system. If that protective system is overwhelmed, free radicals begin to damage cells and other molecules, leading to atherosclerosis, cancer, mental decline and other health problems. Your natural antioxidants are overwhelmed by a lack of fruit and vegetables, an excess of stress and too little exercise.

WHAT'S NEW

• **Free radicals attack LDL cholesterol**
This converts LDLs into a form that triggers or worsens atherosclerosis. The new form can also contribute to plaque bursting; it is this burst plaque that can cause blood clots that block blood flow to the brain or heart.

Excessive amounts of free radicals in your body damage genes, proteins and other body cells by stealing electrons. This can lead to a host of heart-related problems.

The mind-body connection Mental and emotional stress can boost oxidative stress; relaxation can lower it.

DETECTING IT There is no test available to determine the level of oxidative stress going on in your circulatory system, but lifestyle choices pretty much tell the story. Being overweight, having a diet low in fruit and vegetables, smoking and a lack of exercise all raise your risk of oxidative stress.

STANDARD MEDICAL CARE Each year Canadians spend millions of dollars on over-the-counter vitamin and mineral supplements—including popular antioxidants such as vitamins A, C, E and beta carotene, and the mineral selenium. However, research has yet to prove conclusively that they work.

VIABILITY OF SELF-TREATMENT High for most people. Go for natural antioxidants: exercise, stress reduction, colourful fruits and vegetables. Easy food switches that will boost your daily antioxidant intake include drinking apple or grape juice instead of soft drinks, adding broccoli to your salad—and even eating canned vegetables: despite the canning process, they generally retain many of the antioxidants that can be lost from fresh vegetables during storage. Be vigilant, though—vegetables are often canned in salt water, so check the label for sodium.

WHAT WE KNOW TODAY ABOUT YOUR HEART

HEART ATTACK 7
Chronic inflammation

If you cut your thumb while slicing bread, slam the car door on your finger or scald the roof of your mouth on hot coffee, your body will respond.

The response to an injury is warmth, redness and tenderness—in other words, inflammation. This is not a sign of weakness: inflammation is a clever defence mounted by your immune system to repair body damage fast and repel intruders—germs, dirt or toxins—before they pose a threat.

Any "attack" on your body—from cuts and bruises to bacterial or viral infections—triggers this response, which has evolved over millions of years. Your body's defences are already at work when you become aware of signs of inflammation: a hot, red, tender area. What you can't see is going on inside; an army of infection fighters called macrophages, T cells and natural killer cells are engulfing and destroying germs and matter that shouldn't be there, while squadrons of molecular "traffic police" direct the immune system's work.

Inflammation has always been a part of the human healing process but this brilliant system may be doing its job too well for 21st-century humans. The problem isn't the short bouts of inflammation that fight infection or heal a shaving nick in a day or two. The modern threat comes from the sort of inflammation that can't switch itself off. Chronic inflammation is an immune response to being overweight, aging, physical inactivity, less-than-meticulous hygiene, low-grade infection and stress—which attacks the very cells it intends to rescue. As a result, your cells are constantly bombarded by immune system chemicals.

Recent research suggests that these chemicals help to create plaque, the fatty gruel that grows inside artery walls. The chemicals also prompt plaque to rupture, spewing gunk into the bloodstream and causing the formation of blood clots that will block the heart's arteries, thus causing the death of that part of the heart's muscle.

Researchers have long known that inflammation plays a key role in a variety of conditions such as asthma, rheumatoid arthritis, multiple sclerosis and inflammatory bowel diseases such as Crohn's disease. Studies are currently under way around the world to determine the precise process that triggers the body's inflammatory response, and how the body responds to the damage that follows. Recent studies by Harvard Medical School found that one marker of inflammation, an immune system molecule known as C-reactive protein (CRP), is a strong predictor of heart disease. The discovery may help to identify those who are at risk of heart attack despite having apparently healthy cholesterol levels.

The inflammation triggers

How can your body's defence system turn on you in this way? Just as a smoke alarm is easily set off by smoke from frying onions or steam from the shower, inflammation is triggered by forces such as smoking, central fat, a glut of calories, the wrong foods, lack of exercise and perhaps even the daily stress of getting to and from work.

Some medical experts suspect that infection with agents such as *Chlamydia pneumoniae* and *Helicobacter pylori*—might contribute to or even start the inflammatory process. Other possible culprits include smoking, uncontrolled diabetes, high blood pressure and high cholesterol levels. An inflammatory response may also be switched on by seemingly minor infections, such as gum disease or cystitis. Also, because we live longer than ever, our bodies' tissues are simply exposed to more damage. Here is a rundown of chronic inflammation's major modern triggers.

■ **Fast food** A high-fat, calorie-rich meal has a damaging inflammatory effect on vascular function. This is because the level of harmful fats circulating in the bloodstream is much higher than normal for at least 3 hours after eating. The condition is called postprandial hyperlipidemia. So a fast-food diet could keep inflammation turned up indefinitely.

■ **Abdominal or central fat** Fat cells are described by some researchers as "hormone pumps." Among the chemicals they dump into your bloodstream are cytokines, which

What's your risk? Chronic inflammation

C-reactive protein (CRP) is an immune system chemical manufactured by the liver in response to inflammation anywhere in the body. Testing for CRP may help to predict a healthy person's risk of heart attack or other heart conditions. The blood test is designed for accuracy in measuring low levels of CRP.

As yet, there is no agreement about exactly when the test should be used, or who should have it. The presence of other inflammatory conditions will often raise CRP levels. CRP may be requested as one of several tests for a cardiovascular (heart and blood vessel) risk profile, often along with lipid (fat) tests, such as those for cholesterol and triglycerides. Some experts say that the best way to predict risk is to combine a good marker for inflammation, such as CRP, along with a person's LDL cholesterol levels. The theory is that, while LDLs say how much plaque is clogging your arteries, your CRP may tell you how likely that plaque is to burst, causing a dangerous blood clot.

LEVEL (mg/l)	RISK
under 1	low
1–3	average
above 3	high

are inflammatory proteins that help to direct the inflammation process.

■ **Oxidized LDLs** When "bad" LDL cholesterol particles meet the harmful active molecules known as free radicals (caused by factors such as smoking) in the bloodstream, a chemical reaction happens so that LDLs

7 CHRONIC INFLAMMATION
What you need to know

Chronic inflammation occurs when the immune system's powerful defences are switched on—and stay on. Doctors have discovered many things that can cause chronic inflammation in the arteries: everyday infections, such as gum disease or the stomach ulcer bacterium *H. pylori*; substances released by excess stomach fat; and simple aging.

HOW IT HAPPENS Chronic inflammation is bad for the heart because it contributes to plaque buildup in the arteries. This is how it happens. When inflammatory chemicals discover LDL particles in artery walls, they send macrophages to eradicate the unwelcome cholesterol. The by-products of this attack are foam cells (oxidized LDL particles) that form the basis of plaque. As plaque grows, it develops a hard, fibrous cap, but inflammatory compounds can weaken this protective lid, making it susceptible to rupturing and releasing plaque into the bloodstream. Other inflammatory compounds encourage blood to clot and, if constant, low-grade inflammation results in a steady supply of these compounds into your bloodstream, which can also lead to a heart attack.

When your immune system is always in "attack" mode, one of its targets is cholesterol in artery walls. One outcome is larger, more unstable plaque deposits.

WHAT'S NEW Predictive qualities The link between internal inflammation and heart disease has emerged only recently. Now we know that chronic inflammation may help doctors to predict which patients with near-normal cholesterol levels could go on to have heart attacks.

DETECTING IT Doctors are using a blood test for an inflammatory marker called C-reactive protein (CRP); This high sensitivity test is rapidly becoming routine in cardiovascular care.

STANDARD MEDICAL CARE So far, there are no drugs for chronic inflammation, although statins, beta-blockers and low-dose ASA may act as anti-inflammatories. Doctors are also exploring whether long-term, low-dose antibiotics are appropriate for people with low-grade, persistent infections.

VIABILITY OF SELF-TREATMENT High for most people—but only if you take care of your whole body. Regular brushing and flossing, for example, is important to eradicate gum infections. Taking care of your digestion is important to minimize the bacteria that cause ulcers. Also, try and focus on losing stomach fat and eat more inflammation-cooling omega-3 fatty acids (found in cold-water fish such as salmon and in nuts, flaxseed oil and fish-oil supplements).

are more easily sucked in to artery walls. There, they set off an inflammatory response that helps to produce plaque, which is loaded with cholesterol plus immune system cells and other substances. Inflammation then destabilizes the fibrous covering that normally keeps plaque out of the bloodstream. These "hot plaques" are the ones most likely to burst and flood the bloodstream with substances that prompt fast blood clotting and ultimately lead to heart attacks or strokes.

■ Low-grade, chronic infections

Bronchitis, herpes simplex, gum disease, cystitis, a bacterium called *Chlamydia pneumoniae* and another called *Helicobacter pylori* (the bug responsible for most stomach ulcers) provoke inflammation and send inflammatory chemicals into the bloodstream. While we may not realize it, some of us live with low-grade, minor infections all the time but because they cause few symptoms, they go unrecognized, and contribute to an inflammatory response.

■ Stress and anxiety Adrenalin, cortisol and other stress hormones may turn on inflammation. Chronic stress may impair the body's ability to shut down inflammation.

■ Choosing the sofa instead of a walk People who exercise regularly have lower blood concentrations of CRP.

■ Not eating healthy fats "Good" fats— in nuts, flaxseed oil, oily fish such as salmon and fish oil capsules—contain omega-3 fatty acids, the building blocks for inflammation-fighting eicosanoids. Most Canadians need to eat more dietary omega-3s.

■ Too many trans fats These hydrogenated, industrialized fats, routinely baked into cookies, pies and pastries, interfere with the body's ability to produce and use healthy fats.

■ Skimping on fruit and vegetables Do this and you deprive your body of anti-oxidants. Antioxidants, such as the vitamin C and carotenoids in fresh fruit and vegetables, can neutralize the harmful inflammatory effects of unstable free radicals.

People who exercise regularly have lower blood concentrations of CRP.

EMERGING MARKERS
Beyond the big seven

Molecular biologists and cardiology researchers are always looking for new markers for heart disease. Below are four that have been shown to be among the most potentially significant.

1 Homocysteine

At higher-than-normal levels, this amino acid—created when the body breaks down proteins in food, especially animal proteins—is related to a doubled risk of coronary heart disease. A Norwegian study of 587 people with heart disease found that mortality risk was eight times higher in those with high homocysteine levels than those with low levels. A British study found that people who were genetically prone to high homocysteine levels had a higher risk of stroke.

The good news is that research suggests the risk can be reversed by taking folic acid. But large trials are still needed to see whether such treatment would be safe in the long term. And the question remains: does a high level of homocysteine cause or contribute to heart disease, or does it simply indicate some other condition? Will lowering levels cut risk? As homocysteine may damage artery linings and promote blood clotting, many specialists are searching for evidence that raised levels of homocysteine in the blood are associated with an increased risk of cardiovascular disease.

A variety of conditions can lead to raised homocysteine levels including folic acid deficiency—the body uses folic acid and vitamins B_6 and B_{12} to break down homocysteine for use as energy. But you can supply your body with the vitamin by eating a diet rich in vegetables, including asparagus, dried beans and peas, and leaf vegetables (eaten fresh or just lightly cooked to preserve their folic acid), such as spinach, and fresh fruit and orange juice.

Are you at risk? Many experts believe that elevated levels of homocysteine are further evidence of the need to treat raised cholesterol levels and other risk factors.

2 Apo(a) and (b)

Apolipoproteins, known as apo(a) and (b), play an important role in the production and transport of cholesterol around the body. Each type bonds with cholesterol in the blood—apo(a) with "good" HDL molecules and apo(b) with "bad" LDLs. You want more (a)s and fewer (b)s: high apo(b) levels are associated with increased heart disease risk.

Are you at risk? Again, there's no widely used test for this emerging risk factor, but doctors are beginning to suspect that these fat-plus-protein particles may assist in predicting the risk of heart disease, particularly in women and in people with high triglycerides.

The good news is that research suggests that high homocysteine levels may be reversed by taking folic acid—supplied by fruits, vegetables and orange juice.

3 Lp(a)

A renegade variation of LDL cholesterol, lp(a)—or lipoprotein(a)—is a combination of apo(a) and LDL. The particles have cholesterol cores and are wrapped in a sticky protein coating that seems to promote blood clotting. Lp(a) also binds LDLs more easily to artery walls, prompting the formation of plaque. High lp(a) is an important risk factor for early atherosclerosis—over 10 years, it increases your heart risk by 70 per cent, and it can exist in people with otherwise normal cholesterol levels. There is no specific treatment, for reducing lp(a), but knowing that you have it might encourage you to take lifestyle measures to protect your heart.

Are you at risk? Lp(a) seems to be genetic (it appears to be more common among people of Afro-Caribbean descent). In women, higher levels may be linked to higher body weight.

4 Nitric oxide (NO)

This tiny molecule is a big player in heart health: it keeps blood vessels relaxed, which maintains healthy blood pressure, and discourages atherosclerosis by making artery walls more like Teflon so that white blood cells and clot-producing platelets can't stick. Nitric oxide also suppresses overgrowth of muscle cells in artery walls—which keeps blood vessels from thickening—and it helps cut production of free radicals.

It is possible that eating foods rich in arginine (nitric oxide's building block), such as beans, fish, nuts and soya, could boost its production, as will cutting back on saturated fats and exercising—both integral to the plan in this book.

Are you at risk? Your artery linings produce their own supply of nitric oxide. If the lining is not healthy, production drops. At present, there is no widely available test for nitric oxide levels, but you may well be producing less than you should if you are overweight, inactive, a smoker, or if you have high cholesterol levels.

The goal of a healthy heart is best achieved one step at a time. This will make healthy living easy, automatic—and, above all, enjoyable.

Welcome to the
30-Minutes-a-Day Plan

We've organized our advice into six sections. Here's what to expect in each.

What you'll find ahead

Heart-healthy eating

Here we present the 30-Minutes-a-Day Eating Plan—a guide to eating more of the foods that are most beneficial to the health of your heart. It's built around an indisputable fact: foods in their natural state are far healthier than foods that have been processed. Sample menus, shopping and cooking tips, portion guidelines—and even how to order in a restaurant—will make heart-healthy eating as easy and delicious as possible.

Getting active

Sedentary living is known to be dangerous, yet it's very easy to cure. We provide some of the simplest and most enjoyable ways to get moving. There are walking suggestions—ways to sneak in extra steps throughout your day—plus easy stretching and strengthening routines and moves that feel great.

Nurturing a happy heart

You'd be surprised at the amount of scientific evidence there is that links happiness to heart health. We can't make you happy, but we do provide helpful, wise advice for adjusting your attitude and responses to stress in ways that help, not hurt, your heart.

Purging the poisons

Not so long ago, the notion that germs, chemicals and common pollutants could harm the heart was just that—a notion. Today, we know that living in a polluted world does affect heart health. Here, we provide the evidence and show you the best ways to minimize the harmful effects of everyday toxins.

Keeping track

If you have a financial advisor, you probably receive quarterly updates and you know exactly what numbers to watch in order to understand your financial health. The same service is not available for your heart health. In fact, most people don't even know what their most crucial health measurements are. We tell you which numbers you need to monitor for a good indication of your health as well as what you should look at every day.

Resources

From there, we give even more help including extra exercises, recipes, answers to common heart health questions, daily tracking pages and a list of useful resources. Throughout the book are references to the numerous scientific studies that support our advice.

The 30-Minutes-a-Day Plan is a great place to start. If you follow the advice in this book, you will not only give your heart the best protection you can, but you will do so with a minimal sacrifice of time. And the extra benefits will be overwhelming: lower weight, more energy, stronger immunity to infection and a far more positive outlook on life. So get ready and read on.

There are literally hundreds of tiny steps you can take every day that can add millions of beats to your heart's life.

Getting started

The fact that you are reading this book shows you care enough about your heart to start making healthy changes for its benefit. As you'll see in the pages that follow, there are literally hundreds of tiny steps you can take every day that can add millions of beats to your heart's life. That's good news, but for people who have given their health no more than a fleeting thought in recent years, it can also be a little overwhelming to tackle eating, exercise and lifestyle in one fell swoop.

If you are unfit or exercise very little at the moment, or if you have existing health problems or are overweight, you should see your doctor before embarking on the program (see "Involving your doctor" on page 63 and "Keeping track" on page 214 for more on working with your doctor).

Next, answer the quiz overleaf. See where you need the most help and start there. Once you feel confident in that area, continue with the other checkpoints until you've worked through all four.

What if I need help everywhere?

So you've answered the questions and discovered that all your lifestyle habits need improving. Don't despair; that is what this book is for. If eating, exercise and lifestyle all came up as high-priority areas, simply go through the book in the order in which it's written, mastering one section before moving on to the next.

Or you can turn to the section that you feel is most easily tackled first, then work your way through in order of interest. Either way, the total time commitment is low and the rewards are high. It's time you got started.

How's your diet?

1 My favourite breakfast is:
a A bowl of oatmeal or raisin bran.
b Two bacon and egg sandwiches.
c A chicken wrap; I don't eat until lunchtime.

2 Yesterday I ate these fruits and vegetables:
a A wide range of colours: green (broccoli, green salad), orange (cantaloupe, carrots), red (peppers, tomatoes), purple (blackcurrants, grapes).
b A small variety: peas, banana, apple.
c Almost none: the dressing in my burger and french fries.

3 When eating at a restaurant:
a I usually make some special requests, such as substituting baked dishes for fried ones or leaving out the creamy sauces.
b I avoid the obvious bad choices like carbonara or creamy blue cheese sauces, and try to choose wisely, but I don't really know the difference between all the options.
c I'm there to indulge myself. I'll have the chef's special.

4 For nutritional insurance:
a I take a multivitamin whenever I'm rushing or skipping meals.
b I occasionally take a multivitamin.
c I haven't taken a vitamin since childhood.

5 To watch how much I eat:
a I serve small portions at home and eat little more than half of what I'm given when eating out.
b I avoid taking second helpings but still probably eat more than I should.
c I have a hard time resisting seconds, and I usually eat whatever I'm served.

If you circled mostly a's
Your heart jumps for joy whenever you sit down to eat, knowing you always look out for its best interest by eating plenty of fresh produce, reasonable portions and limited amounts of dangerous fat. Adjusting your eating habits is certainly not the highest item on your must-do list, but do flick through "Heart-healthy eating" (page 66) for even more nutritional wisdom.

If you circled mostly b's
Although your heart is often in the right place, the best dietary choices often elude you. Because you are generally motivated to eat well, all you need is a little more know-how to be a "heart-smart" eater. Put "Heart-healthy eating" medium to high on your priority list.

If you circled mostly c's
Put "Heart-healthy eating" high on your priority list; your current eating habits are damaging to your heart. By learning to make little changes, possibly taking a multivitamin, cutting portion sizes, choosing healthier main courses—and even sprinkling cinnamon on your toast—you and your heart can live a longer, healthier life.

CHECKPOINT 2
How active are you?

1 My daily walking habits are:

a I walk to the shower, to the car and to the café near work. I'm too busy for much else.

b I try to get up and move two or three times a day and usually take a nice walk at some point each day.

c I usually try to walk for a few minutes in my lunch hour.

2 My favourite recreational pastimes are:

a Watching my favourite TV programs, reading, renting DVDs and going out to restaurants.

b Walking, cycling and tennis; I like to be outdoors.

c A good game of golf, but we usually take a golf cart.

3 If someone suggested that I lift weights, I'd:

a Laugh; dumbbells are not for me.

b Say that I already do, two or three days a week.

c Be interested. I know lifting weights is important; I just don't know how.

4 When I reach down to touch my toes, I can:

a Barely see my toes, let alone reach them.

b At least reach my shoelaces; on a good day, I can touch the floor.

c Reach my ankles, but I'm definitely not as supple as I used to be.

5 My general attitude about exercise is:

a Ugh; it reminds me of gym class.

b It's the best part of my day.

c I know I should do it, but it's the first thing to go when my day gets busy.

If you circled mostly a's

Dust off your walking shoes, sack your outdated images of exercise, and turn to "Getting active" (page 136). Inactivity is bad for your heart, very bad. The good news is that exercise doesn't have to be boring or time-consuming. Just a few minutes of easy activity a day can dramatically reduce your heart disease risk. Put it high on your priority list.

If you circled mostly b's

Your get-up-and-go is great for your heart. By being active every day, whether by walking, swimming or lifting weights, you're keeping your arteries supple and clear. Although you've already overcome "sitting disease," read chapter 4 when you've finished the others to learn more tips for fitting in the activities you love as well as adding new exercises to your repertoire.

If you circled mostly c's

Try as you might, our sedentary society usually gets the better of you, sidelining your best-laid exercise plans. As you'll soon learn, a little bit of exercise goes a long way toward protecting your heart, especially if you can sneak in small increments throughout the day. Put "Getting active" medium to high on your priority list.

WELCOME TO THE 30-MINUTES-A-DAY PLAN

CHECKPOINT 3
How happy are you?

1 When I go to bed at night:

a I'm usually too wound up to fall asleep quickly. I'm a little groggy in the morning.

b I sleep like a baby and usually wake up before the alarm goes off.

c I'm a night owl. I usually hit the snooze button and I like to sleep in on weekends.

2 I would describe my typical working day as:

a Somewhat stressful. There's a lot of pressure at work and it's hard to relax.

b Busy but manageable. I usually set aside a little time for myself each day.

c Awful. I dread Mondays.

3 When someone cuts me off in traffic, I:

a Swear under my breath and seethe for a minute or two.

b Shrug it off.

c Get furious and sometimes shake my fist, or worse.

4 I would describe my spiritual or community involvement as:

a Fairly active. I don't go to religious services very often but I make time for meditation.

b Very active. I'm involved in my local community and/or I go to church.

c Non-existent. I don't find time to think about it.

5 During a typical week, my alcohol consumption is:

a A few drinks in the week, usually with dinner, but I sometimes overdo it on weekends.

b Usually just a glass of wine with dinner, but sometimes I have two.

c Not daily, but when I do drink, I don't hold back.

If you circled mostly a's

Life isn't bad, but it could be better. You fall into that frazzled no-man's-land of mortgages, loan repayments, job demands and family responsibilities that can suck the fun out of life if you're not careful. Turn to "Nurturing a happy heart" (page 174) early on and learn some quick, easy tricks for relieving your stress and replacing it with calm . . . or even joy.

If you circled mostly b's

You have a smile in your heart most of the time. You've learned how to find calm in chaos and enjoy your life no matter how hectic it gets. By doing so, you'll lower your odds of developing heart disease in the long run. For even more tips on getting the most joy out of life, read the section on "Nurturing a happy heart."

If you circled mostly c's

Like Atlas, you carry the weight of the world on your shoulders—and it's straining your heart. Symptoms of general unhappiness, such as high stress, anger, poor sleep and alcohol misuse, elevate your risk of high blood pressure, obesity and other heart-damaging conditions. Put "Nurturing a happy heart" high on your priority list.

CHECKPOINT 4
How clean is your lifestyle?

1 My dentist would describe my oral hygiene as:

a Awful. It's been so long, he probably doesn't remember my name.

b Good—I even use dental floss regularly.

c Pretty good. I brush regularly but I don't floss as often as I should.

2 During the cold and flu season:

a I'm bound to get at least one nasty cold.

b I have a flu shot and wash my hands frequently.

c I try to avoid ill people, but I could do better.

3 I would describe the area where I live as:

a Busy, with heavy car and truck traffic.

b Rural; my nearest neighbours make milk.

c Just off the beaten track but not far from a large urban centre.

4 When it comes to avoiding environmental pollutants I:

a Don't worry about it; pollution is unavoidable.

b Keep up with reports on high-risk foods and drink filtered water.

c Keep a clean house and kitchen but don't take extra precautionary measures.

5 I would describe my daily alcohol consumption as:

a I drink daily—I just can't seem to get through the day without them.

b I limit my consumption to red wine and I have no more than two glasses per day.

c I am a social drinker, however I sometimes over-consume on the weekends.

If you circled mostly a's

It's time to clean house. You may feel that pollution and germs are inevitable, but with a few clever steps, the worst offenders are avoidable. Environmental assaults from tobacco smoke, viruses, air and water pollution elevate your risk of heart attack—as does excessive alcohol consumption. Put "Purging the poisons" (page 196) at the top of your priority list. And if you are concerned about the amount you drink each day, please seek professional help.

If you circled mostly b's

If your heart were a linoleum floor, it would sparkle. By not smoking, protecting yourself during the cold and flu season and avoiding the worst environmental offenders, you help your arteries to run clean. Also the health benefits of moderate red wine consumption are legendary. For even more clean-living tips, read the section on "Purging the poisons."

If you circled mostly c's

Your approach to monitoring your alcohol consumption and to eliminating everyday toxins is a little like surface cleaning—doesn't quite get the job done. Take extra preventive steps—such as exercising and having a yearly flu shot—to help protect you and greatly reduce your heart disease risk. Put "Purging the poisons" medium to high on your priority list.

WELCOME TO THE 30-MINUTES-A-DAY PLAN

Are you still smoking?

1 When I wake up in the morning:

a Brushing my teeth is the first task of the day.

b I have a cigarette within 5 to 10 minutes.

c I immediately reach for a cigarette and my lighter.

2 At work:

a I enjoy a clean, smoke-free environment.

b I'm often surrounded by the smoke of others.

c I need to leave my desk frequently for a smoke and the relief it provides.

3 In our family:

a No one smokes in the house or the car.

b My children keep asking me to smoke outside.

c There's almost always a cigarette being smoked.

4 When asked about smoking:

a I recognize the importance of quitting and have a plan to do so in the next two weeks.

b I know, I know, I should quit and I will when the price goes up again.

c It's the only stress-reliever I have and I don't really believe it's harmful.

5 I've been thinking about:

a Using a nicotine patch and gum.

b Asking my doctor about help in quitting when I see her in a few months' time.

c How irritable and headachy I feel when without a cigarette for more than an hour.

If you circled mostly a's

Congratulations! You realize the importance of quitting and are taking steps to do so. You've ensured your family lives in a smoke-free environment. Turn to "Purging the poisons" (page 196) for some concrete advice as to how you can dramatically increase your chances of cessation success.

If you circled mostly b's

You're aware of the need to quit smoking and your friends and family are constantly imploring you to do so. It might be helpful to restrict your smoking to certain places and make your home and car smoke-free. And read the section on "Purging the poisons" (page 196) for additional practical advice.

If you circled mostly c's

Like most of today's smokers you are addicted to nicotine and know (better than many) how difficult quitting can be. You'll find the suggestions in "Purging the poisons" (page 196) particularly helpful. Now, more than ever before, there are approaches that can significantly increase your chance of quitting success.

Staying with it

Reaching your goals is exciting. After a few weeks on the 30-Minutes-a-Day Plan, you'll start seeing real results. You'll finish the day feeling as fresh as when you started. Your blood pressure will inch down. Those pants you'd hidden at the back of the closet will fit you. Friends may comment on your healthy glow.

Sooner or later, though, the new you will start being the status quo. When the first thrill fades and the compliments become fewer, then the real work begins. Studies show that half of all people who embark on healthy lifestyle changes start drifting back to their old ways within six months. But if you get past that point, you'll have a habit for life. Below are 22 ways to stay motivated.

1 Wear your heart on your sleeve . . . or on your finger

Literally. Wear a heart-shaped ring or find some other visual trigger to remind you of why you're doing what you're doing. The reason is that motivation is never constant. It comes and goes. If you were sitting in the doctor's office and he was giving you frightening news about your blood pressure, you'd feel very motivated to change. But as days passed, the memory of that fear, and thus the motivation, would fade. So wear a pendant, or pin up a note such as "I want to see my granddaughter graduate from medical school," to keep motivating factors in focus.

2 Create a fan club

When friends and family are behind you, you succeed. One study found that people are more likely to stick to their healthy lifestyle changes if their friends and families support and encourage them. Tell your partner and children that these changes are not easy for you and that you'd love their encouragement. Better still, ask them to join you in some of your healthy new habits.

Wear your heart on your sleeve . . . or on your finger.

3 Create positive motivators

Fear of a heart attack can certainly fuel motivation, but don't focus too much on the negative—worrying can have the opposite effect. A better strategy is to adapt your negative inspirations to sound more positive—for example, "I'm making healthy packed lunches and walking after work to build and maintain a strong heart."

4 Ask for help

Sometimes, the way you handle small obstacles can make the difference between lasting the course and veering off it. If you always make lunch for your partner and he likes fattening foods you can't resist, ask him to make it himself or, better still, convert him. If piles of dishes prevent you from taking your evening walk, delegate this chore to your children. There's always a way around the little things, so don't let them hinder you.

5 Enlist a partner

Remember how, when you were a child, you'd phone all your friends until you found someone to come out and play? Then you'd both run wild until dinnertime. We're not so different as adults. Company makes exercise and eating properly more fun. It also gives you someone to answer to. If you're married, the best 30-Minutes-a-Day Plan partner is probably your spouse. Research has shown that people who take up programs with their spouses are far more likely to be regularly active and far less likely to give up than those who try to get moving alone.

6 Track your progress

We've provided a daily track record on page 233. Please use it. Each time you record your progress, you reinforce your commitment to beneficial change. It's also very encouraging to see your efforts pay off as your weight falls and your blood pressure drops. Knowing that you'll have to write a "zero" under "Movement time" or "Fresh produce consumed" will also make you more likely to fit in some healthy behaviour for the day than if you weren't keeping track at all.

7 Find healthy friends

You don't have to give up friends who smoke or drink to excess, but while you're trying to cement new heart-healthy habits, it's a good idea to limit contact with these people during this vulnerable period. For instance, sitting in a smoky bar, drinking beer and watching the game isn't going to help you to give up smoking. So, for the moment, try to spend more time with people who are already living successfully with the sorts of lifestyle changes you are trying to make.

8 Encourage yourself

Studies show that the more negative your attitude, the worse you'll perform at any given task. If you tell yourself you'll never change, you're throwing in the towel before you've even begun. Think of all the difficult things you've done in your life and say: "If I could do that, I can do this." Remind yourself daily. You are making progress. You ARE a success.

9 Set instantly gratifying goals

Losing 18 kg (40 lb) and controlling your blood pressure are good goals, but they won't happen overnight—and motivation can wear thin along the way. Keep those big goals in mind, but set smaller, easily achievable ones as well. Small objectives throughout the day, such as, "I'm going to have two glasses of

> Sometimes, the way you handle small obstacles can make the difference between lasting the course and veering off it.

water before noon," are doable on even the toughest day and will keep you in a "can do" frame of mind.

10 Think, "I'll just . . ."

When your motivation is rock bottom, lifting weights or preparing a healthy snack can seem like insurmountable tasks. During those low points, fall back on "I'll just" thinking. That is, "I'll just do my arm curls" or "I'll just get the blackberries out of the freezer." Once you take a step in the right direction, your momentum will pick up and pull your motivation along with it.

11 Set up a reward system

Forward-thinking companies reward their employees with incentives for heart-healthy behaviours such as exercising. Do the same for yourself. Think of some goodies you'd like—start small and work your way up to bigger rewards (see sample reward list in the box at right). Have fun with your rewards, and remember, they don't have to cost a thing. You could treat yourself to a Saturday afternoon of window-shopping downtown.

12 Give yourself credit

We have a tendency to dismiss the little things we do well, but all those little things, from choosing a whole-grain breakfast cereal to walking your dog after work, are at the heart of the plan. They add up to life-extending rewards—so praise yourself every time you make a heart-healthy choice.

13 Have a contingency plan

Life is long. You're human. Inevitably, you'll hit a patch where you fall off the plan. If you anticipate the bad spells, they won't destroy your motivation to get back on track. Decide now that when you see your waistline expanding or your blood pressure starting to rise, you'll get back on track by taking three 10-minute walks a day or eating fruit with every meal. It'll help you to get back on the program before you drift too far.

14 Find role models

Everyone knows someone who dropped four dress sizes or stopped smoking and took up tennis after a heart scare. See these people as role models: if they can do it, so can you. If you need inspiration, talk to them; most people are happy to share their stories.

15 Stop, think, act

Before you light that cigarette or eat that second slice of chocolate cake, stop and force yourself to think about why you're doing something you know is bad for your heart.

ACHIEVEMENT	REWARD
Exercise daily for one month	*Lord of the Rings* DVD box set
Lose 5 kg (10 lb)	New shoes
Cholesterol 5.0 or lower	A week by the lake
Clean bill of health	New golf bag

Think what else you could do, drink or eat that might make you feel almost as good, then do that. Before you know it, thinking before you act will become second nature—and so will making healthier choices.

16 Add variety

There are literally hundreds of tips in this book. When you find yourself falling into a rut (nothing kills motivation like boredom), look for something you haven't tried, such as a delicious-looking recipe or a fun exercise.

17 Donate your efforts

If you can't stay motivated to exercise for your own good, do it for someone else. Find a charity group that organizes walks to raise money to support it. These not only give you a reason to keep moving, they give you the satisfaction of working hard to help others.

18 List the pros and cons

If you ever seriously consider giving up, take a couple of minutes, draw a line down the middle of a sheet of paper and list the pros and cons of your decision. This will help to remind you why you started in the first place and the consequences of turning back.

19 Find emotional outlets

Let's be honest: if what we eat and how we behave were nothing more than practical matters of fuelling our bodies and taking care of ourselves, far fewer people would have weight problems or heart disease. We don't plow through a bag of chips or drink one too many glasses of wine because we need the potatoes or grape products. We do it because we're bored, frustrated, anxious or angry. Since those emotions aren't going to go away, you need to find other outlets for those feelings, such as exercise, keeping a diary or pursuing a hobby, or you need to confront them directly rather than masking the problem with bad habits.

20 Take a break

Even if you love your job, you still need a break from its rigours now and then. The same is true of healthy lifestyle changes. Every now and then, spend a long weekend indulging yourself: relax and eat and drink what you want to. If you're true to the 30-Minutes-a-Day Plan most of the time, brief respites won't hurt your results.

21 Become an expert

If you're showing real progress, the chances are you have found one or more aspects of healthy living that you really enjoy. It could be cooking with fresh food, walking or doing yoga. Explore that interest more deeply, perhaps go to classes. There's no reason why you can't become a chef, a master of meditation—or even a marathon runner—once you set your mind to it.

22 Put your calendar to work

Too many of us make a bad job of long-term planning, particularly when it comes to the fun things in life. So change that. Make plans for fun events months ahead. Plan a family trip to the zoo in two months, a weekend by the lake in four months or Christmas in the Caribbean next winter. Then make the bookings, buy the tickets and mark the dates on the calendar. This type of long-term planning gives you positive things to look forward to, as well as the motivation to get leaner and healthier for the activities ahead.

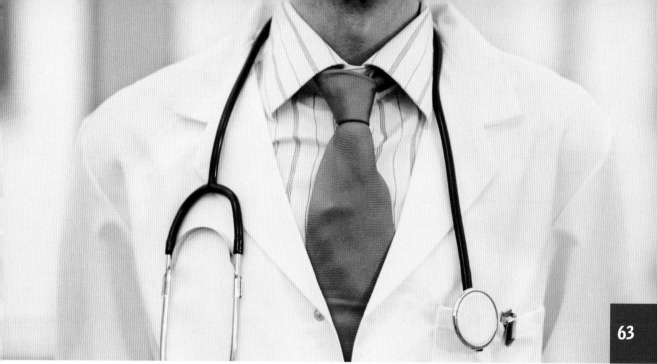

Involving your doctor

You and your doctor are a team working in your heart's best interest.

Your doctor is a key player in your health life. He or she has the unique expertise to perform critical assessments, diagnose problems and provide medicine and advice as needed to keep you well.

Your doctor is also very, very busy. Surveys show that the average family doctor sees three to five patients an hour, spending about 10 minutes—slightly less time than it takes to bake a frozen pizza—with each one. That's not to say that your doctor doesn't want to spend more time with you. It's just that, no matter how competent your doctor is, there are always going to be other patients waiting for the next appointment. There will always be emergencies to fit in.

This is why you can't expect your doctor to be completely accountable for your care.

That's not a doctor's job. A doctor must do the same as any other qualified expert, be it a car mechanic, accountant or lawyer—to occasionally assess your condition, provide remedies when the situation calls for them and detect trouble before it becomes serious. The rest of the time—in fact, most of the time—it's your job to take responsibility for your health. That's where this book comes in.

You're in charge

In these pages, you'll find "take charge" advice that puts you firmly in control of your heart's health. What's more, you'll find advice that few doctors have the time to give you, even if they were to spend twice or even three times the usual available time with you.

Advice on calming stress, finding joy and avoiding toxins—strategies that can slash your risk of heart attack. Advice on which fruits and vegetables are best for cleaning your arteries. How using some spices can lower blood fats. How going outside and walking around the block once or twice a day can literally add years to your life.

It remains very important, however, to maintain an ongoing dialogue with your doctor. Let him or her know of every pill you're taking and the dosage. This includes frank discussions on what supplements you are taking—some may not interact well with prescribed medication. Not all Western doctors are receptive to herbal and nutritional remedies, but nonetheless you must keep them apprised of any supplements you may be taking. This is especially true if you suffer from any chronic conditions, such as asthma, depression or diabetes.

So while a doctor should not be the sole voice in your health care, he or she should always be your primary health advisor. Work with him or her because we all have a duty to ourselves to take responsibility for our own health and well-being.

This book will train you in staying well—and in getting better. Every tip we provide is grounded in scientific research. In fact, researchers around the world have proved innumerable times that taking simple lifestyle steps, such as those outlined in the pages that follow, can play a vital role in protecting your heart.

We all have duty to ourselve to take responsibility fc our own well-being . .

Be honest with your doctor

A healthy doctor-patient relationship is key to getting the most out of medical care. It's easy to blame rushed, brusque doctors if the relationship goes sour, but in fact, we are just as often in the wrong. Our biggest flaw is not telling the truth about our consumption of cigarettes and alcohol.

Don't expect your doctor to help if he or she doesn't know how much you drink or smoke, or whether you rely too heavily on prescription or over-the-counter medications. Discuss any pills you take every day—including vitamins, minerals, herbs and other supplements. Be honest about diet and exercise habits. If you have any worrying symptoms or notice any unusual health developments, be open, even if it scares you to talk about them. Write yourself some notes so you don't forget what you wanted to ask about as soon as you get through the door.

If your doctor doesn't seem that interested or discourages you from being an active participant in your own well-being, make some enquiries locally about finding a different doctor. Unfortunately, the Canadian health care system is currently suffering from a shortage of family doctors, so this might be much harder than it sounds.

Work as a team

It is best to use this plan in conjunction with your doctor's care. Following the advice in this book will probably make pills and medical checkups a smaller part of your life, but it is not intended to replace your normal medical care. You and your doctor are a team working together in your heart's best interest. If you currently have high blood pressure, diabetes or other heart disease risks, you must make sure you keep all regular appointments with your doctor.

Whatever your current condition, even if you're perfectly healthy right now, it's a good idea to have your blood pressure and cholesterol checked if you are over 40 and these haven't been tested before.

The following is a list of tests that your doctor may perform. Some may be offered every three years or so, others annually, or as advised by your family doctor. Older people and those with known risk factors are tested more often.

■ Medical history/physical examination

When you register as a new patient, you usually fill out a form, ticking every condition that you and your immediate family have ever had. Your doctor uses this information to learn about your family history of heart disease and general risk. If you are given a physical examination, your family doctor may listen to your heart, check your pulse and test your blood pressure.

■ Blood glucose

Often known as "testing your sugar," this blood test helps to check for diabetes (a major heart disease risk). Many doctors use small machines called blood glucose meters that can give you a result on the spot by taking a finger prick of blood. Alternatively, you may be offered a simple urine test.

■ Blood pressure

Since blood pressure is a strong indicator of the health of your circulatory system, it is advisable to have it checked every two years after the age of 40, or more often if your doctor thinks it necessary. You can have your blood pressure tested at your local pharmacy, but it is important not to rely solely on the numbers it provides. See a doctor for a more accurate reading.

■ Cholesterol

This blood test measures the levels of good and dangerous lipids (fats) in your bloodstream.

Generally, a checkup every two years after the age of 40 is sufficient, but if you're a man over 45 or a woman over 55 or you have two or more risk factors for heart disease, it's a good idea to have your cholesterol checked every year.

■ ECG

An ECG (electrocardiogram) is a painless test in which you're wired to a machine that measures your heart's electrical activity. The device draws a tracing of the electrical changes occurring in the heart with each beat. Your doctor will only suggest this test if he or she thinks you have risk factors for heart disease. A "resting" ECG can identify current or previous problems, but is a poor predictor of future issues.

■ Stress ECG

This is an ECG performed while you exercise on a treadmill. It is only recommended if your doctor suspects or wishes to eliminate the possibility of heart disease that might be exposed by an exercise test. It can also be used to determine how much exercise is safe for you, particularly during cardiac rehabilitation or after a heart attack.

Few of us understand the difference between fresh food and processed, packaged food, yet almost everyone consumes some processed food daily.

Heart-healthy eating

The 30-Minutes-a-Day Eating Plan

If an apple a day keeps the doctor away, what should you eat to keep the heart surgeon away?

Try lean beef with a touch of garlic, vegetables, a glass of red wine, followed by strawberries and yogourt topped with flaked almonds. Spoil yourself and finish off with a chunk of melt-in-your-mouth dark chocolate.

Thanks to cutting-edge nutrition research, heart experts now know that you don't have to give up all your favourite foods in order to keep your arteries clear and your heart clean and well fuelled.

In the pages that follow, we're going to lay out the essential details of the 30-Minutes-a-Day Eating Plan. We suspect you'll be relieved by what you see: surprisingly few restrictions; plenty of inexpensive, widely available foods and

reassuring doses of moderation. We'll also provide lots of great tips for integrating the right foods into your diet and, in "Heart Healthy Recipes" on page 254, a host of tasty recipes featuring heart-healthy foods.

Throughout this chapter, you'll discover which foods, when eaten on a regular basis, are conducive to good health and those foods that are not. You'll also learn about the Glycemic Index and how it affects blood sugar levels, how to exercise better portion control, how to survive eating out, and more. But let's start at the beginning, with the pillars of the 30-Minutes-a-Day Eating Plan:

■ The five essential food groups for heart-healthy eating
■ Sample meals that show you how to get all these essential foods without difficulty
■ How to adapt your diet if you want to lose weight.

The healthy heart food groups

Here are the five types of food that are essential for good health and are also the keys to a strong, healthy heart.

Base your diet on these groups, getting the number of daily servings recommended, and your risk of heart disease will fall significantly—and almost immediately.

1 PROTEIN Power for a healthy heart

No food group offers more versatile protection from the causes of heart attacks than protein. Lean beef, eggs and pork are packed with homocysteine-lowering B vitamins. Fish delivers omega-3 fatty acids that keep heart rhythm steady and discourage blood clotting. Skinless chicken and turkey are low in artery-clogging saturated fat, and their protein keeps food cravings (and the risk of overeating) at bay. Beans—legumes such as chickpeas, black beans and kidney beans—are not only rich in high-quality proteins but are also one of nature's richest sources of soluble fibre, which transports cholesterol out of your body and helps to hold blood sugar levels steady.

But this food group can also pose a serious threat to your heart. Some protein foods are high in saturated fat that raises your level of harmful LDL cholesterol and your heart attack risk. The solution? On the 30-Minutes-a-Day Eating Plan, you'll find new meat cuts and proteins that will help to keep your total saturated fat intake to about 7 per cent of total calories. The Heart and

Stroke Foundation of Canada recommends that total fat intake be less than 30 per cent of total calories. Here's how to enjoy a range of heart-healthy protein foods.

Make a habit of eating seafood

The healthiest seafood for your heart is cold-water ocean fish because it's so rich in omega-3 fatty acids. The most popular kind is salmon; other choices include mackerel, herring, sardines, anchovies and freshwater lake trout.

Aim to get three or four servings of these fish a week, by having canned salmon or mackerel for lunch twice a week (make your salmon salad with low-fat mayonnaise) and fresh trout for dinner once or twice a week— or have anchovies on your night-out pizza. Alternatively, poach fresh salmon and serve it

The plan Protein

- **On the menu** Fish, chicken, turkey, lean red meat, pork, eggs, beans (pulses).
- **Daily servings** Two to three.
- **Serving sizes** 50–100 g (2–3½ oz) fish, poultry and meats; 6 tablespoons of beans as a main dish or 3 as a side dish; 2 eggs.

with a spicy horseradish and chive sauce (see our recipe on page 271) or make a Spanish-style salad of cooked diced potatoes, finely chopped green onions and flaked smoked mackerel, with olive oil. It's delicious!

Although other seafood may not have as many omega-3s, most types are great sources of protein. So if sautéed sole or shrimp appeals to you more than salmon—or a chicken breast or steak, for that matter—choose the seafood.

None of these suggestions require you to spend a fortune at the fish market or to do any type of exotic or challenging cooking. Today, it's easier than ever to add heart-healthy seafood to your diet. A serving can be part of a side dish or the main course. Do note, however, that Health Canada advises pregnant and nursing women, young children and older women of child-bearing age to eat swordfish, shark, king mackerel and fresh or frozen tuna no more than once a month.

If you really detest fish or can't eat shellfish, simply substitute another type of lean protein—and consider getting omega-3s from ground flaxseed or fish-oil capsules. Better still, include about 125 g (4½ oz) nuts in your week's diet, in studies they have been shown to cut cardiovascular risk. Eating walnuts or almonds will provide essential

minerals and may also help to reduce your cholesterol levels. Other good sources of omega-3s are some dairy products, canola oil and omega-3 eggs.

Rediscover beef and pork

These meats can have a place in your heart-healthy eating plan. Both meats have been made healthier to suit modern tastes, and trimming all visible fat from beef or pork will go a long way to making it much healthier. In one health study, volunteers who ate lean red meat five to seven days a week had the same slight improvements in cholesterol—their LDL levels dropped 2 per cent, and HDL levels rose 3 to 4 per cent—as those who only ate chicken and fish.

It is best to avoid excessive amounts of meat that might displace other important nutritious foods such as whole grains and fruit and vegetables, but remember that the key message has to be: "Enjoy your food."

The lowest-fat cuts available in butcher shops and grocery stores are generally pork tenderloin and lean beef such as round and loin.

Shift the focus to beans

Beans should feature on your lunchtime or dinner menu several days a week. Relatively few people take the trouble to cook bean-dish recipes but if you discover three or four that your family will enjoy, and then prepare one every few days, you will do wonders for your health.

Make meatless chili; create quick, hearty soup by mixing drained and rinsed canned kidney beans and frozen vegetables with a can of low-salt minestrone soup or chicken broth; sprinkle chickpeas or black beans from the salad bar over your lunch salad; or order a bean burrito (but cut out the cheese) when you have Mexican food.

Food myths that hurt your heart

MYTH: Shrimp are high in cholesterol.

THE TRUTH: Most of the cholesterol in our blood is made by the liver from foods that are high in saturated fat—only about 25 per cent comes from foods high in cholesterol. Although shrimp and other shellfish do contain relatively high levels of cholesterol, they are low in fat and particularly low in saturated fat. Too much cholesterol, however, can raise LDL levels in some people. Limiting your cholesterol intake to less than 300 mg a day is suggested. A 90 g serving of shrimp has 140 mg of cholesterol, so enjoy shrimp from time to time, but don't overdo it. Shrimp also contain trace elements and minerals such as selenium, iodine and zinc.

MYTH: Eggs are heart attacks in a shell.

THE TRUTH: Research found that people who eat up to one egg a day have no increased risk of heart disease or stroke. Eggs are one of the few dietary sources of vitamin D and provide good amounts of vitamins A, B_2, B_{12} and E. As with shrimp, it's not the amount of cholesterol in the food that matters—it's the amount of saturated fat that is converted to blood cholesterol by the liver.

Eggs are one of the few dietary sources of vitamin D and provide good amounts of vitamins A, B_2, B_{12} and E.

2 GOOD FATS
Better than low-fat

Why use butter that has saturated fat or crunch on questionable snacks packed with trans fatty acids when you could eat as if you spent your days beside the Mediterranean—spreading fruity olive oil on crusty bread or drizzling it over fresh vegetables and snacking on delicious almonds? Many studies have shown that these cornerstones of the Mediterranean diet protect your heart. That's why olive oil and walnuts, which are good sources of omega-3 fatty acids, get top billing in this plan, too.

All are rich in monounsaturated fats. Eat them instead of saturated fats to lower LDL cholesterol, slightly increase HDL levels and reduce triglycerides. While you should eat very little saturated fat, monounsaturated fats should be part of your daily calorie intake. Just watch your portions—oils, nuts and nut butters are calorie dense, so a little goes a long way. Here's how you can rebalance your fat budget.

Say "no" to saturated fats

Remove skin from chicken and turkey before eating; trim excess fat from all meats; choose dressings with no more than 1 g of saturated fat per tablespoon (look for versions made with canola oil); and replace cream in recipes with yogourt. For baking and cooking, substitute canola or olive oil for butter by using a quarter less oil than the amount of butter called for in a recipe (for example, use ¾ tablespoon of oil instead of 1 tablespoon of butter).

Banish trans fats

Avoid packaged snacks and baked goods with partially hydrogenated fats or oils listed as ingredients. Switch to margarine that is free of trans fats, if possible, or use olive oil

The plan Good fats

- **On the menu** Olive oil, canola oil, nuts.
- **Daily servings** One to three of each.
- **Serving sizes** ½ to 1 tablespoon oil; 30 g (1 oz) nuts.

instead. Trans fat are still present in some low-fat, spreadable margarines. As long as the level of trans fat is very low (about 5 to 7 per cent), the effect on cholesterol will be negligible. For more on why cutting down trans fats is important, see "It's all in the processing" on page 84.

Use monounsaturated fats

Invest in an olive-oil sprayer (they can be found in the kitchenware section of most department stores) to give toast and vegetables a light, tasty coating instead of using butter or margarine. Make olive and canola oils your first choice for salad dressings, marinades and cooking. (Other oils have lower levels of monounsaturates.) Try olive oil for scrambling eggs, browning meat and sautéing vegetables. For coating bakeware to prevent sticking, use a commercial olive or canola oil spray.

The plan Fruits and vegetables

■ **On the menu** All fruits and vegetables—fresh, frozen, dried or canned in natural juices.

■ **Daily servings** Three or four of fruit; four or five of vegetables.

■ **Serving sizes** 75 g (3 oz) vegetables, raw, cooked, canned or frozen; 1 dessert bowl of salad; 1 medium fruit such as apple, orange, banana or pear; 1 large slice of melon or pineapple; 2 small fruits such as plums or apricots; 1 cup of raspberries or strawberries; $\frac{1}{2}$ cup fresh or frozen raw fruits or vegetables; 1 tablespoon dried fruit such as raisins; $\frac{1}{2}$ cup fruit or vegetable juice; 3 tablespoons cooked legumes.

Say goodbye to chips—hello to nuts

The monounsaturated fats in nuts (and omega-3s in walnuts) make them excellent snacks. But to guard against overeating, limit yourself to one serving and put the rest away. And choose unsalted nuts to help keep your blood pressure under control.

Diversify your nut portfolio

Apart from peanuts, almonds and walnuts, try pistachios, pecans and hazelnuts. Sprinkle them on cereal and salads and add them to cake mixes, yogourt and crumbles.

Don't forget the peanut butter

Peanut butter has impressive amounts of monounsaturated fat, protein, vitamin E and fibre. Try to find a low-salt and non-trans fat brand and spread some on toast for breakfast, or enjoy a peanut butter and jelly or jam sandwich for lunch (on whole-wheat bread, of course), or use a tablespoonful as a dip for baby carrots, apple slices or pears as a snack.

3 FRUIT AND VEGETABLES
Nature's cholesterol cure

Our ancestors existed on wild produce, so researchers suspect that the human body evolved to expect large daily doses of the antioxidants, cholesterol-lowering phytosterols and soluble fibre found in fruits and vegetables. Without them (and most of us get too few servings of fruit and vegetables a day) heart risk rises. Here's how to get nine servings a day, both at home and at work.

Take a juice break

Sip 100 per cent orange juice or grape juice as one of your daily fruit servings, or mix juice concentrate with olive oil for a sweet salad dressing. A small glass of juice is one fruit and vegetable portion.

Whiz up a smoothie

Toss frozen strawberries, orange juice and a banana, pear or sliced peach into the blender for a triple serving of fruit, smoothie-style. Add plain yogourt with a sprinkle of wheat germ or chopped nuts, and you've got breakfast.

Stock up with fridge-fruits

Buy a cantaloupe or small watermelon, cube the fruit and keep it in a sealed container in the fridge for an easy, antioxidant-rich snack when you're looking for something sweet to nibble.

Keep fruit and vegetables handy

Keep a bowl of cherry tomatoes or a bowl of bananas or apples on the kitchen counter. If you see them, you'll eat them.

Redefine fast food

Grocery stores have a huge selection of ready-to-use salad greens. In just a few minutes, you can pick up a bag of baby spinach or mixed greens, cherry tomatoes, grated carrots, mandarin orange slices and chopped nuts and raisins for a salad that instantly offers two to three fruit and vegetable servings.

Follow a new "second-helpings rule"

Allow yourself to take second helpings only of vegetables at mealtimes. You'll cut calories from fat and boost fibre intake.

Eat a rainbow

From blackberries to carrots, and tomatoes to pineapple, eat as many different-coloured fruits and vegetables as possible daily for the widest variety of nutrients.

Splurge like a chef

Don't stick to the same old favourites when you buy fruit and vegetables. Be adventurous and try something new. Look for ideas for new ways to cook them—such as broiling, poaching or baking fruits.

Invest in your cupboard and freezer

This means canned (in juice) and frozen fruit and vegetables for times when you run out of fresh or don't have time to wash and chop. Some frozen produce has more nutrients than fresh versions because it's frozen immediately after harvesting.

Tuck in extras

Keep a bag of grated carrots in the fridge to toss into soups, stews, casseroles, sauces and tuna salad and add extra frozen vegetables to soups and stews.

Wash and blot, but don't peel

Wash all produce thoroughly and blot it dry. Then eat it all, skin included—the skin is full of fibre, and the fruit or veggie flesh just below the skin contains extra nutrients.

4 WHOLE GRAINS
High fibre, high value

Simply eating a high-fibre, whole-grain breakfast could help to reduce your risk of heart attack, as can switching completely from refined to whole grains. Whole grains are packed with vitamins and a wealth of heart-protecting phyto-chemicals, plus insoluble fibre to help digestion. Some, such as barley and oatmeal, also have cholesterol-lowering soluble fibre.

In the next chapter, you'll learn more about grain processing and why refined grains aren't as healthy as whole grains. Here's how to fit in five or more whole grains every day.

Think fibre in the morning

Breakfast on oatmeal or another high-fibre cereal and each gram of soluble fibre will cut your LDL cholesterol substantially, says the American Heart Association. One bowl a day could make a big contribution to keeping your LDL levels heart-healthy.

Boil once, then freeze the leftovers

Brown rice, barley and bulgur are delicious. To save weekday preparation time, cook up a big pot on the weekend and freeze extras in

The plan Whole grains

■ **On the menu** Whole-wheat bread, whole-wheat pasta, barley, bulgur; brown rice; whole-wheat and high-fibre cereals, including oatmeal.

■ **Daily servings** At least five.

■ **Serving sizes** 1 slice whole-wheat bread; ½ cup cooked cereal; ½ cup cooked rice, bulgur or pasta.

5 DAIRY FOODS
Better bone protection

Having milk on your morning cereal, a small container of yogourt as a mid-afternoon snack and grated low-fat cheese on your chili or pasta at dinner, boosts your intake of calcium, a mineral vital for healthy bone development. It also provides high-quality protein and essential B vitamins, zinc and phosphorus.

Use the following tips to get the calcium advantage of dairy foods without adding saturated fat.

Get the skim-milk habit

If you drink homogenized milk, switch to 2% milk for a while, then try skim. Or use skim milk for cereal and soups, where the taste difference is less noticeable, and use 2% milk in tea, coffee and hot chocolate.

Add fruit

A small pot of low-fat yogourt topped with chopped fruit and a tablespoon of nuts makes a filling snack. Try vanilla yogourt topped with banana slices and a dusting of cinnamon; add sliced strawberries and chopped walnuts to strawberry yogourt.

Replace the water

Use skim milk instead of water when cooking oatmeal or making soups. Swirl a little low-fat plain yogourt into a bowl of tomato soup for taste and presentation.

Top it with cheese

A tablespoon of reduced-fat cheese is delicious melted on toast or as a topping on pasta, chili or a baked potato.

single-meal portions, then defrost in the microwave as needed. Add to ground poultry for extra body when making meat loaf or burgers.

Always buy baked goods with the word "whole" in it

Choose breads with "whole wheat" leading the ingredient list and with at least 3 g of fibre per serving. Substitute whole-wheat toast for bagels, and low-fat whole-wheat muffins for pastries. Make sandwiches with whole-wheat breads or rolls. Choose whole-wheat pita breads instead of white ones.

The plan Dairy foods

- **On the menu** Skim or 1% milk, low-fat yogourt and reduced-fat cheese.
- **Daily servings** Two to three.
- **Serving sizes** 1 cup milk; 50 g (2 oz) reduced-fat cheese; 175 g low-fat yogourt.

Healthy heart sample meals

Now that you know the foods that make up the 30-Minutes-a-Day Eating Plan, here are lots of sample meals, with the right portion sizes, for you to try.

BREAKFASTS

Here are eight breakfasts to choose from. Each has between 300 and 500 calories. (All milk is skim or 2%.)

1 Yogourt and muffin morning
■ 1 cup mixed fresh fruit (melon, banana, apple, strawberries and peaches) topped with 1 small container (175 g) low-fat yogourt and 25 g (1 oz) almonds.
■ 1 small whole-wheat muffin.
■ ¾ cup milk.

2 Oatmeal and fruit
■ A bowl of oatmeal, mixed with 1 to 2 tablespoons or wheat germ, or 2 tablespoons raisins, or ½ to ¾ cup strawberries, raspberries or blueberries, or 1 small chopped banana.

3 Mushroom sauté
■ Stir-fry 50 g (2 oz) mushrooms in a little oil, and serve with 1 whole-wheat muffin spread with 1 teaspoon margarine.

4 Cereal-plus breakfast
■ Try 3 tablespoons whole-grain cereal (choose one with at least 3 g fibre per serving) with ⅔ cup milk, 2 tablespoons chopped walnuts and a few strawberries, raspberries or blueberries.

5 Peanut butter bagel
■ Lightly toast 1 whole-wheat cinnamon bagel and spread with 1 tablespoon crunchy peanut butter. Top with a sliced banana.
■ ¾ cup milk.

6 Tropical muesli
■ Stir 3 tablespoons of sugar-free muesli into 175 g low-fat yogourt and add 1 diced mango.
■ ¾ cup milk.

7 Smoothie
■ Whiz 1 cup orange juice, 75 g (3 oz) frozen strawberries and a small container (175 g) low-fat vanilla or plain yogourt in a blender.
■ 1 slice whole-wheat toast with 1 teaspoon margarine (2 slices of toast for men).

8 Scrambled eggs on toast
■ Scramble 2 eggs in a little olive oil. Serve with broiled tomatoes and a slice of toast.
■ 1 small glass (⅔ cup) fruit juice.

Workday snacks

Resist the vending machine. Tuck these sweet and savoury snacks into your desk drawer, briefcase or the office fridge. For extra heart protection, take an afternoon stroll around your office building.

NUTS Fill small plastic bags with 25 g (1 oz) portions—about 24 almonds, 14 walnut halves, 18 cashews or 50 pistachios (in the shell). And make sure your nuts are unsalted.

DRIED FRUIT Bag up 50 g (2 oz) portions of raisins, dried apricots, dried cranberries and dried prunes.

SINGLE-SERVING FRUIT Take a portion of fruit salad in a small plastic container, or buy a ready-prepared fruit salad. Remember to take along a spoon.

WHOLE-WHEAT CRACKERS Store them in a plastic bag or container to keep them fresh. About 3 crackers make a healthy snack.

FRESH FRUIT OR LOW-FAT YOGOURT Pack any of these into a small cooler bag or label it and put it into the office refrigerator.

LOW-FAT CEREAL BARS There's a wide variety of these to choose from, so make sure you choose one that's low in fat, sugar and salt, and high in fibre.

LUNCHES

Here are seven lunches, each under 500 calories. All are healthy and delicious.

1 Soup and roll

■ **Tuscan bean soup** Finely chop 1 red onion and sauté in a teaspoon of olive oil. Add a crushed clove of garlic, 1 sliced stalk of celery and cook for 5 minutes. Add half of 1 can (540 ml) chopped tomatoes and 1¼ cups low-sodium vegetable stock. Bring to a boil, then reduce the heat and simmer for 20 minutes. Add 4 tablespoons drained, rinsed mixed beans and simmer for a further 10 minutes.

■ 1 small whole-wheat roll.

2 Salmon choices

Salmon salad in pita Mix 100 g canned salmon with 2 tablespoons chopped walnuts, 2 thinly sliced green onions, ½ diced red pepper and 1 grated carrot; add 1 tablespoon reduced-fat mayonnaise mixed with 1 tablespoon plain yogourt. Spoon into a small whole-wheat pita.

. . . or Salmon melt Mix 100 g of canned salmon with 2 tablespoons chopped celery and 1 small grated carrot. Add 1 tablespoon each reduced-fat mayonnaise and low-fat yogourt. Spoon mixture over 2 halves of a whole-wheat muffin and top each with 1 tablespoon grated reduced-fat Cheddar. Broil for a few minutes.

3 Mexican bean wrap

■ Mix together 3 tablespoons each drained, rinsed mixed beans, grated, reduced-fat Cheddar and tomato salsa. Spoon the mixture into the middle of a warmed whole-wheat wrap, top with shredded lettuce, and roll up.

■ 1 piece of fruit.

4 Poultry options

Tandoori chicken salad sandwich Chop 100 g (3½ oz) precooked tandoori chicken breast and mix with 3 tablespoons tzatziki. Spread 2 slices of whole-wheat bread with mango chutney and a large handful of watercress. Fill the sandwich with the chicken mixture.

. . . or chicken and avocado sandwich Spread 2 slices of whole-wheat bread with whole-grain mustard, a layer of sliced chicken, ½ small avocado and 2 thick slices tomato.

Heart-smart toppings for soups, sauces, salads and stir-fries

For both flavour and health, add the following liberally to your favourite meal.

GROUND FLAXSEED This is the richest plant source of heart-protecting omega-3 fatty acids. Buy preground or milled flax and store it in the freezer. Add 1 to 2 tablespoons to food.

CHOPPED NUTS Add 1 to 2 tablespoons to cereal, salads, or fruit for extra fibre and monounsaturated fat (walnuts also provide omega-3s). Chopped nuts stay fresh longer in the freezer.

WHEAT GERM It's a great natural source of vitamin E, an antioxidant that may discourage artery-clogging plaque. Add 1 to 2 tablespoons per serving to cereal and when you bake. Store in the fridge or freezer to preserve freshness.

CINNAMON Some studies suggest that cinnamon may help to control blood sugar levels and lower cholesterol. Sprinkle it over breakfast cereal, stewed fruit and fruit salad, and add it to smoothies.

FRESH GINGER Add this powerful antioxidant to stir-fries, fruit salad and stewed fruit. You can keep fresh ginger in the freezer and simply grate what you need.

CHOPPED GARLIC This popular flavour enhancer can help to lower cholesterol levels. Add it to salad dressings, meat dishes, veggies and dips.

5 Veggie burger
■ Pan-fry a veggie burger and serve in a whole-wheat roll with 2 slices of tomato, and 2 tablespoons reduced-fat coleslaw.

6 Hummus salad pita
■ Mix 60 g (2¼ oz) reduced-fat hummus with ½ diced red pepper and 1 small grated carrot. Spoon mixture into a whole-wheat pita.

7 Smoked mackerel and pasta salad
■ Flake 1 small smoked mackerel fillet and mix with 4 tablespoons cooked, whole-wheat pasta, 4 halved cherry tomatoes and 1 teaspoon honey and mustard dressing.

DINNERS
Here are seven choices. Each delicious meal provides about 600 calories and is good for your heart.

1 Variations on salmon and salad
Broiled or pan-fried salmon Allow 125 g (4½ oz) salmon fillet per person.

. . . or Broiled citrus trout (see recipe on page 272).

■ **Quick spinach salad** Mix a good handful of baby salad leaves, 1 grated carrot, 2 tablespoons roughly chopped walnuts and a handful of dried cranberries or raisins; toss with 1 tablespoon dressing made with 2 teaspoons olive oil, the juice of 1 orange and a pinch of salt.

■ ¾ cup cooked brown rice or bulgur wheat, or 1 slice whole-wheat bread.

2 Pick poultry
Roast turkey breast with garlic sauce (recipe on page 274).

. . . or Herb-stuffed chicken breasts (recipe on page 275).

. . . or New-style chicken salad (recipe on page 277).

■ 1 baked sweet potato.

■ **Cauliflower provençale** (recipe on page 291). Omit if serving the salad.

Two perfect pizzas
You can still enjoy pizzas on the 30-Minutes-a-Day Eating Plan. For guilt-free, heart-healthy versions, try these.

At a restaurant Ask for half the cheese, double the tomato sauce, and all the vegetable toppings on a thin whole-wheat crust.

At home Create individual gourmet pizzas by topping whole-wheat pitas with sauce, precooked vegetables (use up leftovers), fresh basil, oregano, crushed black pepper, garlic purée and fresh tomatoes. Add reduced-fat mozzarella or cut the fat even further by using grated Parmesan.

3 Here's the beef
Lean steak Allow 100 g (3½ oz) per person.

. . . or beef kebabs Slice 100 g (3½ oz) lean beef into cubes. Mix 2 tablespoons olive oil, 2 tablespoons balsamic vinegar and 1 crushed garlic clove. Pour it over the beef and allow to marinate for 30 minutes. Thread beef onto metal skewers, alternating red pepper pieces with onion chunks, whole, small mushrooms and cherry tomatoes. Brush with remaining marinade and place under broiler for 8 to 10 minutes, turning often, until beef is cooked.

4 Legumes
Spicy beans (recipe on page 286).

. . . Black-eyed pea casserole (recipe on page 288).

. . . or Chicken with three-bean salad Drain and rinse a 540 ml can of mixed beans; mix with 3 sliced green onions, 2 finely chopped stalks of celery and 4 halved cherry tomatoes. Whisk 2 teaspoons olive oil, 2 teaspoons lemon juice, a small pinch of salt, 1 crushed clove of garlic and ½ teaspoon chopped fresh herbs; pour over the beans and serve with cooked chicken breast.

■ Mixed green salad leaves with 1 tablespoon olive oil dressing.

- Whole-wheat roll or 1 slice whole-wheat bread
- Steamed broccoli.
- Cherry tomatoes with olive oil dressing.

5 Other meat options

Spaghetti Bolognese Make it with 100 g (3½ oz) extra lean ground beef per person or use less and add in lentils or red kidney beans.

. . . **or Mediterranean lamb stew** (recipe on page 281).

. . . **or Pork loin stuffed with winter fruits** (recipe on page 283).

- **Oven fries** (recipe on page 292) or baked sweet potato.
- Steamed vegetable mix.

6 Go vegetarian

Mediterranean lentils with mushrooms (recipe on page 284).

. . . **or Vegetable and three cheese lasagne** (recipe on page 285).

. . . **or Warm goat cheese salad** (recipe on page 287).

- Mixed green salad leaves with 1 tablespoon olive oil dressing.
- **Nutted lemon barley** (recipe on page 289).

7 Pasta pleasures

- 1 cup cooked whole-wheat spaghetti or pasta shapes per person, tossed with a choice of:
- 100 g (3½ oz) shrimp sautéed in 1 tablespoon olive oil, 1 crushed clove of garlic, lemon juice, and herbs to taste.

. . . **or** 150 ml of your favourite tomato sauce mixed with 3 tablespoons mixed canned beans, rinsed and drained.

. . . **or** 100 g canned salmon, 2 teaspoons olive oil, 1 crushed clove of garlic, ½ diced small red pepper and herbs to taste.

- Mixed salad greens with olive oil dressing.

DESSERTS

Here are nine delicious desserts for everyday and special occasions. Each one is under 200 calories a serving.

1 1 cup strawberries (fresh or frozen, no added sugar) topped with 1 scoop of reduced-fat ice cream or frozen yogourt.

2 Mixed fruit (fresh, frozen or canned in its own juice and drained) topped with a sprinkle of coconut, chopped nuts, cinnamon and ½ teaspoon brown sugar.

3 Homemade berry fool In a blender or food processor, combine 1 cup frozen summer berries and 175 g low-fat yogourt. Purée until smooth. Add sweetener to taste and process until smooth but not runny.

4 Cinnamon baked apple Core 1 apple (Granny Smiths work well) and loosely fill the centre with cinnamon, raisins, nuts and ½ teaspoon brown sugar. Pour 2 tablespoons water into the bottom of a microwaveable bowl and add the apple; cover and microwave for 5 minutes or until soft. The time depends on the size of the apple and the setting of your microwave.

5 Fresh or gently thawed frozen raspberries topped with 1 tablespoon chocolate syrup or 25 g (1 oz) melted dark chocolate.

Lower your LDLs with food

The smart food choices in the 30-Minutes-a-Day Eating Plan can help to lower your cholesterol naturally. This strategy may help you to avoid medication or, if you do take a cholesterol-lowering drug, help to lower the dose you need. Heart researchers think reductions in LDLs are possible if you take the following key steps: cut back on saturated fat, replace any butter you have with healthy oils, and get plenty of soluble fibre (from oatmeal and barley).

6 Cantaloupe with raspberry sauce (recipe on page 295).
7 Walnut raisin pudding (recipe on page 296).
8 Apricot and pear compote (recipe on page 298).
9 Lemon-walnut frozen yogourt (recipe on page 299).

BEVERAGES

What you drink is just as important as what you eat. Sip these for a healthy heart.

■ **Water.** Aim to drink 6 to 8 glasses of water a day. You may need more when the weather is warm. Remember to drink before and after exercise.

■ **Green and black tea.** Have 1 to 3 cups a day. Antioxidants in tea reduce levels of LDL cholesterol and make arteries more flexible.

■ **Red wine.** Red wine contains a heart-protecting antioxidant called resveratrol. Occasionally, enjoy a glass of red wine. However, regular alcohol consumption is not advisable as a preventative health measure.

■ **Cocoa.** Chocolate has antioxidants, too. Choose plain cocoa and make your own hot chocolate, or have 25 g (1 oz) of rich, dark slab chocolate.

■ **What to avoid.** Colas and other soft drinks, energy drinks, sweetened fruit juices. If you drink cappuccino or latte, ask for it to be made with skim or 2% milk.

HEART-HEALTHY EATING

. . .researchers suspect that the human body evolved to expect large daily doses of the antioxidants and soluble fibre found in fruits . .

Losing weight the 30-Minutes-a-Day way

Weight loss begins with a deceptively simple formula that no fad diet can disprove: to lose weight, you must burn more calories a day than you eat. So why, if it's that simple, are so many Canadians overweight? Stress, food cravings, fatigue, temptation, office parties and lack of time contribute to weight gain—and make losing weight a challenge.

By following the 30-Minutes-a-Day Eating Plan as well as the advice in the rest of this book, you'll not only eat proper portions and get the calorie-burning exercise your body needs, you'll also discover ways to relax, and feel happy that will help real change to take place.

Successful, lasting weight-loss is rarely achieved by diet alone. It requires a gradual shift to healthy living in all its forms. But to start, here are two basic keys to eating for weight loss.

1 Get to know what you need

How many calories do you need to eat in a typical day? Very few people know their calorie requirements, although most know their weight and some will also know their blood-pressure levels.

If we knew more precisely how much food we should eat, we probably wouldn't need to worry about other numbers. Here are some guidelines for working out what your body needs each day.

What is a calorie?

The word "calorie" is often misused. Strictly, it is a very tiny measure—the amount of heat required to raise the temperature of 1 g of water by 1°C. The more accurate term for the calories we eat or burn in exercise is "kilocalories" or "kcal," equivalent to 1,000 calories.

IF YOU'RE INACTIVE You need about 28.6 calories per kg (13 per lb) of bodyweight. For a 68 kg (150 lb) woman, that's about 1,950 calories a day. For a 79.5 kg (175 lb) man, it's about 2,275 calories a day.

IF YOU'RE SLIGHTLY ACTIVE (fewer than three exercise sessions a week, but regularly on your feet): You need about 31 calories per kg (14 per lb) to maintain your weight. For a 68 kg (150 lb) woman, that's about 2,100 calories, and for a 79.5 kg (175 lb) man, around 2,450 calories.

IF YOU'RE ACTIVE (getting 30 to 60 minutes of exercise at least three times weekly): You need about 33 calories per kg (15 per lb) of body weight. For a 68 kg (150 lb) woman, around 2,250 calories; for a 79.5 kg (175 lb) man, about 2,625 calories.

To lose about 0.2 kg (½ lb) a week—a realistic goal for people who make small healthy lifestyle changes—you need 250 calories less per day. It's easy to eat 125 fewer calories; by, for example, having fruit instead of ice cream for dessert or by resisting an afternoon cake.

It's just as easy to add 125 calories of exercise with a 15-minute walk at lunch and another after dinner. Or you could wash the car, rake leaves and use the stairs instead of the elevator.

2 Forget about calorie counting

Counting calories can be depressing. Even worse is trying to count grams of fat or grams of carbohydrates or trying to add up the calories in the foods you eat, as so many diet plans insist you should do.

Instead, do what your common sense tells you: eat a bit less and move a little more. Do that every day and you'll lose weight. For steady, healthy, lasting weight loss, there's no better way. And the best foods for a healthy heart are ones you need for a healthy weight. Here are some simple guidelines for making the change to lifelong healthy eating.

LET PORTIONS BE YOUR GUIDE Using the perfect portion size-guide on page 101, keep track of serving sizes. You may find you're eating more fruits and vegetables than you thought (which is good), or you may be underestimating how much pasta, ice cream or snack foods you eat, and consuming more calories than you realized.

START WITH BREAKFAST Skipping a morning meal leaves you so hungry that you can justify eating anything later on. Weight-loss winners tend to eat in the morning.

DON'T MISS LUNCH OR DINNER The main reason for nighttime binges is not eating enough during the day. Try filling up on the "slimming" parts of your meal—salad, vegetables and broth-based soups. Eat more caloric meats and starches last so you need a little less of them.

DRINK WATER, UNSWEETENED TEA OR DIET DRINKS Cutting out one sweetened drink a day—whether a soft drink or sweetened tea—could help you to lose just over 11 kg (25 lb) in a year.

KEEP A FOOD DIARY FOR A WEEK It will reveal what you're really eating and help you to spot the times of day when you're skimping or overdoing it.

DON'T BE AN ISLAND Join a weight-loss support group online or locally. Enlist the support of family and friends. Plenty of research shows that dieting with a friend helps both of you to stick with it, especially in the tough first few weeks.

Don't eat out of boredom, stress or habit. It's amazing how many people do. We tend to nibble while watching TV, while at the computer, or just when we need to take a break.

Find healthier ways to take breaks or deal with the stresses of everyday life. The best choice is a short walk followed by a glass of cold water or a cup of hot tea or coffee.

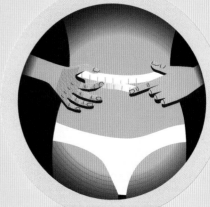

Processed foods have often lost the nutrients designed by nature to protect your heart ...

It's all in the processing

Take a can of soup, a box of crackers or a cheese sauce mix from the cupboard, a package of hot dogs or any precooked ready-meal from your fridge and examine the fine print on the ingredient lists. You'll find food additives in almost every one.

Repeat the experiment with any packaged food in the grocery store. Nearly all contain something that wasn't part of nature's original package. Technological advances have dramatically increased the variety of processed foods, but compared with the foods our bodies were designed to eat, they are not always as healthy.

No one likes to admit to eating lots of foods filled with additives and artificial flavourings, but processed, packaged foods have become a much greater part of our daily diet. Studies throughout the Western world show that we are consuming far less fresh fruit, vegetables, seafood, lean meats, dairy, grains and bread. In fact, much of today's average household food budget goes toward the purchase of convenience foods. We are leading busier lives, with longer work hours and less free time to cook.

Few foods reach today's supermarket free of additives

Additives—substances that do not occur naturally in a food but are added for various reasons—include preservatives to prevent spoilage; emulsifiers to prevent water and fat from separating; thickeners; salt and sweeteners to improve taste; and more. The majority of processed foods are designed for maximum taste impact. Nutritionally, some of these products do not measure up to fresh home-cooked meals. In fact, some critics blame our growing reliance on processed or convenience foods, which are typically loaded with sweeteners and fats, for the ever increasing size of Canadian waistbands.

The trouble with processed foods is not just what has been added to them. Processed foods have often lost the nutrients designed by nature to protect your heart, such as soluble fibre, antioxidants and "good" fats found in nature's bounty. In addition, processing may strip vitamins and minerals from foods.

Combine that with additives known to endanger your cardiovascular system, such as sugar, sodium and trans fatty acids, and you begin to see why a diet made up primarily of processed foods is bad for your health. No doctor, nutritionist or other health care professional would disagree that eating fresh, wholesome foods is best for you.

A major tenet of the 30-Minutes-a-Day Plan is to put whole, natural foods back onto your plate, but without requiring you to spend hours shopping, chopping or cooking.

Plan of action

Achieving this kind of diet may be harder than it sounds. Most of us are so used to eating food out of boxes, packages and cans. Processed foods are convenience foods, and they certainly fit into our busy lifestyles. However, they were not intended to replace fresh or homemade meals on a daily basis. If this is happening to you, then slow down and take time to improve your diet.

In this chapter, we'll highlight the four ingredients you should focus on first and foremost and try to limit their consumption. Then, in the chapters ahead, we'll detail the foods you should eat most of and provide tips and recipes to make it as easy as possible to do so.

The health dangers How processing can damage your food

Many of the foods we eat are no longer in a natural state. Fish often come from fish farms instead of from algae-rich wild waters and many fruit and vegetable concoctions are robbed of their fibre and nutrients. To make matters worse, unhealthy doses of salt or sugar are often added during processing. Modern processing technology can make food less healthy by:

■ Adding heart-threatening trans fats and saturated fats.

■ Adding blood pressure-raising sodium (salt).

■ Adding blood glucose-elevating sugars.

■ Removing natural fibre.

■ Removing vitamins, minerals and antioxidants.

■ Adding chemical preservatives, flavours, colours and sweeteners.

■ Including so many varied additives, thereby increasing the risk of contamination.

■ Replacing naturally balanced nutrients with a more limited range of man-made vitamins and minerals in fortified foods.

Vitamins in a bowl Are fortified foods nutritious?

Everyday foods often have pumped-up nutritional profiles—breakfast cereal with added vitamins and minerals, and orange juice with bone-building calcium. They all look like health superstars, but do you need them?

The answer is yes and no. While fortified and enriched foods may help to fill nutritional gaps, they aren't better than a healthy, balanced diet, according to nutrition experts. Here's what you need to know.

■ Fortified foods should still be nutritious in their own right. Look for natural nutrients first and consider fortification a bonus. Choose calcium-rich skim or 2% milk and whole-grain, high-fibre breakfast cereals (if they have added nutrients, it's a plus). A little extra nutrition is fine but it shouldn't be the reason to choose a food.

■ If you are eating a good healthy diet, you should not need to take a daily multivitamin (unless a medical or allergic condition means you are not eating certain foods). But you do need fibre, good fats and the hundreds of protective phytochemicals in fruits and vegetables—and they don't come in pill form.

Producing processed foods

Processed food arrives at the store in a sealed package, and in a form different from its original, natural state. That includes most canned, frozen, bottled, boxed or dehydrated food items such as soup, frozen pizza, candy, bottled pasta sauce and savoury snacks.

Of course, not all prepackaged foods are a problem. Milk, yogourt and cheese all arrive

at the store in their final packaging after some type of pasteurizing process, and some very healthy organic spaghetti sauces and energy bars have few, if any, unnatural, unhealthy ingredients.

The problem is mostly with foods that have been dramatically altered for convenience, taste or long shelf life. These are the foods with lengthy ingredient lists that include chemicals the typical person has never heard of. Among the additives we typically consume each day are food dyes and colourings, preservatives, emulsifiers, acidity regulators, gelling agents and more.

North American food processors use up to 2,800 different additives, all of which have gone through extensive studies before being put on the market. Nonetheless, many additives are not specified on the label or are listed simply as "flavouring."

Food additives are not new: natural ingredients such as salt, vinegar and sugar have been used for hundreds of years to help preserve food. The worrying fact is that modern food processing relies more and more heavily on additives, and their use has increased greatly in the past 50 years.

Are they safe?

The vast majority of additives have undergone extensive testing and are considered safe. Often additives are used only to enhance the taste of the food we are buying. The amount of fruit added to most fruit yogourts, for instance, is insufficient to add much flavour or colour, so the perception of fruitiness may be achieved by colouring and flavouring additives. And although people do have allergic reactions to some of these unseen additives, allergic reactions to wheat and milk are 100 times more common.

Food colourings are more controversial. Many processed foods contain food colourings: Soft drinks, candies, jams and some margarines, as well as many processed meats and surprisingly the skins of oranges. Some people say they are unnecessary and have caused allergic reactions.

Chemicals aside, food processing often entails stripping down natural foods to their components before creating the final product. When whole grains are refined this way, the healthiest part of the grain is often left behind.

This is often true even in seemingly innocuous processes. For example, a whole orange has much more fibre than a cup of freshly squeezed orange juice, so even this simple, natural "processing" reduces the health benefit of the original, natural food.

It would be nearly impossible today to eat a diet devoid of chemicals and untouched by modern processing methods. It is possible, however, to reduce your consumption of the additives and refinements known to cause the most damage to your health and heart.

Here, then, are the big four. Focus your efforts on these, and you'll take a major step toward protecting your heart.

1 TRANS FATS
A man-made disaster

Trans fats are the phantom fats in many processed cakes and pastries and in hard blocks of margarine, which some people may think are a "heart-healthy" alternative to the saturated fat in butter. Look for the term "hydrogenated" on the ingredients list as hydrogenation is the process that converts oils into trans fats.

In recent years, trans fats have been denounced as more dangerous for your heart than saturated fat. In fact, the Heart and Stroke Foundation of Canada would like to see processed trans fats eliminated from the Canadian food supply. A Dutch study suggests that doing so would reduce deaths from heart disease by 20 per cent. That would mean 15,000 fewer premature deaths in Canada every year.

The trouble is, trans fats are everywhere—in cookies, icing, potato chips, snack foods, margarine, doughnuts and muffins, plus commercially prepared fries, onion rings and fried chicken and fish. Here's what you need to know about avoiding foods with trans fats.

THE DETAILS

■ **What are they?** Trans fats are produced during hydrogenation: a chemical process that manufacturers use to convert vegetable oils into semi-solid fats. Hydrogenation helps to extend the shelf-life of fats and gives food a creamier taste. But it also changes their natural configuration.

■ **How trans fats attack your heart** They boost levels of "bad" LDL cholesterol and decrease "good" HDL cholesterol. Some researchers also suspect that trans fats further threaten your heart by increasing inflammation and making cells resistant to insulin.

■ Label detective All processed foods sold in Canada must list levels of trans fats on the Nutritional Facts table, which allows all shoppers the opportunity to see what they are about to purchase.

Trans fats are most commonly found in processed foods such as cookies, cakes, pastries and meat pies. Even some "health" foods such as cereal bars and vegetarian dishes contain trans fats. Trans fats are less likely to turn rancid, so are often used for deep-frying in fast-food outlets. There is no way of knowing what type of fat is used in takeout foods and in restaurants and cafés, although you can always ask.

■ Avoid trans fats for this heart bonus
Cutting out trans fats could reduce Canadian deaths from heart disease by 20 per cent.

8 ways to escape the trans fat trap

1 Choose soft margarines rather than hard block margarines and look for brands with no trans fats. It may be shown as hydrogenated fat or oil.

2 Use olive oil for sautéing.

3 Sprinkle flaked or chopped nuts or sunflower seeds on salads instead of bacon bits.

4 Snack on a small handful of unsalted nuts or a box of raisins rather than potato chips. Or try peanut butter on celery stalks, carrots or rice cakes.

5 Shop around the perimeter of the grocery store. Most processed foods, which contain a lot of trans fats, are on the inner aisles.

6 When you do buy processed foods, choose trans-fat-free versions of cookies, cereals and desserts.

7 Skip fast-food fries. Order a side salad, a plain baked potato or a healthy alternative such as fresh fruit (now becoming available at more fast-food chains).

8 When you have time, make your own scones, waffles and cakes instead of using store-bought versions or a mix packed with trans fats. Make extra and freeze some. (See "Heart-healthy recipes" on page 254 for recipes for Strawberry bran waffles, Tomato and basil scones, and French apple cake.)

Make your own muffins instead of using store-bought versions or a mix packed with trans fats.

2 REFINED CARBOHYDRATES
Stripped of goodness

If your three meals a day include white bread, white rolls, sugary cereal, white rice or traditional white pasta, you're not alone. Most, if not all, of the six to seven helpings of grains most of us eat every day are refined; less than one is an unrefined, heart-boosting whole grain.

Choosing refined over whole grains boosts your heart attack risk by up to 30 per cent, so it's time to start shopping more wisely: you may think you're eating healthy whole grains when in fact that brown bread or multi-grain cereal on your table is an impostor. Look at the label and don't be fooled. Often, they're just the same refined products that raise the risk of high cholesterol, high blood pressure, heart attacks, insulin resistance, diabetes and abdominal fat.

This is not just a 21st-century malady. In ancient Egypt, rich people feasted on breads made from hand-sieved grain. In European manor houses, the kitchen staff filtered wheat flour through silken sieves to remove the gritty (nutrition rich) brown bits. Here's what we know today.

THE DETAILS

■ **What are they?** Grains are commercially milled and polished these days—in fact, 27 kg of wheat leaves the mill as almost 20 kg of white flour.

What's left behind? Wheat bran—the brown, fibre-rich outer layer of the wheat grain, filled with niacin, thiamine, riboflavin, magnesium, phosphorus, iron and zinc— along with wheat germ, the grain's rich inner layer, that not only contains more of these nutrients, but also, vitamin E, some protein and fat. Together, the bran and germ contain up to 90 per cent of the grain's nutrients. Refining merely offers a longer shelf life.

6 ways to go whole grain

Aim for three or more servings of whole grains per day. Here's how to exchange refined grains for the good stuff.

1 Switch to a high-fibre cereal such as muesli, oatmeal, Cheerios, bran flakes, Shredded Wheat, Spoon-Size Shredded Wheat, Weetabix or Grape-Nuts.

2 Substitute whole-grain toast for white toast or bagels and enjoy low-fat multi-grain muffins in place of pastries.

3 Make sandwiches with whole-grain breads or rolls.

4 Expand your grain repertoire with whole grains such as kasha, brown rice, bulgur and whole-grain tortillas.

5 Use barley in soups, stews, casseroles and salads.

6 Add whole grains, such as cooked brown rice, or whole-grain bread crumbs to ground meat or poultry for extra "body."

■ How whole grains protect your heart

At least seven major studies show that women and men who eat more whole grains (including dark bread, whole-grain cereals, brown rice, bran and other grains, such as bulgur and kasha) have 20 to 30 per cent less heart disease. Those who opt for refined grains have more heart attacks, insulin resistance and high blood pressure.

This is because blood sugar levels climb higher and faster after you eat a slice of white bread or a scoop of white rice. Raising blood sugar levels raises insulin levels, which in turn decreases levels of "good" HDLs and increases triglyceride levels. It also raises your risk of insulin resistance and Type 2 diabetes. If you opt for whole-grain bread or brown rice, the increase in blood sugar is not as high and is stretched over a longer period.

When nutritionists measured the waistlines of 459 people, they found that those who ate the most refined grains saw their midriffs expand by a ½ inch a year. Abdominal fat releases heart-threatening hormones and fatty acids 24 hours a day. It also deprives arteries of a huge range of protective substances found in whole grains, including cholesterol-lowering soluble fibre and antioxidants.

■ **Safe upper limit** Try to cut out refined carbohydrates. Aim for at least three whole-grain servings a day.

■ **Label detective** Read the ingredient list on packaged grain products; top of the list should be whole wheat or another whole grain, such as oats, and the fibre content should be at least 3 g per serving. And remember: Wheat bread is not necessarily whole wheat and neither is brown bread. And wheat flour does not mean whole-wheat flour.

3 SALT
Addictive flavour, extra trouble

Here's a mystery: you shake a few grains of salt on your scrambled eggs, add a pinch to your mixed green salad at lunch and then scatter a bit more on dinner's baked potato and roasted chicken. The total? Scarcely ½ teaspoon. Yet somehow, most people actually consume nearly 2 heaping teaspoons of blood pressure-raising sodium chloride daily. Where does it all come from?

Three-quarters of the sodium in our diets isn't from a salt shaker. It's hidden in processed foods, such as canned vegetables and soups; condiments, such as soy and Worcestershire sauce; fast-food burgers (and fries); and cured or preserved meats, such as bacon and sliced ham or turkey.

Some occurs naturally in unprocessed edibles, such as milk, beets and celery. That's a good thing: sodium is necessary for life. It helps to regulate blood pressure, maintains the body's fluid balance, transmits nerve impulses, makes muscles—including the heart—contract, and keeps your senses of taste, smell and touch working properly. You need a little every day to replace what is lost to sweat, tears and other excretions.

But is more salt harmful? Scientists—and the salt industry—have debated this for decades but medical evidence suggests that it is. Medical experts around the world agree: Most people eat too much salt. There is a strong link between a high salt diet and the development of high blood pressure. Reducing blood pressure lowers your risk of stroke and heart disease.

THE DETAILS

■ **What is it?** Since prehistoric times, humans have used salt to enhance flavour, improve texture and make food last longer. Today, food manufacturers put millions of

Medical experts believe excess salt is a cause of hypertension and heart disease.

tons per year into processed foods. It's in everything from bread to breakfast cereal, canned foods to frozen dinners, soups to sauces and butter to margarine.

■ **How salt attacks your heart** Your body needs a precise concentration of sodium; so excess salt prompts it to retain fluid simply to dilute the extra sodium in your bloodstream. This raises blood volume, which forces your heart to work harder; at the same time, it makes veins and arteries constrict, raising blood pressure.

Bones benefit from less salt too, because excess salt causes the leaching of calcium, which leads to bone thinning and a higher risk of osteoporosis and fractures.

While 30 to 60 per cent of people with high blood pressure and 25 to 50 per cent of people with normal blood pressure can lower their blood pressure by cutting back on salt, some researchers believe that nearly everyone could cut their blood pressure at least a little by eating fewer processed foods and by losing the habit of automatically sprinkling salt over their meals. As well as eating fewer salty foods, you should also ensure you have at least five portions of fruit and vegetables a day. These are a good natural source of the mineral potassium, which has the opposite effect to sodium or salt.

■ **Safe upper limit** Nutritionists recommend reducing sodium intake to no more than 2,300 mg per day, the equivalent of 6 g of salt. A whopping 75 to 80 per cent of our salt intake comes from processed foods. Be extra vigilant when shopping for groceries and when ordering a restaurant meal.

7 ways to shake the salt habit

You don't need to be addicted to salt. Try these salt-reduction strategies, and within a week or two, you won't miss it at all.

1 Omit salt from recipes or automatically reduce sodium by 25 per cent by measuring out the same amount of coarse salt instead—the coarse granules of these salts don't pack as tightly into a measuring spoon.

2 Take the salt shaker off your table. If it's not there, you may not think about adding salt to your meal.

3 Use other flavourings, such as herbs and spices, lemon or mustard to flavour your foods. Use spices such as coriander, caraway and fennel seeds to add flavour to fish dishes and cooked vegetables.

4 Choose the "no added sugar or salt" varieties of canned foods such as kidney beans, chickpeas and sweet corn. If you can't find beans packed in water, rinse them thoroughly before using them, to remove some of the salt.

5 Processed foods, such as canned soups, often contain very high levels of salt. Invest in a blender or processor so that you can make your own.

6 Give unsalted or reduced-sodium pretzels, chips, peanuts and condiments a try.

7 Instead of adding salt, give cooked vegetables a bit of a lift by adding the zest (grated rind) and juice of a lemon.

HEART-HEALTHY EATING

Many everyday foods contain "hidden" salt, and too much of it can cause high blood pressure.

■ Label detective Only the Nutrition Facts table, found on most products, will give you the real sodium or salt count. Don't be fooled into thinking that "reduced sodium" means "low sodium"—it may be much higher than you think.

■ Avoid excess salt for this heart bonus Reducing your daily sodium intake by just 0.3 g (300 mg)—the amount in about two slices of cheese—can cut systolic pressure (the first number in a blood pressure reading) by 2 to 4 points and reduce diastolic pressure (the second number) by 1 to 2 points. Reduce your intake even more, and your blood pressure may drop even lower.

4 ADDED SUGARS
Rogue sweetness?

When you ask most people what makes food sweet, they'll usually say sugar. But these days, added sugars come in many different chemical forms that you may not instantly recognize on a label and are present in a huge variety of foods, including canned vegetables and some breads.

THE DETAILS

■ What are they? These are all the sugars that are added to foods, with names such as glucose, fructose, maltose, hydrolyzed starch, invert sugar and corn syrup.

■ How added sugars attack your heart Cambridge University researchers, who studied more than 10,000 people aged between 45 and 79 over five years, discovered that people with high blood sugar levels were at even higher risk of heart disease than people with diabetes (there is a proven link between heart disease and diabetes). Obesity, and its alarming increase in the general population, is a key issue here.

Excess sugar consumption … has been implicated in the development of diabetes as well as heart disease.

■ **Safe upper limit** A report by the World Health Organization and the Food and Agricultural Organization of the United Nations stated that an individual's intake of added sugars should be limited to less than 10 per cent of calories consumed daily. Excess sugar consumption is a factor in weight gain and has been implicated in the development of diabetes as well as heart disease.

■ **Label detective** On Nutritional Facts labels, look for the "Carbohydrates (of which sugars)" figure. More than 10 g sugar per 100 g is a lot; less than 2 g is a little.

The ingredients contained in a product are usually listed from largest to smallest so beware if sugars (under any name) are high on the list. And watch out for sugar in all its guises, such as sucrose, glucose, fructose and maltose.

■ **The heart bonus for avoiding sugars** By rejecting added sweetness you can lower your blood sugar, insulin and triglycerides. You may also find it easier to achieve weight loss.

4 ways to reducing the added sugars in your food

Here are four ways to reduce the added sugars in your diet.

1 Enjoy natural sweet treats such as fruit— fresh, frozen (without syrup), canned in its own juice, or dried (provided it's not sugar coated). Fruit brings you a wealth of fibre, vitamins, minerals and antioxidants as well.

2 Limit processed fruit juice or soft drinks. If you must have a soft drink, choose the diet version. Try soda water or sparkling mineral water with a splash of orange or lemon juice; or just enjoy refreshing plain water.

3 Take your reading glasses, if necessary, to the grocery store. So many products such as apple sauce, stewed tomatoes, baked beans and pasta sauce contain added sugars—but there may well be a more natural version available.

4 Try to cut the sugar you add to cereals, tea or coffee. Many cereals are already sweetened (check the label) and you'll probably find you quickly get used to unsweetened beverages— in the end you may even prefer the taste.

Most experts agree that for good health you need a healthy, balanced diet that includes carbohydrates.

The truth about carbohydrates

Net carbs. Impact carbs. Fit carbs. Smart carbs. The mania for restricted-carbohydrate eating programs has brought a whole new vocabulary to the world of nutrition, hundreds of competing diet plans and cookbooks to bookstores, and hundreds of "low-carb" products to grocery store shelves in recent years. Without question, this has stirred controversy among nutritionists, doctors and governments—and confusion for the consumer. There are even those who advocate a no-carb diet with freedom to eat as much and as many proteins as one desires. Most experts agree that for good health you need a healthy, balanced diet that includes carbohydrates—at least a third of daily calories should come from carbohydrates— as well as healthy fats and proteins.

Among the new offerings are numerous cookbooks with recipes for indulgent low-carb desserts and low-carb slow-cooker dinners, a rescue manual for low carbers who've fallen off the wagon, and even books to help you choose the best low-carb diet book. On store shelves: low-carb breads and pastas, chocolate candy and creamy cheesecake, energy bars, beer, and even a reduced-carb substitute for fat-free milk. (We ask: Does anyone need a substitute for fat-free milk?)

Behind the low-carb craze is one central claim: faster, easier weight loss thanks to lower, steadier blood sugar. In reality, it's not nearly that simple. No one denies the claim that it is sensible to cut down on the refined carbohydrates in your diet—such as pastries and white bread, white rice and potato chips—but many diets pose an immediate threat to your heart by demonizing all carbohydrates.

Blacklisting fruit, vegetables and whole grains robs your cardiovascular system of the health protectors you need every day: soluble fibre, vitamins, minerals and antioxidants. And replacing them with a high intake of saturated fats poses untold dangers to your heart and blood pressure. Research shows that in the long run, a moderate-carbohydrate diet that includes fruit, vegetables and whole grains may be as good as, or even better than, a low-carbohydrate diet, for losing weight.

As for high-priced, processed low-carb foods, remember that a chocolate bar claiming "2 net carbs" sounds slimming, but it probably has as many calories and as much fat as its normal-carbohydrate equivalent.

The promises on low-carb products make them seem healthier, leaner, almost magic— but a chocolate bar is still a chocolate bar, governed by nature's first rule of weight gain—eat too many calories, and you will gain weight.

Myths and truths

The premise of all low-carbohydrate foods and associated diet plans begins with nutrition-science basics. Carbohydrates do raise blood sugar, because they provide so much of the body's preferred source of fuel: glucose. When glucose levels rise, your pancreas releases a flood of insulin that prompts cells to store sugar.

Advocates say that eating a diet low in carbohydrates makes weight loss easier because low, steady blood sugar conquers food cravings. But the next step in the low-carbohydrate equation is open to debate: proponents say these diets also change your metabolism so that your body breaks down

The new "Carb" glossary

Carbohydrate information can be confusing, so here are some useful terms. Some are used more widely than others, but you will see them on products, in diet plans and in magazines.

■ **Carbohydrates** One of the three main forms of food in the human diet (the other two are fats and protein). Carbohydrates are a wide range of organic compounds, created by plants, that include carbon, hydrogen and oxygen. Starches and sugars are among the carbohydrates we eat.

■ **Complex carbs** Carbohydrates with a more intricate chemical composition, which require more time to break down into basic sugars during digestion. Plant-based foods in their raw or natural form are mostly composed of complex carbohydrates, as well as fibre, plant-based fats and nutrients. It is this winning combination of nutritious ingredients and slow digestion that makes plants, in their natural form, among the healthiest foods available to humans. Diet experts often call these "good carbs."

■ **Simple carbs** These are chemically simple, so they digest quickly into glucose, or blood sugar. While some plant foods—such as potatoes and carrots—contain lots of simple carbohydrates, most of the simple carbohydrates in our diet are a result of refining done by manufacturers. White flour, refined sugar and white rice are the most common simple carbohydrates. The process that simplifies carbohydrates often removes the fibre, plant fats and micronutrients from the original plant, thus stripping it of much of its nutrition value. Diet experts may call these "bad carbs."

■ **Net carbs** (also known as "smart carbs" or "impact carbs") This is a recently devised concept; essentially, net carbs are complex carbohydrates minus their fibre and certain natural sweeteners. The theory is that net carbs are the parts of the carbohydrate that affect blood sugar levels, but most nutritionists consider these measurements to be gimmicky, invalid and not at all useful.

Most potatoes are easily digested but you can improve their GI rating by choosing new potatoes . . .

more fats, and so fewer of the calories you eat are stored as body fat. But are they?

Low-carbohydrate weight-loss plans do work—for a while. Weight falls quickly at first because burning stored carbohydrates (called glycogen) releases water. Quite simply, you lose excess water weight.

Nutritionists say, though, that this type of weight loss is not metabolic magic, just the working-out of nature's first rule of weight loss: eat fewer calories and you will lose weight. Some dieters say this special way of eating eliminates cravings but others suffer headaches and feel nauseous. Burning fat without carbohydrates produces substances

Glycemic Index tricks

The Glycemic Index ranks carbohydrates according to their effects on blood sugar levels. Carbohydrates that break down quickly in the body have the highest GI ratings; those that are digested and absorbed slowly, releasing sugar gradually into the bloodstream, are low on the GI index. Research has shown that eating low-GI foods can lower "bad" LDL cholesterol, raise "good" HDL cholesterol, help you to lose weight and to cut your risk of diabetes, heart disease and even cancer.

The trouble is, the GI index is a rather strange list: carrots have a higher GI than pound cake, for example. Also, computing a food's ultimate effect on blood sugar requires you to consider portion size, other foods eaten at the same meal (fat and protein slow down sugar absorption) and how the food is prepared—for example, a slow-rising bread has a lower GI than one made with rapid-acting yeast.

This sounds far too complex, so experts suggest that you forget the formula but keep the GI idea in mind by following this advice to lower the GI of any meal.

■ Eat breakfast cereals based on oats, barley and bran, as well as whole-grain breads, rather than refined white breads.

■ Choose whole fruits rather than juices, which have a higher GI.

■ Eat lots of vegetables and include plenty of legumes such as lentils, chickpeas and beans. In recipes, legumes can help to lower the total GI of a dish.

■ Most potatoes are rapidly digested but you can improve their GI rating by choosing new potatoes (medium GI), making mashed potatoes with low-fat milk or cooking sweet potatoes instead.

■ Pasta and noodles are low GI so both can make an ideal alternative to rice and potatoes which are both high GI foods.

■ Choose vinaigrette dressing for salad. Researchers have found that vinegar reduces a meal's Glycemic Index rating significantly.

■ Have some fat and protein. For instance, if you are nibbling baby carrots or apple wedges, add a dab of unsalted peanut butter.

called ketones, which can decrease appetite, but sustained high ketone levels may deplete mineral stores in bones, leaving them fragile. Here's the rest of the story.

What the evidence shows

Carbohydrate-conscious eating may speed up early weight loss, but not much more. End results are often less than exciting. In a year-long study of 63 dieters, University of Pennsylvania researchers found that low-carbohydrate dieters lost 4 per cent more weight than those following a conventional low-calorie plan in the first six months—but both groups had achieved nearly identical weight losses after one year.

When researchers at the National Weight Control Registry in the United States looked at the diets of 2,681 successful dieters who had maintained at least a 13.5 kg (30 lb) weight loss for a year or more, they found that only 1 per cent of the total group were low-carb dieters and concluded that low-carb plans didn't produce a lasting metabolic change that kept weight off.

British researchers studied a group following four different weight loss programs including the Atkins Diet. All were effective to some degree but the researchers concluded that different types of diet suit different people, and there was no single outstandingly successful diet.

The high-fat, very low-carb threat

Dr. Atkins' diet—the oldest and most famous of the low-carbohydrate regimens—allows a mere 20 g of carbohydrates a day in the earliest, strictest phase, putting most grains, beans, fruits, breads, rice, potatoes, pastas and starchy vegetables off-limits. At the same time, it allows generous amounts of beef, pork, chicken, eggs and butter and all that saturated fat can raise levels of heart-threatening LDL cholesterol—and at the same time deprive you of the antioxidants from fruits, vegetables and grains that protect arteries from plaque formation.

Low-carbohydrate diets are also high in protein, which makes them risky for people with diabetes because they can speed the progression of diabetic kidney disease.

Low-carbohydrate isn't low-calorie

Many low-carbohydrate products undermine weight-loss efforts because they're packed with as many—or even more—calories than normal versions. Many are also higher in fat. This is especially true of reduced-carbohydrate comfort foods such as ice cream, bread, pasta and snack bars.

Heart experts say that it is the calories, not the carbohydrates that count. People are gaining weight because they are eating more calories than they can burn because they are getting less exercise.

Low-carb junk food is still junk

Indulging in a low-carbohydrate snack food in the belief that it's a better weight-loss choice than a piece of fruit or a serving of vegetables puts you in double jeopardy: you will have robbed your body of a host of heart-healthy nutrients and fibre, and you may have eaten a number of empty calories.

Here's an example: for 40 g of carbohydrate a day, you could eat 1 apple,

1 banana and a slice of whole-grain toast (a total of just 200 calories but also a hefty dose of antioxidants, vitamins and minerals). But if you choose to get those 40 g from low-carbohydrate snack foods, you may find you are consuming three times as many calories and very few nutrients.

Low-carbohydrate lessons

What about refined carbohydrates—candy, white bread and white rice? Refined carbohydrates have been stripped of the good stuff that slows digestion, so they can cause sugar levels to soar. As a result, your pancreas pumps out extra insulin to help cells to absorb the extra sugar, and your body endures an excess of insulin that wreaks havoc with triglyceride levels.

Eating lots of refined carbohydrates doubled heart risk in the landmark Nurses' Health Study, for which researchers at the Harvard School of Public Health followed more than 74,000 women from 1984 to 1996. It showed that a diet high in refined carbohydrates boosts triglycerides, suppresses levels of heart-helping HDL cholesterol, and may contribute to high blood pressure and artery-threatening inflammation.

Buried in all the low-carbohydrate hype is a second truth: eating fat and protein is important. Both keep blood sugar levels steady, thus cutting food cravings. "Good fats" won't raise your LDL cholesterol but will keep HDL levels from dropping (a danger on low-fat diets).

Protein that is low in saturated fat, such as lean beef, chicken, turkey, or pork tenderloin, supplies heart-protecting nutrients and amino acids to rebuild heart muscle cells and other cells throughout your body.

The 30-Minutes-a-Day way

With this plan you should be able to include satisfying good fats, protein and "good" carbs in every meal.

Good carbohydrates—such as fruit, vegetables, and whole grains—are essential guardians of heart health. A University of Minnesota review of ten studies involving 91,000 men and 245,000 women found that for every 10 g of fibre from fruit that volunteers ate every day, the risk of fatal heart disease dropped a staggering 30 per cent. For every 10 g of cereal fibre, risk dropped 15 per cent.

That's not much food for a lot of protection: you'd get 10 g of fibre a day if you ate an apple, a pear and two dried apricot halves. You'd get 10 g of cereal fibre from a bowl of bran flakes and one slice of whole-grain toast. Vegetables count, too: for each additional serving of vegetables you eat daily, heart risk drops 4 per cent.

Fruits and vegetables are packed with heart helpers, including fibre to cut cholesterol and discourage blood clots; antioxidants; and folate and vitamin B_6—all key nutrients for lowering levels of homocysteine, an amino acid that can damage artery walls and increase the risk of heart disease.

Good carbohydrates can also help you to control your weight. As part of the Nurses' Health Study, researchers found that women who consistently consumed more whole grains weighed less than women who consumed fewer.

The thinking is that the fibre in complex carbohydrates aids weight loss by keeping you feeling full for longer (they hold more water in your digestive system), slowing down digestion and whisking some calories out of the body, unabsorbed.

What is a healthy serving?

Overeating is one of the prime causes of Canada's obesity epidemic, yet most of us don't even realize that we overeat—or just how crucial serving size really is.

There is good evidence that over the past 50 years, portions in many restaurants and stores have super-sized, growing with our expanding waistlines. And—disturbingly—many people have just got used to eating larger portions.

Not realizing how calories mount up?

Most fast food is very dense in calories so you need to eat only a little for a huge caloric intake. These energy-dense foods can fool people into taking in more calories than they need. Similar foods, cooked at home, are far less energy-dense. And some people also think that eating certain types of food while avoiding others is more central to their weight-control efforts than eating less food. They're wrong—for weight control, it's total calories that count.

We eat whatever is put in front of us In the past we were taught to eat everything on the plate, whether we were hungry or not. When the portions we were told to finish were small, there was no problem, but, according to the *Journal of the American Medical Association,* in the last 20 years, fast-food chain burgers jumped from 172 g to 204 g and soft drinks nearly doubled in size, adding almost 50 calories.

We think more food is a better bargain Getting more for your money isn't good for your waistline or your health. People think they are getting a bargain when they get more

Leave the "clean plate" club.

food for just a few pennies more. What isn't a bargain are the extra calories and fat that come with these "added value" meals. The World Cancer Research Fund says that the food and drink industry is contributing to obesity by offering consumers ever-larger portion sizes. There is a call for the industry to make it easier to make healthy choices by not promoting "super-sized" portions.

Health Canada began a new labelling program in 2003. It obliges companies to include a Nutritional Facts table on food products, listing the number of calories and 13 ingredients deemed important by health professionals, scientists and consumers. According to the health experts, particular attention should be paid to the saturated fat and trans fat content.

Most weight-loss success stories are the result of cutting portion sizes. It's a simple fact: if you eat less, you'll lose excess weight.

Cutting portions down to size

Here's how you can reduce your portions and still feel satisfied.

Wait 10 minutes Your stomach needs about that long to signal to the brain that it's full, so wait before helping yourself to more mashed potatoes or lasagna. Keep the conversation going, tell a joke or, if you're dining alone, read the newspaper or do the crossword. If you're truly hungry after the delay, have seconds of the vegetables or salad.

Leave the "clean plate" club Most of us eat everything we're served no matter how big the portions. A better strategy is to eat a healthy portion (see "Perfect portion size guide," right), then stop. It's better to waste a little food (or save it for tomorrow) than to overload your body.

Never eat straight from the bag, box or carton If you are having takeout, put the right portion on a plate and put the package away, then sit down and enjoy your meal, taking your time over it.

What to do if you like big portions Overload your plate with vegetables, or a salad with a smidgen of dressing, or have a big, steaming bowl of broth-based soup. These water-rich, low-fat foods are low in calories, so a big portion isn't a problem. Use a smaller plate for your meal. Less space on the plate means automatic portion control.

When ordering food or drinks or buying packaged food at the grocery store, program yourself to choose or order the smallest size of any high-calorie items. (The exceptions are salads and vegetables without added fat.) Get the small latte, the half-sized filled baguette instead of the big one, the small muffin instead of the big chocolate chip version. Calories you haven't bought can't end up around your waist.

Choose single-serve Buy or make high-calorie foods in individual serving sizes. Instead of family-sized cartons of ice cream, buy single serving cartons; make cupcakes instead of a big cake; and buy single-serving bags of chips.

But read the label first. Many packaged foods and drinks may look as if they provide one serving but are actually meant to serve two or more people and the calories and other nutrition information on the label are for just one serving. So read the number of servings per container first, then be sure to eat or drink just one serving per person.

Put away leftovers before eating It's easy to sit down to a healthy plate of food. The trouble starts when your plate is empty and you have more of each food sitting in front of you in alluring serving bowls. The answer is to package and store leftovers before you sit down to eat. That way, taking a second helping is more of a conscious effort and feels more inappropriate.

Round off the meal with fruit or vegetables As you make the transition to more modest portion sizes, you may find yourself craving more food with your meal. The answer is to have a large, crunchy serving of celery, carrots or peppers, or a sliced tomato with your meal. And there is no easier, healthier way to add volume to a meal than with an apple, an orange, or a big helping of watermelon or cantaloupe at the end of it.

Perfect portion size guide

Most of us underestimate portions and, therefore, calories by at least 25 per cent—meaning that you could eat hundreds of extra calories every day and not even know it. Here's how to estimate the perfect portion size every time. We give you two comparisons: one compares the portion size to everyday objects and the other to parts of your hand, for a take-anywhere system.

THE PERFECT PORTION	LOOKS LIKE THIS	OR THIS
90 g (3 oz) meat	a mini-pack of tissues	your outstretched palm
90 g (3 oz) fish	a chequebook	your outstretched palm
3–4 tablespoons beans	a tennis ball	a cupped handful
40 g (1½ oz) cheese	3 dice	your thumb
2 heaping tablespoons rice or pasta	a full cupcake wrapper	a rounded handful
1 portion of mashed potatoes	a drink coaster	your palm
25 g (1 oz) roll	a bar of soap	half of your palm
1 small bun	the round part of a light bulb	half of your fist
8 cm piece of cake	a pack of cards	about ¾ of your palm
1 teaspoon butter or margarine	a postage stamp	the tip of your thumb
1 tablespoon oil or dressing	the base of a teacup	the centre of your cupped hand
potato chips	a tennis ball	a cupped handful
nuts or dried fruit	a golf ball	a small cupped handful

Superfoods to the rescue

Luscious strawberries dipped in rich, dark chocolate. Grilled salmon. Mashed sweet potatoes dusted with cinnamon. Spinach salad tossed with cranberries and walnuts. Definitely a gourmet's delight but also a huge dose of heart health—from good fats and fibre to powerful antioxidants and essential vitamins and minerals.

Foods, such as the 18 described in this section, work better than supplements to lower your risk of heart disease. Not only do they delight your taste buds, but they also do battle with all seven deadly heart attackers at the same time. Specifically, the foods in this chapter can help to:

■ Reduce your risk of artery-clogging atherosclerosis.
■ Whittle away at cholesterol.
■ Lower your blood pressure.
■ Cool inflammation.
■ Neutralize damaging free radicals.

■ Reduce your chances of developing metabolic syndrome by keeping blood sugar lower and steadier.
■ Help you to lose weight, when eaten in healthy portions.

You don't have to go to a health-food store to find them; just push your shopping cart around the aisles of your local grocery store and seek out the fresh fruit and vegetables, meat, fish and dairy products. Or take a trip to your local farmers' market for the freshest of fresh garden produce.

More good news: we've pulled together the quickest, tastiest ways to cook and serve these healing foods, from tried-and-trusted favourites to fresh, new ideas.

Eating as healthily as this doesn't have to take extra time out of your busy day—reaching for a slice of watermelon or a bag of walnuts can be just as quick as grabbing a bag of chips. And the taste and rewards are well worth it.

> People who ate two apples a day had fewer oxidized, artery-attacking LDLs than non-apple eaters.

1 ALMONDS

- **Super nutrients** Monounsaturated fat, magnesium, calcium, potassium, fibre.
- **Serving size** 30 g (1 oz)—about 24 almonds; 160 calories.
- **Benefits** A single serving of these crunchy, protein-packed nuggets provides 9 g of monounsaturated fat to help cut LDL ("bad") cholesterol and boost HDL ("good") cholesterol. Simply choosing almonds instead of a doughnut, chips or pretzels for two snacks a day could cut LDL levels by nearly 10 per cent. A serving of almonds also gives 10 per cent of your daily calcium quota and 25 per cent of the magnesium you need.

Bonus You get 60 per cent of the recommended amount of vitamin E, an artery-protecting antioxidant, as well as 2 g of fibre. Just be sure to stop at one handful at snack time—advice that holds true for all nuts because they're calorie-dense.

2 APPLES

- **Super nutrients** Antioxidants, fibre.
- **Serving size** 1 medium; 85 calories.
- **Benefits** Red Delicious, Granny Smith and Gala apples are among the foods richest in antioxidants, thanks to large quantities of the flavonoid quercetin. (Flavonoids are natural chemicals in plants that, in your bloodstream, remove free radical molecules, fight inflammation and impede cancer.)

Bonus Apples are a rich source of pectin, a soluble fibre. In a recent study at the University of California, people who ate two apples a day had fewer oxidized, artery-attacking LDLs than non-apple eaters—endorsing the old "apple a day" theory.

Good ideas — Almonds

- For a serving of almonds into a small plastic container and slip it into your handbag or briefcase for a healthy snack during the day.

- Toss some flaked almonds into salads, stir-fries, fruit salad or hot or cold cereal.

- Keep flaked almonds on hand (store them in the freezer for freshness) to add to vegetable dishes, baking and salads.

Good ideas — Apples

- Cut up an apple and add it to hot cereal.

- For a portable snack or lunch dessert, cut up an apple and place the slices in a plastic bag with 2 teaspoons of cinnamon. Carry it with you in an insulated lunch bag (or pop it in the office fridge). It tastes like apple pie, without the crust or the sugar.

- For a quick baked apple, core an apple, pack the centre with raisins and walnuts, and dust with cinnamon. Place it in a bowl with ¼ cup of orange juice, apple juice or water and microwave on high for about 5 minutes.

3 AVOCADOS

■ **Super nutrients** LDL-lowering mono-unsaturated fats, folic acid, vitamin E, potassium.

■ **Serving size** ½ medium-sized avocado; about 150 calories.

■ **Benefits** In a Mexican study, people who ate one avocado a day for a week had reductions in total cholesterol of 17 per cent. While their levels of unhealthy LDLs and triglycerides fell, beneficial HDLs actually rose—thanks, perhaps, to avocado's high levels of monounsaturated fat. Avocados are also full of a cholesterol-cutting nutrient called beta-sitosterol. (But do note that avocados are high in fat and eating too many could lead to weight gain if the energy isn't used up with physical activity.)

Good ideas: Avocados

■ Use mashed avocado in place of cheese, butter or cream cheese. Although avocados provide good fats, there are almost 30 g in a whole fruit (as much as in a large hamburger), and they're loaded with calories. That's why it's a good idea to use it in place of another high-fat item instead of just adding half an avocado to your diet.

■ Spread mashed avocado on bread.

■ Mix it with lemon juice, garlic and chopped coriander for homemade guacamole. Serve with low-fat chips or tortilla chips.

■ Slice and add to salads.

■ Add slices to sandwiches.

Good ideas: Bananas

■ Spread banana slices with peanut butter for a luscious snack.

■ Blend a peeled banana with a little milk or yogourt for a delicious smoothie.

■ Add banana chunks to hot cereal while it is cooking.

■ Freeze peeled ripe bananas in tinfoil for a delicious and healthy alternative popsicle.

4 BANANAS

■ **Super nutrients** Potassium, vitamin B_6.

■ **Serving size** 1 medium; 95 calories.

■ **Benefits** Researchers from India found that people who ate two bananas a day lowered their blood pressure levels, thanks to this fruit's artery-relaxing potassium. Potassium also helps to regulate sodium and water content in the bloodstream—high levels of both raise blood pressure. Also, one 115 g (4 oz) banana has 2 g of dietary fibre, instrumental in lowering blood cholesterol levels. (A warning: if you have diabetes, check your blood sugar after eating a banana—its high carbohydrate count could send your glucose soaring.)

Frozen berries make it possible to enjoy some sort of berry every day.

5 BERRIES

■ **Super nutrients** Antioxidants, vitamin C, fibre.

■ **Serving size** ½ cup; about 25 calories.

■ **Benefits** From cranberries to strawberries, raspberries, blackberries and blueberries, these tiny fruits would be high on any list of antioxidant-rich foods. Inside each juicy berry are beneficial plant-based compounds such as quercetin, kaempferol and anthocyanins (which give berries their brilliant red and blue hues). They act as antioxidants that can reduce the oxidation of LDLs and cool inflammation. Berries also contain salicylic acid, the same anti-inflammatory substance found in aspirin. Frozen berries make it possible to enjoy some sort of berry every day, regardless of the season.

Good ideas — Berries

■ Keep frozen berries in your freezer and add them to smoothies, hot cereal and fruit salads.

■ Make healthier smoothies by liquidizing together frozen berries, skimmed milk and sugar substitute (if needed).

■ Add berries to tossed green salads or make an all-berry salad and dress it with lemon vinaigrette.

■ Enjoy a sophisticated and luscious dessert: simply top raspberries with 25 g (1 oz) of melted dark chocolate.

■ Add berries to all your baking. Blueberries go well in breads made in bread machines, and raspberries add a unique twist to little cakes. Also add berries to pancake, waffle and muffin batters. Be sure to compensate for the moisture they add to the recipe by slightly reducing the other liquids.

6 BROCCOLI

■ **Super nutrients** Antioxidants, calcium, folate, glucoraphanin.

■ **Serving size** 1 medium head; 50 calories.

■ **Benefits** A serving of broccoli is very low in calories, but rich in heart-healthy nutrients. It provides 75 mg of calcium, 1.2 mg of iron, 5 g of protein and 3.5 g of fibre. Most of these nutrients remain after broccoli is steamed or stir-fried until crispy tender, but not when boiled. Flavonoids in broccoli also cool inflammation and discourage formation of blood clots. Numerous studies have shown that broccoli consumers also tend to have a reduced incidence of cancers.

Good ideas — Broccoli

■ Sprinkle finely chopped broccoli florets over casseroles, soups and salads.

■ Cook fresh broccoli and top it with grated Parmesan and a little olive oil.

■ Steam and refrigerate extra broccoli; you can use it with a slice of low-fat cheese as an omelette filling or serve it as an accompaniment at lunch.

■ Purée cooked broccoli with olive oil, garlic and crushed red pepper flakes to use as a sauce for pasta.

9 surprising uses for CINNAMON

A little cinnamon each day—½ teaspoon sprinkled on your morning toast—could cut your triglycerides and total cholesterol by 12 to 30 per cent, according to American researchers.

This pungent spice makes muscle and liver cells more sensitive to the hormone insulin and may help to reduce the insulin resistance that can throw blood fats (and blood sugar) out of kilter. Here are ways to work more of this heart-healthy spice into your diet.

1 Sprinkle a little in your morning coffee or hot chocolate.

2 Double the amount suggested in cake, pie and cookie recipes.

3 Use it in place of salt and pepper on baked sweet potatoes.

4 Create a zero-carbohydrate cinnamon-sugar: make a 2-to-1 mixture of cinnamon and a sugar substitute to use on oatmeal, toast and pancakes.

5 Add it to chili and curries for an authentic flavour.

6 Create a sweet breakfast rice by stirring raisins, nuts and cinnamon into reheated leftover brown rice.

7 Stir it into marinades for beef, pork or lamb.

8 Stuff a chicken with chopped apples, cinnamon, onion and a little sage.

9 In a small baking dish, toss 200 g (8 oz) of pecans with 3 teaspoons of canola oil, 2 teaspoons of cinnamon and 1 teaspoon of sugar substitute or sugar. Bake at 350°F (180°C) for 8 to 10 minutes.

7 CARROTS

■ **Super nutrients** Good source of beta-carotene, an artery-protecting antioxidant.

■ **Serving size** ½ cup cooked; 30 calories.

■ **Benefits** Carrots contain very high levels of beta-carotene, an antioxidant that guards against artery-clogging oxidized LDL cholesterol. Only foods like carrots offer this protection—recent studies suggest that antioxidant pills don't help protect your heart.

Cooked carrots have twice the antioxidant power of raw carrots because heat breaks down tough cell walls so that your body can use what's inside. Carrots, which are rich in fibre, also provide blood pressure-lowering potassium, homocysteine-lowering folate; vitamin B_6; and the antioxidants alpha carotene and beta carotene.

Good ideas   Carrots

■ Set out a bowl of baby carrots as a healthy snack that won't fill you up with unwanted calories or wreck your appetite.

■ Buy sliced and shredded carrots in the fresh fruit and vegetables department; add them to soups, salads and casseroles.

■ Instead of chips, serve carrot sticks with a low-fat dip.

■ Add finely grated carrots to muffins, and tuna or salmon salad.

■ Microwave baby carrots, stir in a teaspoon of honey and sprinkle finely chopped parsley over the top for an unusual vegetable dish.

■ Roast carrots in the oven with olive oil, along with parsnips and baby onions.

Could CHOCOLATE be a health food?

Just 25 g (1 oz) of luscious, dark chocolate contains as much as 41 mg of flavanols—the powerful antioxidants that guard against plaque buildup in artery walls. That's more antioxidants than a cup of green tea, an apple or a glass of red wine and it's one that may also reduce blood clotting and help to keep arteries flexible.

But don't rush out and buy any old chocolate bar—to get chocolate's benefits, choose one with the highest cocoa content—at least 70 per cent cocoa solids. But remember, that as well as its heart-healthy antioxidants, chocolate has a lot of fats and sugars. Dark or plain chocolate has less fat and more antioxidants than milk chocolate but it has more sugar. To get the benefits without adding too much fat, limit yourself to 25 g (1 oz) a day. Here are some ways to stretch your chocolate budget.

■ Add citrus to unlock more of chocolate's antioxidant powers. Dip orange sections into melted chocolate.

■ Start with pure cocoa powder (rather than a mix) when baking or making hot chocolate. It contains even more antioxidants than a chocolate bar.

Good ideas — Lean beef

■ Look for the words "lean" or "extra-lean" on the label or ask the butcher for lean cuts. And trim any visible fat from the beef.

■ Sauté thin slices of steak with onions, garlic and fresh basil. Serve with brown rice.

■ Add ground beef to tomato sauce and serve over pasta.

■ Skewer beef cubes with your favourite vegetables, then brush with a little olive oil, and broil.

■ Layer thinly sliced, cooked lean steak on split, toasted whole-grain bread rolls; top with roasted peppers and onions for a delicious open-faced sandwich.

■ Coat steaks with crushed peppercorns before barbequing.

8 LEAN BEEF

■ **Super nutrients** Vitamin B_6, vitamin B_{12}, stearic acid, iron, zinc.

■ **Serving size** 100 g (3½ oz); 177 calories.

■ **Benefits** In addition to its protein, a 100 g serving of lean beef provides more than 100 per cent of the RDA for vitamins B_{12} and B_6. The body needs both to convert homocysteine into other, benign molecules (high homocysteine levels are associated with increased risk of heart attack and stroke, and with osteoporosis). And while beef is a major source of saturated fat, a third of it is stearic acid, which has a neutral or even beneficial effect on blood cholesterol levels.

A WELL-BALANCED DIET should include lean beef

Beef contains a type of fatty acid called conjugated linoleic acid (CLA). CLA has been shown to improve cholesterol ratios (the ratio of LDL or "bad" cholesterol to HDL, or "good" cholesterol), at least in animals. Studies in animals have also found that CLA can delay the development of atherosclerosis and possibly even help with weight loss.

9 GARLIC

■ **Super nutrients** Contains allicin and other sulphur compounds which may help to lower blood pressure and cholesterol.

■ **Serving size** One or two small cloves, approximately 4 g (⅛ oz); 4 calories.

■ **Benefits** Your heart may benefit from regular garlic consumption. The compounds in garlic can be good for the heart, helping to lower blood pressure and to suppress production of harmful LDL cholesterol in the liver. In Germany, processed garlic is the basis of a drug used for lowering blood pressure. Garlic also adds a delicious flavour to food for very few calories and may well help you to cut your salt intake.

HYDRATE your heart

Sparkling or still, bottled or straight from the tap, water is kind to your heart. H_2O's super power lies in the fact that it's absorbed readily into the bloodstream, so it keeps blood diluted. Other liquids require digestion, a process that draws fluid out of the bloodstream, thickening the blood and increasing the risk of clots.

Water's other great benefit is the minerals that occur in it naturally. If you live in a hard water area and use a water softener, make sure you have one tap that supplies hard water for your cooking and drinking water: you'll benefit from the calcium in the hard water and avoid the high level of sodium that's produced in the water-softening process.

If you prefer to buy bottled water, and think that all bottled water is pretty much the same, think again! The array of choice on the store shelves includes everything from imported mountain spring water to tap water in a bottle. Make sure you read the fine print so you're getting what you want in terms of source, content and taste.

Your heart may well benefit from regular garlic consumption . . . In Germany, processed garlic is the basis of a drug used for lowering blood pressure.

Eating beans four times a week ... could lower your risk of coronary heart disease.

Good ideas — Kidney beans

■ Rinse canned kidney beans before using them to remove salt. Toss them into chili, casseroles and soups.

■ Make a better three-bean salad: combine kidney, black and white beans, then mix in chopped tomatoes and green onions. Dress with olive oil, lemon juice and black pepper.

■ In a food processor or blender, combine cooked kidney beans with garlic, cumin and chili peppers for a delicious spread that can be used as a dip for crudités or a sandwich or pita bread filling.

10 KIDNEY BEANS

■ **Super nutrients** Soluble fibre, folate, potassium, magnesium.
■ **Serving size** ½ cup; 118 calories.
■ **Benefits** Eating beans four times a week—as baked beans, in dips, chili or a salad sprinkled with chickpeas or black beans—could lower your risk of coronary heart disease. Make some of them kidney beans; they're rich in LDL-lowering soluble fibre and homocysteine-controlling folate, as well as blood pressure-easing potassium and magnesium.
Bonus Thanks to healthy doses of fibre and protein, beans give you steady energy, not a sudden rise (and fall) of blood sugar that raises your risk of metabolic syndrome and weight gain.

11 WALNUTS

■ **Super nutrients** More omega-3 fatty acids than any other nut.
■ **Serving size** 25 g (1 oz)—14 halves; 160 calories.
■ **Benefits** One serving of walnuts contains 2.6 g of alpha-linolenic acid (ALA), an omega-3 fatty acid that helps to prevent blood clots and promote a healthy heartbeat. Walnuts are also rich in vitamin B_6, which helps to control homocysteine. In one study, people who ate 40 g (1½ oz) walnuts every day for six weeks cut levels of extra-harmful very low density lipoproteins by 27 per cent. These delicious nuts also provide the amino acid arginine, which helps your body to produce nitric acid, a molecule that relaxes constricted blood vessels.

Good ideas — Walnuts

■ Chop walnuts in a food processor with a splash of olive oil and a generous helping of cinnamon. Spread over sliced fruit in a baking dish and bake for 45 minutes at 350°F (180°C) for a healthy dessert.

■ Keep a jar of chopped walnuts in the freezer to toss into cold or hot cereal, baked foods, salads, pancakes and waffles.

■ Treat yourself to a nut snack mid-morning or mid-afternoon: seal 14 walnut halves into a plastic bag and take them with you if you're going out.

Snacktime superstar: the PEANUT

A handful of roasted peanuts packs 62 mg of phytosterols—plant compounds that prevent your body from absorbing cholesterol and may help to explain why people who regularly eat peanuts or peanut butter and other nuts have a 30 to 50 per cent lower risk of fatal heart attacks. Peanuts are also a good source of homocysteine-lowering folate. But opt for unsalted nuts and don't eat too many—they are also high in fat.

12 OATMEAL

■ **Super nutrients** Cholesterol-lowering soluble fibre, slow-release carbohydrates that won't make your blood sugar spike.

■ **Serving size** ½ cup dry; 150 calories.

■ **Benefits** Beta-glucan, the soluble fibre in oats, acts like a sponge in your intestines, absorbing cholesterol-rich bile acids and eliminating them. The result is lower LDL cholesterol. Having a big bowl of oatmeal each day could cut cholesterol by 2 to 3 per cent. Soluble fibre may also help to lower blood pressure.

Good ideas — Oatmeal

■ Flavour it yourself: cook old-fashioned oats and top with a little honey, dried or fresh fruit, nuts and 2% or skim milk.

■ Use oats to thicken soups and stews by just tossing in a handful.

■ For a heart-healthy crumble topping for fruit, combine chopped walnuts, a little canola oil, oats and brown sugar to taste. Spread over cut fruit in a baking dish and bake at 350°F (180°C), for 30 to 45 minutes.

■ When making stuffing for a chicken, use half the amount of bread crumbs, and make the weight up with oats. The stuffing will be lighter and more interesting in texture.

■ Replace up to one-third of the flour in pancake recipes with oats; grind it into a fine powder first in the blender.

13 SALMON

■ **Super nutrients** Richest source of omega-3 fatty acids.

■ **Serving size** 100 g (3½ oz) grilled salmon; about 200 calories.

■ **Benefits** Among omega-3–rich fatty fish, salmon is king: one serving contains nearly 2 g of eicosapentaenoic acid (EPA) and docosahexaenoic acid (DHA), both important omega-3s that help reduce LDLs (especially very low density lipoproteins that clog arteries easily); cool inflammation; and may even discourage atherosclerosis and the formation of blood clots.

Most nutritionists recommend that everyone eat at least one or two portions of oily fish a week because eating oily fish is a simple way for people to reduce the risks of heart disease.

Good ideas ♥ Salmon

Most Canadians do not get enough omega-3 fatty acids in their diet. Eating salmon is one of the best ways to change that.

■ Choose canned salmon. Use it to make salmon salad, toss it with pasta, add it to casseroles or mix it with mashed potatoes to make salmon fish cakes. Don't pick out the little bones—they are so soft by the time they have gone through the canning process that they are easy to eat and add extra calcium to your diet.

■ Keep fish fillets in the freezer so that you always have some on hand; separate each fillet with cling wrap or parchment paper before you freeze them, so that you can take out as many fillets as you need.

■ Fish thaws and cooks very quickly (especially in the microwave), so use it when you have to rustle up a meal for unexpected guests or when you get home late.

■ Don't forget sardines, a handy cupboard standby and also rich in omega-3s. Serve on toast for a healthy and delicious snack.

Mercury in the food chain

Most fish contains traces of mercury and around the world there has been some concern about the potential effects of mercury contamination as a result of eating fish such as swordfish, king mackerel, tuna and shark. They are long-lived fish, and as a result, have the increased potential to be laden with heavy-metal contaminants. Health Canada advises:

■ all adults to limit consumption of swordfish, shark and fresh or frozen tuna to one meal a week.

■ pregnant and nursing mothers, women trying to become pregnant and children under five should avoid shark, marlin and swordfish and should not eat fresh and frozen tuna more than once a month.

Among the lowest levels of mercury in seafood are flounder, shrimp, haddock, pollock, sardines, wild salmon, crab and scallops. When choosing canned tuna, select "light" over "white" varieties and trim the fat from swordfish and other high-fat predator fish.

Soy for beginners

Soy foods—from milk to soy nuts—may help lower heart-damaging LDLs, thanks to unique plant estrogens called genistein and daidzen. Soy is no longer a food for vegetarians only. It has become so mainstream that the Heart and Stroke Foundation of Canada recommends it as part of a heart-healthy diet. Some soy products carry their Health Check™ symbol on their labels.

Yet not everyone's sold on soy. While some experts recommend two to four servings a week, in 2006 the American Heart Association released its review of a decade-long study on the health benefits of soy. It concluded that soy-based foods and supplements don't lower cholesterol. But nutrition experts agree that eating soy-based foods is a good idea because they contain less saturated fat than meat and provide healthy doses of fibre, vitamins and minerals. If you're new to soy, here are six ways to get you started:

EDAMAME That's the Japanese name for fresh soy beans. They resemble peas in shape, size and colour and come in pods just like green peas. Usually, you buy them frozen. Steam them and eat the beans unadorned or with a pinch of salt. Not only are they absolutely delicious, but in this form, soy most closely resembles ordinary vegetables.

MISO SOUP This delicate soup made from soy beans is often the first course of a Japanese dinner. Most grocery stores carry miso soup packages that are as cheap and easy to make up as any dry noodle product. Just pour the contents of the package into a cup of hot water, stir, and you have a wonderful, quick soup.

CALCIUM-FORTIFIED SOY BEVERAGES High in protein, calcium and isoflavones (plant chemicals that act like the hormone estrogen in the body), fortified soy can be a substitute for cow's milk in coffee, tea or on cereal.

SOY NUTS Dry-roasted soy nuts are among the richest sources of soy isoflavones. Have a handful as an afternoon snack or toss some into a salad. You can find them in health-food stores and grocery stores.

SOY BURGERS Grocery stores have delicious soy-based burgers, sausages, pâtés and other deli-type foods. Check the ingredient information, before you buy, though, because some soy-based foods may be high in fat, loaded with trans fats and/or contain very few isoflavones.

TEXTURED VEGETABLE PROTEIN (TVP) It may not sound appetizing but TVP can be a very useful source of protein—particularly for vegetarians—and is packed with isoflavones. TVP is defatted, dehydrated soy flour compressed into tiny clumps and chunks. If you soak it (stir 1 cup of TVP into an almost-full cup of hot water or broth and drain after 5 to 10 minutes) you can use it in dishes such as chili con carne or spaghetti bolognese. It has the chewy texture of ground meat. Uncooked TVP will keep in a cool, dark cupboard for months.

14 SPINACH

- **Super nutrients** Folate, magnesium, potassium.
- **Serving size** ½ cup cooked; 22 calories.
- **Benefits** ½ cup of cooked spinach contains 130 mcg of folate. Getting 300 mcg per day of this essential nutrient could cut your heart disease risk by 13 per cent. And ½ cup cooked spinach also supplies 440 mg of potassium (about one-third of the daily amount recommended).

Good ideas — Spinach

- No time to painstakingly rinse and trim each leaf in a bagful of fresh spinach? A microwaveable bag of prewashed spinach is worth the added expense. Slit the bag, add a drop of olive oil and some chopped garlic, then follow the heat-and-eat directions.

- For a tasty spinach salad, rinse some pre-washed baby spinach, then toss it with walnuts, dried cranberries and sliced pre-cooked chicken for a fast, healthy dinner.

- Add spinach to homemade soup or jazz up canned soup. Stir it in just before you turn off the heat. It wilts very quickly.

- Instead of lettuce, layer baby spinach leaves into sandwiches.

- Wilt baby spinach leaves over cooked sausages, raisins and pine nuts, and splash with balsamic vinegar for a new look, healthier supper. Serve with mashed potatoes, made with 2% or skim milk.

15 TURKEY

- **Super nutrients** Protein, vitamin B_6, vitamin B_{12}, niacin.
- **Serving size** 100 g (3½ oz); 153 calories.
- **Benefits** Don't save roast turkey for Christmas. A 100 g serving of turkey breast provides more than 50 per cent of the protein you need in a day, with only half the saturated fat found in most cuts of red meat. And it's packed with homocysteine-lowering niacin, plus vitamins B_6 and B_{12} that help your body to convert protein, fats and carbohydrates into energy. These days there is no need to wait until Christmas to reap these benefits as turkey is widely available in smaller portions, fillets, ground or freshly sliced.

Good ideas — Turkey

- Use ground turkey instead of ground beef or chicken in recipes for chili, meat loaf and burgers.

- Broil or roast a turkey breast instead of a whole chicken. Slice, then refrigerate or freeze leftovers to use in turkey salad (toss diced turkey with low-fat mayonnaise, chopped apples, walnuts, celery and grapes).

- Make a festive salad: place some cubed turkey, sliced cooked sweet potato, cranberries and walnuts on a bed of spinach and drizzle with your favourite olive oil dressing.

- Keep skinless, boneless turkey steaks in the freezer for quick meals. Thaw them in the microwave, then sauté with a little olive oil and your favourite seasonings.

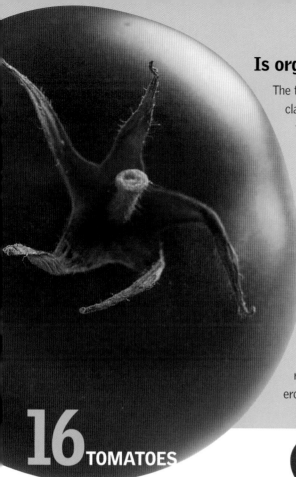

Is organic food safer?

The term "Certified Organic" is not meant to be a nutrition claim. Nor does it mean that the food is any less likely to be contaminated with pathogens that cause food-borne illness. Organic chickens, for example, can be contaminated with salmonella just like conventional chickens.

Synthetic pesticides, herbicides, fungicides, insecticides and other agricultural chemicals can certainly have adverse health effects on the farm workers who use them. But the evidence is not conclusive about their effect on consumer health. So there's no clear evidence that there is a risk to eating conventional food, or a benefit to eating organic ones. Environmental benefits, however, are more established. Agriculture that relies on organic methods can help to prevent soil erosion, protect groundwater and preserve wildlife.

16 TOMATOES

■ **Super nutrients** Lycopene, fibre, vitamin C.

■ **Serving size** 1 medium (113 g, 4 oz) tomato; 26 calories. 150 ml homemade tomato sauce; 70 calories.

■ **Benefits** Fresh from the vine, cooked down into a thick sauce or sun dried, tomatoes are highly nutritious. Eating seven or more servings per week may cut the risk of cardiovascular disease. The heart-healthy factor is probably the antioxidant lycopene or tomatoes' high levels of vitamin C, potassium and fibre. An interesting note: tomatoes that have been cooked for 30 minutes (as they are for sauce, purée, paste and salsa) have significantly higher levels of lycopene than raw tomatoes. And ¼ cup of sun-dried tomatoes has more potassium than a medium banana.

Good ideas — Tomatoes

■ For a change from regular tomatoes, try plum or on-the-vine types in the fruit and vegetable section of your grocery store.

■ Toss a handful of sun-dried tomatoes into chili, your favourite bolognese mixture or casseroles—or while sautéing chicken or salmon. They're also delicious cooked with chopped garlic, a little olive oil and a splash of white wine.

■ For a quick chili, combine the following ingredients in a glass bowl and heat in the microwave: canned, rinsed black beans, tomato sauce, frozen sweet corn and a dash of cumin and oregano.

■ Blessed with a bountiful harvest from your vegetable garden? Core big tomatoes, add a scoop of tuna or salmon salad, and serve.

17 SWEET POTATOES

■ **Super nutrients** Beta carotene, fibre, antioxidants.

■ **Serving size** One medium(150 g, 5½ oz) baked sweet potato; 173 calories.

■ **Benefits** A sweet potato is nearly a meal in itself—full of protein, fibre, artery-protecting beta carotene, blood pressure-controlling potassium and the antioxidant vitamin C. Unlike white potatoes, sweet potatoes are slowly digested and low on the Glycemic Index (GI), so they won't send your blood sugar soaring.

Good ideas ♥ Sweet potatoes

■ Wash and pierce the skin of two sweet potatoes and microwave on high for 6 to 8 minutes. Mash with a little olive oil for a savoury treat or with cinnamon and a teaspoon of brown sugar for a sweet treat.

■ Toss a peeled, cubed sweet potato with a little olive oil into a small baking dish. Roast at 450°F (230°C), stirring frequently until slightly browned.

■ Whip up a healthy, tastier alternative to regular fries . Slice four sweet potatoes, toss them in 3 tablespoons of canola oil, spread on a baking sheet, and bake at 425°F (220°C) until tender, for about 20 minutes. For sweet fries, sprinkle with cinnamon. For savoury fries, sprinkle with a mixture of 1 teaspoon each of cumin and salt plus ½ teaspoon ground red pepper.

The art and science of TEA

Tea—whether green or black—may be a heart helper. Antioxidants called catechins in green tea may play a role in reducing the negative effects of bad cholesterol, lowering triglyceride levels and increasing the production of good cholesterol.

Drinking three cups of black tea a day could lower heart attack risk. Laboratory studies suggest that theaflavins—antioxidants found even in regular grocery store tea brands—can cut levels of "bad" LDL cholesterol by 16 to 24 per cent.

WHICH TEA? Let your taste buds decide. Delicately flavoured, green tea is less processed, less caffeinated, more subtle and paler than black tea. If you're new to green tea, try a variety flavoured with fruit, honey or spices. You're probably used to regular black tea, so, for variety, experiment with naturally flavoured types such as flowery Earl Grey or citrusy, spicy Russian Caravan. To prepare iced tea, add three tea bags to 2 cups of cool water, cover and refrigerate overnight. Serve with crushed ice, mint and a slice of lemon.

18 WATERMELON

■ **Super nutrients** Lycopene, potassium.
■ **Serving size** Medium slice (about 200 g, 8 oz); about 62 calories.
■ **Benefits** Don't save delicious watermelons for summer; the fruit and vegetable section in your grocery store probably stocks it for much of the year. One 200 g slice packs about 275 mg of blood pressure-lowering potassium. Also inside is lots of the antioxidant lycopene.

Good ideas   Watermelon

■ Add cubes or balls of watermelon to fruit salad. (Buy a melon-ball cutter—scooping out balls is quicker than cutting up a melon.)

■ Freeze chunks of watermelon, then whirl in a food processor with sugar substitute for fresh watermelon sorbet.

■ Make melon kebabs by alternating cubes of watermelon, cooked low-sodium turkey breast, and low-fat cheese on wooden skewers.

■ Add watermelon chunks to chicken salad or green salads.

Four   heart-healthy switches

Make these easy food adjustments, and you'll automatically cut your risk of heart disease significantly.

1 Cook and bake with olive and canola oils. Canola oil is rich in protective omega-3 fatty acids; other vegetable oils contain high levels of omega-6 fatty acids that can promote inflammation—a potential marker for heart disease. And they don't offer as much monounsaturated fat, which protects "good" HDL cholesterol, as olive oil. When baking, experiment with the least amount of butter or margarine you can use. Try replacing half with canola oil.

2 Go for brown starches. Buy brown rice, whole-grain cereals and whole-grain pasta (or a whole wheat/refined wheat mix) instead of the white varieties. You'll get heart-healthy fibre and antioxidants, such as natural vitamin E, and you will help to control sharp rises in blood sugar that lead to hunger and ultimately raise the risk of heart disease and diabetes.

3 Always add extra vegetables to soups, stews and casseroles. When heating canned soups, stir in some frozen vegetables. If you're making homemade soup or stew, prepare twice the amount of vegetables called for. Cook and purée half and add them to the dish, then cook the rest as directed.

4 Keep a covered container of washed, bite-sized fruit (cut fruit or grapes or berries) in the fridge. Visit the fruit bowl, rather than the cookie jar, when you need a bite to eat.

Cooking cures

It may be no surprise to learn that people tend to consume more calories, fat and salt when they eat out than when they eat meals at home. When you sit down with your family, you are also more likely to eat more fresh fruit, vegetables, whole grains, beans and other nutrient-packed, heart-healthy foods than you would at a burger chain or restaurant.

But even if you always eat at home, you may not always have a healthy breakfast, lunch or dinner. Among the excuses are a busy schedule, a hungry family who want instant meals and a tendency to rely on processed, ready-made convenience foods. But these are not insurmountable obstacles.

The cooking cures suggested here won't take any more time (and may actually take less) than you're spending now to make a meal. What's more, most of them could save you money because they rely on healthy, quick-cooking, minimally processed foods instead of expensive processed main meals and snacks.

Invest in a slow cooker

Walking into the kitchen on a cold day and sniffing the aroma of a homemade soup or stew is one of life's simple pleasures—and one you can easily enjoy if you invest in a slow cooker. It is fuel-efficient and turns a few ingredients into a one-pot feast while you're out and about.

The most successful slow-cooker dishes have a high moisture content, such as soups, stews and casseroles. A slow cooker's low heat, generally between 160°F (70°C) and 275°F (140°C) tenderizes lean cuts of meat or poultry.

For a basic meal: use bite-sized chunks of meat. If you have time, brown the meat the night before, then refrigerate. In the morning, add vegetables to the cooker first (they cook more slowly than meat and need to be closer to the heat source), then add the meat and some low-sodium chicken stock, garlic, fresh herbs and a little white or red wine. Cover and cook on low for 8 hours, or on high for 5. Before serving, stir in a little Dijon mustard for an added tang.

STRATEGY 1

USE LOTS OF READY-PREPARED FRUITS AND VEGETABLES, FRESH OR FROZEN

THE CURE FOR fast-food dinners that feature no vegetables or fruit because you don't have the time or energy to buy, clean, prepare and cook it.

HEART-HEALTHY BONUS as frozen vegetables and fruits have as many, if not more, nutrients than fresh, because they're usually frozen soon after picking, when nutrient content is highest. Precut is also usually as nutritious as fresh.

THE PLAN is to load your refrigerator with pre-cut, pre-washed and frozen vegetables, as well as frozen berries. These convenient foods can be cooked quickly in the microwave and having a variety on hand could double or triple a meal's vegetable servings because it's so easy to open the bag, heat and eat. Wise choices include baby carrots (easy to munch raw or cook in the microwave); sliced carrots, pre-cut broccoli and cauliflower and frozen peppers. Many grocery stores offer miniature, bite-sized vegetables that need no preparation.

Frozen berries don't even need to be defrosted; just let them thaw while you eat dinner, or mix the contents with other, room-temperature fruits.

STRATEGY 2

STOCK UP FOR HEART-HEALTHY "MAGIC MEALS"

THE CURE FOR nights when you're too tired to even think about what's for dinner, and you've prepared nothing in advance.

HEART-HEALTHY BONUS as fibre helps to lower cholesterol, spices and flavourings are rich in antioxidants, good fats please the palate and protect against atherosclerosis.

THE PLAN is to think like a gourmet cook and think ahead. You could then sit down to a cheese omelette with a spinach, mandarin orange and pecan salad on the side; or pasta with clam sauce and mushrooms and a glass of red wine; or bean burritos with guacamole—all made in just 15 minutes.

The key is your imagination and a cupboard stocked with healthy basics and a few high-flavour extras. By keeping quick-cooking items on hand (such as eggs rich in omega-3 fatty acids; whole-wheat pastas; nuts; canned beans; canned seafood; whole-grain breads; and reduced-fat cheese), you'll be able to whip up something quick

and tasty even on nights when you're tired—when you most need a good meal and are most likely to eat badly. Here are four more fast, ideas.

■ **Supercharged soup** Add rinsed canned beans and frozen vegetables to low-sodium canned minestrone or vegetable soup. Serve with whole-grain toast and follow with a fruit salad (made from canned fruit mixed with frozen berries).

■ **Baby spinach with chicken** Rinse some ready-prepared spinach, arrange it on a plate and top with nuts, pre-cut carrots and cherry tomatoes. Add strips of pre-cooked chicken breast and dress with olive oil and balsamic vinegar. Have sliced melon for dessert.

■ **Simple pasta with white beans** Cook some whole-wheat spaghetti, then toss it with a spoonful of olive oil (or pesto), Parmesan cheese, black pepper and canned white beans, rinsed and heated. Serve the spaghetti with steamed broccoli and finish off the meal with fresh fruit.

■ **Turkey melt with cranberry sauce on whole-grain bread** Arrange sliced turkey on a slice of whole-grain bread and top it with a little cranberry sauce and one slice of reduced-fat, low-sodium cheese. Microwave the open sandwich until the cheese melts. Serve with a green salad, then round off the meal with mixed berries and a dollop of low-fat frozen yogourt.

"READY-FOR-ANYTHING" fridge, freezer and cupboard foods

With the following items on hand, you can prepare healthy dinners in a flash.

IN THE FRIDGE

■ **Condiments** (whatever you like, such as horseradish, salsa, mustards, low-sodium soy sauce, low-fat mayonnaise, fat-free sour cream, cranberry sauce, pesto in a jar, olives, capers, roasted red peppers packed in water, artichokes packed in water, chutney, jars of chopped garlic and ginger)

■ **Eggs** (look for brands with extra-high levels of omega-3 fatty acids)

■ **Lots of fresh fruit**

■ **Lots of fresh vegetables** (including pre-cut and pre-washed)

■ **Low-fat or fat-free yogourt** (plain or flavoured)

■ **Parmesan cheese**

■ **Reduced-fat cheeses**

■ **Skim or 2% milk**

IN THE FREEZER

■ **Fish**

■ **Frozen fruits** (especially berries)

■ **Frozen vegetables**

■ **Lean meats and poultry**

IN THE CUPBOARD

■ **Brown rice**

■ **Canned beans** (black, navy, pinto and kidney beans; chickpeas)

■ **Canned fruit in its own juice**

■ **Canned salmon** (red salmon is tastiest)

■ **Canned tomatoes**

■ **Canola oil**

■ **Dried fruit** (especially raisins)

■ **Garlic** (fresh and/or a jar of puréed)

■ **Low-sodium chicken, beef or vegetable broth**

■ **Olive oil**

■ **Onions**

■ **Pasta sauce** (no more than 7 per cent saturated fat per serving)

■ **Peanut butter**

■ **Salad dressings** (with canola or olive oil)

■ **Whole-wheat pasta**

■ **Whole-grain cereals** (including oatmeal)

MAKE SMALL CHANGES

THE CURE FOR a pretty good diet that could be slightly more nutritious. More fruit and vegetables, more fibre, more good fats, more dairy produce—or whatever else applies to your present diet.

HEART-HEALTHY BONUS as these changes are small enough, and tasty enough, for you to make them part of your cooking repertoire, giving your cardiovascular system a steady dose of antioxidants, good fats, and vitamins and minerals.

THE PLAN is to eat for a healthy heart without overhauling your kitchen and cooking style. Start with these nutritious cooking solutions.

■ Garnish fruit salads, green salads and cooked vegetables with chopped nuts for an extra helping of monounsaturated fats. Toss a handful into muffin and pancake recipes or add some to yogourt. For some extra flavour, first toast the nuts under the broiler until golden.

■ Top salads with avocado slices, rich in monounsaturated fat. Skip the crispy bacon bits and croutons, which are loaded with saturated fat and trans fats.

■ Instead of ice cream topped with a few strawberries, have a bowl of berries crowned with 2 tablespoons of Greek yogourt, frozen yogourt or sorbet. You'll triple the antioxidants and cut your fat and sugar intake in half.

■ Cook or serve vegetables with a drizzle of olive or canola oil. Fat helps your body to absorb more of the antioxidants, vitamins and minerals in vegetables.

■ Think in colour. Serve fruits or vegetables in contrasting colours: red peppers with broccoli, carrots with peas and blueberries with peaches. There is some new scientific research which suggests that the antioxidants in vegetables and fruits are more effective when they're combined.

■ Use canned salmon instead of tuna in your lunchtime salad, as salmon, unlike tuna, retains its omega-3 fatty acids when canned.

■ Toss rinsed, canned beans into everyday foods—chickpeas into salad and kidney beans into spaghetti sauce. Beans are rich in appetite-controlling fibre.

■ Keep a jar of puréed garlic and a jar of puréed ginger in the fridge. Use each at least once a week to season vegetables, meats or soups. Garlic, as mentioned earlier, may help to lower cholesterol and cut the rate of plaque buildup in arteries, and antioxidant-rich ginger can fight inflammation and may discourage the formation of blood clots.

■ Boost your iron intake by cooking regularly in cast-iron pans and casseroles. Long-simmering soups, stews and sauces absorb the most iron, but even scrambling an egg in a cast-iron frying pan increases the egg's iron content. Your body needs adequate iron to deliver oxygen to cells, including heart muscle cells.

■ In recipes, halve the amount of salt or cut it out entirely. Replace it with antioxidant-rich spices, garlic or a salt-free seasoning mix.

... you can eat gourmet food that delights your heart and your taste buds.

How to survive eating out

In Canada, it is estimated that one meal in three is eaten away from home. When you prepare food yourself, you know exactly what has gone into that meal—you can choose what type of fat—and how much of it—you use. You can control how much salt you add, and you can determine the portion sizes that go onto your plate.

The same is not true of food eaten outside the home. Restaurant food may have hidden fats and salt, takeout and fast foods often contain unhealthy trans fats, and special "buy-one-get-one-free" deals can tempt you into buying foods you wouldn't normally eat.

We're not suggesting that you avoid eating out at restaurants or choose the most boring "healthy" dish on the menu.

On the 30-Minutes-a-Day Plan, you can eat restaurant and takeout food when you want to—and enjoy your meal. You won't have to phone in advance to quiz the chef about calorie counts, limit yourself to a low-calorie special or pack your own salad dressing and sugar substitute. By employing a few tricks, you can relax and enjoy a special dinner out, a business lunch or Saturday night pizza. If you're properly prepared you can eat gourmet food that delights your heart and your taste buds. Here's how.

Before you leave home

Putting yourself into a healthy mindset before you sit down (or pick up the phone) guarantees success. You can avoid the pitfalls of restaurant food without feeling deprived, by refocusing on all the possible options.

Imagine your meal Picture your plate before you pick up the phone to order a takeout, before you make a dinner reservation or before going into the restaurant. Think about the healthy choices on most menus—the thin-crust pizza loaded with vegetables, the fancy mixed-greens-and-pecans salad with vinaigrette or the mouth-watering grilled fish at your local seafood restaurant.

Have fun treating yourself to delicious, healthy choices that you might not cook at home, from roast beets to wild salmon to wonderfully crunchy Chinese vegetables, such as snow peas, bok choy, baby corn and water chestnuts.

And, if you absolutely must have a sweet treat once in a while, plan to share one when you go out to eat—your sweet tooth will be satisfied and you won't have to deal with the temptation of leftover desserts in your own kitchen.

Don't skimp on breakfast and lunch
Starving yourself before a big night out sounds reasonable, but this plan has a flaw: you're ravenous and ready to overeat by the time you arrive at the restaurant (or open the pizza box at the kitchen table). A better plan is to satisfy your appetite by having adequate daytime meals and then a piece of fruit, or some yogourt and whole-grain toast, an hour or so before going to the restaurant.

Worried about the extra calories and fat? Consider this: a healthy snack at home is bound to have fewer calories and more nutrients than most restaurant appetizers.

TRANSFORM YOUR TAKEOUT MEALS Keep flavour but cut calories and fat

SANDWICHES Eat 'em open-faced to save 80 to 90 calories. Skip the mayo and go with mustard as your first choice or olive oil and herbs as your second. Ask for extra tomatoes, lettuce and onions. Lean toward turkey, chicken or roast beef, since processed meats such as salami are extremely high in fat.

PIZZA Choose healthy toppings and avoid fatty meats such as pepperoni or sausage. Seafood, tomato or vegetables are best. Go for thin-crust (whole wheat, if possible), rather than deep-pan, and add a side salad with low-fat dressing.

CHINESE Avoid deep-fried dishes such as spring rolls, breaded shrimp or anything in batter. Sweet-and-sour dishes can contain as much as 8 teaspoons of sugar. Chicken with cashew nuts or peppers, stir-fried noodles and seafood are healthier, with boiled rice or noodles, rather than egg fried rice. Steamed dim sum and fish are also good choices.

THAI Avoid dishes with coconut milk which is high in saturated fat. Soups such as tom yum soup and sweet-and-sour soup, or chicken or beef satay are good starters. Thai fish cakes are usually quite low in fat. Chicken, pork or fish-based noodle dishes are good choices as are salads and vegetable dishes. Choose dishes that are stir-fried or steamed.

Starving yourself before a big night out sounds reasonable, but this plan has a flaw . . .

FAST FOOD survival guide

Some fast food outlets, once notorious for the high calorie and fat content of their foods, are starting to take nutrition more seriously, so you will often find quite healthy salads and fruit-packed desserts on their menus, such as you would expect to find in a vegetarian restaurant or in a café at a health-conscious leisure club. Conversely, you should also be wary. Some apparently health-conscious outlets may have high-calorie, high-fat foods on their menus.

TREAD CAREFULLY Finding the nutritional gold mines—and avoiding the minefields—of these everyday eating places requires a smart plan of attack. Here's how to limit the calories, fat and salt—and get a healthy dose of fruit, vegetables, lean protein and low-fat dairy products at the same time.

INFORMATION Some of the well-known fast-food chains now provide customers with leaflets giving a detailed nutritional breakdown of their foods. Check the calorie and fat content before you order.

SMART CHOICES If you choose a burger, go for a small one, without cheese. Order the grilled chicken sandwich rather than the fried chicken or the fried fish.

Surprisingly, veggie burgers contain considerable fat and calories, but compared to a beef burger, they will have more fibre, which helps to keep the digestive system working well.

The lettuce leaves and pickles that accompany most burgers don't provide more than just a garnish, so ask for extra lettuce, onion and tomatoes instead of cheese, bacon, special sauce or mayonnaise. Better yet, order a salad. But remember, some vinaigrettes can be high in fat, so make sure you order one with a low-fat dressing and pass on the bacon bits and croutons. Choose orange juice, rather than a diet cola or a shake, to boost your vitamin C.

Extra credit: walk to the restaurant If you can walk from your home to your destination, do so. Other options are to arrive early, then take a walk with your dinner companions, or go for a short walk afterwards. You'll burn extra calories and place the emphasis where it belongs: on the socializing, not just on the food.

At the restaurant

When ordering, don't feel shy about asking questions and making special requests to ensure that your meal is exactly what you want. Your waiter is the link between table and kitchen. Make him or her your ally. This will help you to avoid empty calories, leaving you free to enjoy your meal without guilt.

Banish the bread basket To avoid extra calories of blood sugar-raising refined carbohydrates and artery-blocking saturated fat, ask the waiter to take the bread-and-butter basket away. (Or just take one piece.)

Start with water After that, limit yourself to one glass of wine and have it with your meal. For many people, alcohol triggers extra eating, so sipping while you wait means your resolve about the bread may just weaken.

Ask lots of questions Is the chicken in the salad grilled or in batter and then fried? What's in the mashed potatoes? Can you have two vegetables instead of the fries? Can the fish be broiled? Most restaurants will be happy to accommodate you; if there's a small extra charge, it's usually worth it.

Always ask for sauces and dressings separately You don't need lashings of creamy dressing on your salad. When possible, choose dressings and sauces made with good fats such as olive oil instead of with cream and butter. Spoon a little over your food or dip the ends of your fork into the sauce before spearing a forkful of food. Plan to leave most of the dressing or sauce uneaten.

Choose a sensible starter Avoid calorie-laden starters such as pâté or anything deep-fried. You are much better off choosing something fruit- or vegetable-based, like melon, vegetable-based soup, salad, shellfish or smoked salmon.

Outsmart super-size portions Did you know that some china manufacturers have re-sized their tableware to accommodate restaurant portions that are now two to seven times bigger than before? Even the healthiest menu choice can become unhealthy for your heart in those quantities. Learn how to downsize extra-large servings.

■ Look at the portions served to other people in the restaurant. If they look huge, order two starters instead of a main course. Make one protein-based and the other vegetable-based.

■ Decide whether you would rather have a starter or a dessert and then order one or the other. Or agree to share your dessert with one of your dining companions.

■ Share the main course and order a small salad to go with it, for yourself.

■ Check with the waiter to see which vegetables come with your dish. You may want to order an extra portion of vegetables or a side salad.

■ Be a kid again. While sit-down restaurants may often prohibit it, fast-food restaurants don't care if grown-ups order children's meals for themselves. Today, a child's meal at major fast-food chains is often the size an adult portion was 20 years ago. A hamburger, small fries and a low-fat milkshake or orange juice are surprisingly filling and contain a fraction of the calories of "super" adult meals. They're not particularly nutritious, but for those who can't break their fast-food habit, they're a good compromise.

Secrets of the restaurant trade

What tricks do restaurants use to make their food taste so good? You may not be surprised to discover that some of them are not particularly healthy.

BUTTER In the soup. In the sauce. On the meat. On the vegetables. Using butter is the easiest, quickest way to make things taste rich and wonderful. Most restaurants go through huge amounts, despite the fact that it's almost pure saturated fat.

OIL Another way to make foods taste richer is to use lots of oil. Sometimes it's olive oil, and sometimes it's more exotic nut oils for unique flavour. At lower-grade restaurants, it's old-fashioned vegetable oil. (Take note of what collects on the bottom of the container the next time you get takeout.) This is also why fried foods taste so good: they're sponges for the oil they're cooked in.

ANIMAL FAT The next time you see restaurant steaks or hamburgers described as juicy, remember: meat "juices" are mostly melted fat. Sauces made "au jus" are often extremely calorie dense and unhealthy for your heart.

SALT Cook at home and you can limit or, at best, omit the salt. At a restaurant, it's often used liberally to extract maximum flavour.

SUGARS Ever had a side dish of vegetables that tasted almost as sweet as the dessert that followed the meal? That may be from added sugar. And the sticky chocolate pudding, chocolate mousse and other delights of the dessert trolley are equally loaded.

The 30-Minutes-a-Day restaurant guide

CHINESE

Go for: Stir-fried (request little or no oil) or steamed dishes with lots of vegetables, steamed rice or poached fish, or entrées that contain chicken, seafood or just vegetables.

Avoid: Fried food such as crispy wonton appetizers, egg or spring rolls, fried rice and shrimp toast. Limit sodium by asking for low-sodium soy sauce and no monosodium glutamate (MSG) in your food.

ITALIAN

Go for: Red, clam, or non-creamy seafood sauces and grilled or roasted chicken or fish.

Avoid: Entrées smothered in cream and butter sauces, such as fettuccine Alfredo; anything topped with carbonara or served "parmigiana" (with melted cheese); and pasta stuffed with cheese or fatty meat.

MEXICAN

Go for: Fajitas—you build them yourself, piling grilled veggies and chicken, shrimp or beef on a flour tortilla. Add lettuce, tomato and peppers; skip or limit the shredded cheese and guacamole. Also good: simple burritos and soft tacos, grilled chicken and fish, and black beans. The best sauces to choose are salsa and pico de gallo.

Avoid: Fat-drenched refried beans, fried items such as chimichangas, and cheese-covered nachos and entrées.

JAPANESE

Go for: Sushi and sashimi, soba or udon noodles, yakitori (chicken teriyaki), shumai (steamed dumplings), tofu, sukiyaki and kayaku goban (vegetables and rice).

Avoid: Shrimp or vegetable tempura, chicken katsu, tonkatsu (fried pork), shrimp agemono and fried tofu (bean curd).

UPSCALE CAFÉ

Go for: Seafood broiled with lemon and herbs, pan-roasted meats, interesting vegetable dishes and mixed green salads, but with dressing on the side. Choose broth-based, not creamy, soups.

Avoid: Items made with cheese, fatty meats, cream and butter.

BREAKFAST SPOTS

Go for: Whole-wheat pancakes, topped with fruit; vegetable-filled omelettes; whole-wheat or rye toast with jam; poached or boiled eggs; lots of fruit; low-fat cottage cheese; orange juice.

Avoid: Butter (used on eggs, toast, pancakes and hash browns); whipped cream on your waffles or pancakes; regular bacon or sausage; cream in your coffee; white bread toast; waffles or pancakes made with bleached, refined flour.

What to choose and what to avoid when eating out.

Although no supplement can ever replace a balanced diet, chances are, almost everyone feels the need to take a multivitamin from time to time.

And supplements?

You will be enjoying heart-healthy, nutrient-packed food on the 30-Minutes-a-Day Eating Plan. So do you need to add supplements? In most cases, the answer would be "no."

Conventional wisdom has long held that as long as people who are healthy eat well enough to avoid nutritional deficiencies, they do not need to supplement their diet. The only thing they have to do is consume a diet that meets the recommended dietary allowances of various nutrients.

But in today's fast-paced world, some people find it difficult to meet those nutritional requirements. In a recent survey, only 36 per cent of Canadians said they ate five daily servings of fruits and vegetables—the amount recommended for obtaining the

minimum level of nutrients believed necessary to prevent illness. A recent Canadian Heart and Stroke Foundation report revealed that only 14 per cent of children have four or more daily servings of fruits and vegetables, although 98 per cent knew that five to ten is good for the heart.

Supplements are not a substitute for healthy living. The best way for Canadians to improve their diets is to increase fruit and vegetable intake. The best nutrition comes from the interactions of the thousands of nutrients found in fruits and vegetables. If you want to analyze your diet, ask your doctor to recommend a dietitian to consult. The following pages, however, concern vitamins and other supplements that may be of interest.

Choosing a multivitamin

If you do choose to take a multivitamin, look for these levels of important nutrients.

100 per cent of the Recommended Dietary Allowance (RDA): Make sure your multivitamin has 100 per cent of the RDA for thiamine (vitamin B_1); riboflavin (vitamin B_2); niacin (vitamin B_3); folic acid; and vitamins B_6, B_{12}, C, D and E.

Less than 1,500 IU of retinol-based vitamin A: Getting more than 5,000 IU of vitamin A daily from retinol may increase your osteoporosis risk. Your supplement should contain no more than 1,500 IU.

No more than 100 per cent of minerals: You don't need more than 100 per cent of the RDA for any mineral. Most people get plenty of chloride, phosphorus and potassium from a healthy diet but surveys show that some people don't get the RDA for magnesium (300 mg) from food, which is significant as there is some evidence that magnesium reduces cardiovascular risk. Trace elements, such as boron, nickel, silicon, tin and vanadium, aren't necessary.

Vitamin K:
(CAUTION: Talk to your doctor if you take a blood-thinning drug.)
In Canada, vitamin K (which promotes blood clotting) supplements are not available over the counter and vitamin K is not found in multivitamins. To ensure you get the RDA of 120 mcg, eat green leafy vegetables.

Iron—your age and sex matter:
Premenopausal women should look for a product containing 18 mg (100 per cent of the RDA for iron). Postmenopausal women and men should look for supplements with a lower iron content.

Final note: Some multivitamin makers sell premium versions that include "proprietary blends" of herbs, minerals, extracts and amino acids. Be cautious about these. While many of the individual ingredients may have research that supports them, no one has looked at the efficacy of these blends. You might pay extra money for a mix of ingredients of little or no value.

No time for five to ten servings of fruits and vegetables daily?
Try a delicious multivitamin citrus drink made with oranges, limes and kiwi.

1 MULTIVITAMIN

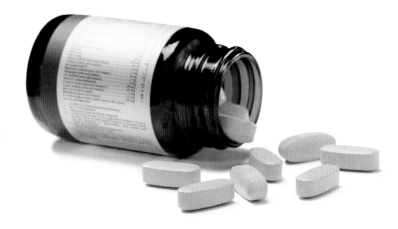

Is taking a daily multivitamin a good way to ensure you get these essential nutrients? A number of leading medical practitioners have advocated this approach; however, not everyone is convinced. Most health experts continue to emphasize the importance of a healthy diet.

■ **BENEFITS** Taking a multivitamin may help to make good any deficiencies in your diet.

■ **HOW IT WORKS**

The B vitamins may reduce homocysteine levels according to some researchers. However, the evidence for this is inconclusive. Homocysteine, an amino acid produced when your body breaks down protein, is an emerging risk factor for heart disease and stroke. Your body needs the "three Bs"—vitamins B_6 and B_{12} and folate (or folic acid, the supplement form)—to convert homocysteine into a form that cells can use to build new proteins. Otherwise, homocysteine levels rise and so does heart risk. As we age, our bodies absorb less of the B vitamins in food, but luckily, those in supplements are well absorbed.

Provides protective vitamin D. Among other duties, vitamin D helps the body to absorb and retain calcium, which is important for healthy blood pressure. It may also guard against the buildup of artery-hardening calcium deposits, and research from Belgium suggests that it reduces inflammation. Your body produces vitamin D naturally when exposed to sunshine, but if you don't go out in the sun or live in a northern climate, you may not get enough sun exposure to make enough of the vitamin.

■ **BEST KIND TO BUY** Not necessarily the most expensive multivitamin—plenty of brands offer the same complete range of vitamins and minerals, at the right doses, for far less money. Shop carefully.

■ **BEST DOSE** One per day.

■ **WHEN TO TAKE IT** With food for best absorption.

■ **SIDE EFFECTS** Mild nausea. This is less likely if you take a multivitamin with a meal.

■ **CAUTIONS** Take only the recommended dose. If you have a medical condition, and wish to investigate whether or not a multivitamin might help, it is extremely important to talk to your doctor before taking any kind of supplement.

■ **SMART TIP** Take your multivitamin with a full glass of water for better absorption.

2 FISH OIL

Even two fish meals a week could help to cut heart attack risk.

Research suggests that even two fish meals a week could help to cut heart attack risk and most nutritionists advise at least one or two portions of oily fish, such as salmon or mackerel, every week. These fish are particularly rich in two heart-friendly omega-3 fatty acids—eicosapentaenoic acid (EPA) and docosahexaenoic acid (DHA)—and most people don't get enough of them. Can fish oil in capsules or cod liver oil fill the gap? Although some studies show that it can cut the risk of a second heart attack, heart specialists disagree on whether heart patients who do not eat fish regularly should take fish-oil capsules. Talk to your doctor before making a decision.

■ **HEART BENEFITS** The omega-3 fatty acids in fish oils appear to cut heart attack risk dramatically when consumed daily as part of a diet low in saturated fat and full of fruit, vegetables and whole grains. They also reduce triglyceride levels; high levels are thought to be a risk factor for heart disease.

■ **HOW IT WORKS**

▉ **Lowers triglycerides** Triglyceride levels rise after eating a meal high in saturated fat—which may explain higher heart attack rates following a big breakfast, lunch or dinner. In one U.S. study, the triglyceride levels of men who took fish-oil supplements were 35 to 50 per cent lower than normal after eating big meals— a decline that could save your life. It is speculated that fish oil helps muscle cells to break down triglycerides more efficiently, vacuuming them out of the bloodstream.

▉ **Keeps hearts on the beat** Wildly irregular

heartbeats (arrhythmias) can trigger sudden cardiac death. In a study published in *The Lancet*, British researchers found that fish oil significantly protected the hearts of women and men who wore pacemakers to guard against heartbeat irregularities. When the scientists tried to induce arrhythmias in the volunteers, seven out of ten had irregular beats before taking fish oil; after taking it, only two did.

■ **BEST DOSE** Experts suggest getting a total of 1 g, combined, of EPA and DHA. How many capsules is that? Read labels; the dose varies by brand. Talk to your doctor about the best dosage.

■ **WHEN TO TAKE IT** With food.

■ **SIDE EFFECTS** Fishy burps, mild nausea and bloating. Some experts suggest avoiding fish liver oils, such as cod liver oil, because they are also a concentrated source of vitamins A and D.

■ **CAUTIONS** Fish oil's anticlotting powers could be dangerous for people with bleeding disorders and those who take anticoagulant medications such as warfarin. Talk to your doctor before starting to take fish-oil or any other supplement.

■ **SMART TIP** Refrigerate the capsules or take them on a full stomach to eliminate fishy burps.

3 SOLUBLE FIBRE

Oatmeal and beans, barley and oranges, grapefruit and strawberries are all rich in soluble fibre—an indigestible carbohydrate that forms a thick, cholesterol-trapping gel in your digestive system. You need at least 10 g a day of soluble fibre, out of a total fibre intake of 25 to 35 g per day, but unfortunately most of us take in barely 15 g total fibre daily (about the amount in a bowl of oatmeal and a handful of strawberries).

That's why your doctor may advise a soluble fibre supplement—not as a substitute for fibre-rich grains and produce but because getting extra soluble fibre is a safe, drug-free way to achieve a small reduction in cholesterol levels. Top fibre researchers in the United States say that about 15 per cent of the people whose doctors recommend statin drugs to lower slightly elevated cholesterol could get the job done with a healthier diet and a soluble fibre supplement.

■ **HEART BENEFITS** Soluble fibre can cut total cholesterol by 7 per cent and LDL cholesterol by 5 per cent, which translates into a 10 to 15 per cent reduction in heart disease risk. Fibre supplements may help people who want to prevent future heart problems; if you have diagnosed heart disease, don't use them in place of recommended drug therapy.

■ **HOW IT WORKS** Soluble fibre forms a thick gel that moves slowly through your intestines and binds to cholesterol-packed bile acids, ushering them out of the body. Your liver manufactures bile acids to help to break down fats for digestion.

Usually, 95 per cent of the cholesterol in these acids is reabsorbed. If soluble fibre helps to eliminate more of these acids and less is reabsorbed, the liver is forced to draw cholesterol from the bloodstream to manufacture more bile acids. As a result your cholesterol levels drop.

■ **BEST KIND TO BUY** Fibre supplements usually come as flavoured powders to mix with water. They're made from psyllium husks or seeds. You can also buy cereal with psyllium.

■ **BEST DOSE** To help lower cholesterol, aim for 7 to 10 g of supplemental soluble fibre daily. Check the fibre content of the supplement.

■ **WHEN TO TAKE IT** Take half in the morning and the rest in the evening.

■ **SIDE EFFECTS** A bloated feeling, gas and constipation.

■ **CAUTIONS** You should discuss fibre supplements with your doctor before taking them, particularly if you have a bowel obstruction, an ulcer or chronic constipation. High intakes of fibre may also reduce the effectiveness of some drugs. In rare cases, psyllium can cause an allergic reaction. Seek emergency medical help if you develop fast or irregular breathing, a skin rash, hives or itching after taking a psyllium product.

■ **SMART TIP** If you take a prescription drug, take your fibre supplement at least 2 hours before or after your medicine. Always take a fibre supplement as directed, with at least one or preferably two glasses of water. If you're new to fibre supplements, it may be advisable to take it slowly. For the first week, take one dose a day, then work up to your goal over a month or so to avoid discomfort.

Antioxidant supplements: no extra protection

For years, some experts have recommended getting megadoses of vitamin E and beta-carotene to help to protect your heart. The reasoning made sense as antioxidants neutralize plaque-promoting free radicals—destructive particles released naturally when you breathe, digest a meal or are exposed to toxins such as cigarette smoke. Getting extra antioxidants should equal extra protection.

But, for reasons not fully understood, pills don't help. Taking antioxidant vitamins is at best a waste of money; at worst, it may actually raise your risk of a deadly heart attack. When scientists at the Cleveland Clinic in Ohio examined seven big studies on vitamin E and eight large studies on beta-carotene and heart health, they concluded that E offered no protection. Even more troubling: beta-carotene raised the risk of death from cardiovascular disease. A 2004 study showed that high doses of vitamin E raised similar risks.

The best advice is to get vitamin E from three servings of whole grains and wheat germ a day and fill up on beta-carotene (and hundreds of other antioxidants) by loading your plate with fruit and vegetables.

4 COENZYME Q10

A vitamin-like substance found in all parts of the body, coenzyme Q10 (CoQ10) boosts the effectiveness of enzymes that help cells to produce energy and is especially abundant in the heart. It is found naturally in a variety of foods.

■ **HEART BENEFITS** There have been a number of studies to see if CoQ10 can be a helpful supplement, especially for people suffering from heart failure or weakened hearts. It acts as an antioxidant, helping to neutralize free radical damage which has been linked to heart disease. However, the evidence for benefit is inconclusive.

■ **HOW IT WORKS**

■ In the 1950s, researchers first noticed that people with heart disease had low levels of CoQ10. Experts suspect that it helps mitochondria, the tiny power-generating plants inside cells, to produce energy. In a 12-month study of 2,500 people with heart failure, 80 per cent of those who took CoQ10 noticed an improvement; they retained less fluid, experienced less shortness of breath and slept better. (Not all studies have shown a benefit.)

■ It may offset statin problems. However, always consult your doctor if you consider a supplement, and are on medication.

■ **DOSE** 50 mg twice a day.

■ **WHEN TO TAKE IT** With a meal. CoQ10 is fat soluble, so your body will absorb much more if you take it with a fat-containing food, such as the oil in salad dressing.

■ **SIDE EFFECTS** Rarely, it can cause mild insomnia, stomach upset, or loss of appetite. Talk to your doctor before taking any supplement.

■ **CAUTIONS** May reduce the effectiveness of blood-thinning medicines such as warfarin.

Hawthorn

Hawthorn berry extract is an age-old heart tonic with some new science to support it. In the *Journal of Family Practice*, researchers noted that this herbal extract is a good add-on therapy for people with heart failure because it seems to improve blood flow to the heart and help to stabilize out-of-rhythm heartbeats. Hawthorn is not a substitute for heart medication or for any of the other supplements in this chapter, but as an added therapy, it may be helpful. But consult your doctor first. Hawthorn may interact in a harmful way with other heart medications.

■ **SMART TIP**—Essential tip. If you're being treated for high blood pressure or heart failure, you must discuss CoQ10 with your doctor; it is not a substitute for medication.

5 ASA

ASA (acetylsalicylic acid) is not a nutrient. However, it is easily available, and widely publicized with respect to its ability to reduce risk of heart attack in some people. It is important to know that daily use of ASA should only be taken with your doctor's approval.

■ **HEART BENEFITS** Long-term ASA use has been shown to reduce the risk of heart attacks in some people. But daily doses are not appropriate for everyone and no one should take it without first consulting a doctor.

■ **HOW IT WORKS** ASA inhibits the clumping action of blood platelets, cells responsible for blood clots that may cause a heart attack or ischemic stroke.

■ **BEST DOSE** Talk to your doctor.

■ **WHEN TO TAKE IT** As prescribed by your doctor.

■ **SIDE EFFECTS** No medicine is completely safe. The risks associated with daily ASA use may outweigh any benefit. Your doctor will review your history and discuss this with you. In some people, ASA can cause stomach bleeding or kidney failure or raise the risk of a less common type of stroke called hemorrhagic stroke.

■ **CAUTIONS** If you take the pain reliever ibuprofen, wait 2 hours before taking ASA: ibuprofen can interfere with ASA's heart-protective powers. If you take ibuprofen regularly and would like to add ASA to your heart-healthy regimen, talk to your doctor about switching to an alternative painkiller, which may not interfere with ASA.

■ **SMART TIP** Always talk to your doctor first before taking regular doses of ASA.

911 Emergency! ASA can be a lifesaver

If you or someone you're with has sudden heart attack symptoms, thoroughly chewing and swallowing one regular-strength ASA tablet immediately while you wait for the ambulance to arrive could be a lifesaver.

Chewing the tablet will deliver ASA to the bloodstream quickly; by contrast, swallowing the ASA whole delays the effect.

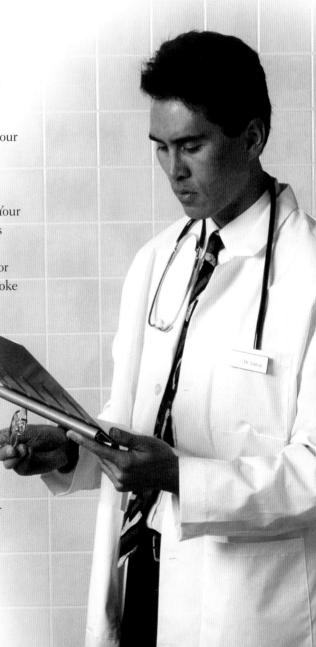

6 FLAXSEED OIL

Flaxseed (linseed) contains essential fatty acids, among them alpha-linolenic acid (ALA), an omega-3 fatty acid, known to protect against heart disease. Although ALA is not as potent as the omega-3 fatty acids in fish oils, it is a good source for vegetarians. You can sprinkle ground seeds on yogourt, muesli or any other cereal.

■ **HEART BENEFITS** Flaxseed oil is thought to aid in lowering cholesterol, and may be beneficial for the heart.

■ **HOW IT WORKS** Flaxseed contains 50 per cent ALA (compared to 3 to 11 per cent in walnuts) so is an excellent plant source. ALA is an omega-3 fatty acid, which the body partially converts into eicosapentaenoic acid (EPA), an omega-3 fatty acid found in fish oils. Research has shown that EPA may have an anti-coagulant effect. Flaxseed may lower blood cholesterol, protect against angina and help to control high blood pressure.

■ **BEST KIND TO TAKE** Canadians get most of their ALA from soybean and canola oils. Alternatively, sprinkle flaxseeds on food or mix the oil with juice, yogourt, cottage cheese or other foods and drinks.

■ **DOSE** 1.1 to 1.6 g per day. A typical Canadian consumes at least that much in their diet.

■ **WHEN TO TAKE IT** Take flaxseed with food to enhance absorption by the body.

■ **SIDE EFFECTS** Flaxseed appears to be safe although those taking the seeds may experience some initial flatulence.

■ **CAUTIONS** The seeds should not be taken by anyone with an intestinal blockage or prostate cancer. Flaxseed should not be combined with other drugs, laxatives or stool softeners. If pregnant or breastfeeding it is probably best to avoid flaxseed. Do not take it if you are prescribed warfarin, which also thins the blood.

Niacin: the vitamin that acts like a drug

In large doses—500 to 1,000 mg per day—the B vitamin niacin has been shown to raise "good" HDL cholesterol by 15 to 35 per cent while lowering triglycerides by 20 to 50 per cent. But high-dose niacin has side effects, including severe facial flushing. Large doses can also damage your liver.

If you have low HDL cholesterol and high triglycerides, talk to your doctor about a time-released, prescription-strength niacin supplement. It reduces flushing and is easy on your liver. Niacin works but it is essential to take it only on the advice of your doctor; never take high doses on your own.

■ **SMART TIP** Ground flaxseed is a better choice than flaxseed oil because the former contains fibre, omega-3 fatty acids and phytochemicals called lignans. The oil contains the beneficial fats, but not the fibre or lignans.

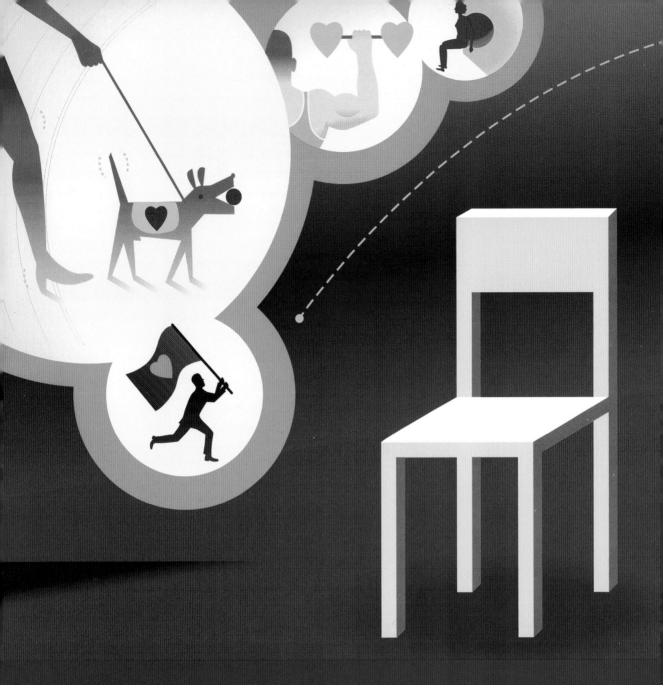

How did exercise become so hi-tech? All you really need to do is just get up and move. After a healthy diet, nothing is better for your heart than being on your feet.

Getting active

Rise up against "sitting disease"

If you are sitting down as you read this, you are engaged in an un-activity that most of us now spend an amazing amount of time doing. No one keeps accurate statistics on our cumulative sitting time, but the available data reveal that the average North American is seated for 12 to 14 hours each day: behind the wheel of a car (1 to 2 hours); watching television (3 hours); and parked behind a desk, working either on the job or at home (7 to 9 hours). Add an hour of sitting at mealtimes and 7 hours of shut-eye, and you're looking at an astonishing 19 to 22 hours of almost complete downtime. For many, the numbers are worse. Think about the most sedentary people you know. Can you honestly say that they are on their feet for three hours a day? Probably not. Ironically, our ancestors would have been thrilled with this chair-centric lifestyle. They toiled from sunrise to sunset just to have a meal to sit down to at the end of the day. Today, we barely budge from our seats to get breakfast.

Through the genius of remote controls, dishwashers, washing machines, electric gadgets, email and Internet shopping we've engineered physical activity out of our lives almost completely—so much so that some experts estimate that we burn up to 700 fewer calories each day than we did just 30 years ago. That adds up to well over 0.45 kg (1 lb) a week.

Consider the energy savings of a single email: if you were to walk across your office building and back to talk to someone instead of spending the same 2 minutes sending an email, you could save nearly 5 kg (11 lb) over 10 years—and that's just one email a day.

Because our modern lives require so little physical effort, exercise tends to be a leisure-time activity—walking, gardening or sports—but woefully few of us find time for that, either. Surveys report that up to one-quarter of adults—and a full one-third of women—engage in absolutely no leisure-time physical activities.

In recent years the levels of walking and cycling have fallen. Given these realities, it's hardly surprising that too many of us tip the bathroom scales into the danger zone; that too many of us have high blood pressure; and that too many of us die from illnesses linked to sedentary living.

Vitamin X for a healthy heart

Just as white bread and cereals are now refined, then fortified with vitamins and minerals, so we must fortify our bodies with activity lost thanks to modern labour-saving

Time investment

Your goal is to reduce your sitting time every day by 1 hour (including the time you spend with the easy exercise plans outlined in this section). That doesn't mean you have to block out a big chunk of your daily schedule or add anything to your to-do list, although you can if you like. By exchanging sedentary moments for moving moments, you'll move more, feel better and live longer.

gadgets and machines. This daily dose of vitamin X (for exercise) is every bit as essential for heart health as the nutrients you get through a healthy diet.

The importance of exercise is that when you walk, pull dandelions or swing a 5-iron, your heart becomes more efficient, pumping more blood with every beat and performing work with less stress and strain. Regular daily exercise also fends off heart disease on some specific fronts.

It brings down blood pressure

Physical activity flushes out your arteries, cleaning them and keeping them clear and supple. In a recent study of more than 500 men and women aged 40 to 60, researchers found that physical activity is inversely related to the progressive buildup of plaque in the carotid arteries. Even people who played golf or gardened just a day or two a week had clearer arteries than those who did no leisure-time activity.

It burns off blood sugar

Recent Czech research showed that three months' strength training improved insulin sensitivity in men with insulin resistance. And a British study confirmed that exercise was linked to reduced metabolic syndrome—

and that people who were unfit to start with benefited even more from the physical activity than those who were reasonably fit when they started.

It controls weight

Exercise burns calories so you lose, or at least don't gain, weight. A recent study showed that among people whose BMI averaged 41 (that's morbidly obese), those who lost just 7 per cent of their body weight through regular exercise regained healthy blood pressure and triglyceride levels, and the inflammation in their arteries dropped by between a quarter and a third, even though their BMI still averaged 38 (still too high). Numerous studies have confirmed that you don't need to be skinny to be physically fit.

It cuts total cholesterol

The major and most important effect of exercise is to raise levels of "good" HDL cholesterol, thus reducing total cholesterol levels. An international review of multiple studies revealed that adding exercise to a weight-loss diet not only raised HDL cholesterol but also increased the benefits of the weight-loss program and reduced triglycerides and blood pressure.

It reduces your heart rate

Every 60 seconds, the average couch potato's heart beats 70 to 75 times—more than a beat per second. An active person's heart, on the other hand, is so strong that it can pump the same amount of blood in only 50 beats. That's 36,000 fewer beats every day and 13 million fewer by the end of just one year. Exercise strengthens your heart and saves it having to work at a higher rate all the time.

It lifts stress and sadness

The positive effects of exercise on mood were demonstrated in a groundbreaking study in Britain in the late 1980s. Sedentary adults were randomly assigned to moderate intensity aerobic exercise, stretching exercises or none at all, for 12 weeks. Those in the moderate intensity group reported reduced tension, anxiety and confusion. The others did not.

A Berlin study revealed that just 30 minutes a day of exercise can be more effective than antidepressant drugs in treating mild to moderate depression. Exercise stimulates the brain to produce endorphins—the body's "feel good" hormones. It has two other advantages: it acts immediately (unlike drugs) and has few harmful or dangerous side effects.

It breaks bad habits

In a study of 280 women, U.S. researchers found that those who gave up smoking and started exercising were twice as likely to stay smoke-free—and gained half as much weight—as those who gave up without exercising.

It could save your life

According to the World Health Organization, inactivity causes 2 million deaths worldwide annually and is a major factor in breast and colon cancer, diabetes and heart disease. The World Heart Federation believes that inactivity is as bad for you as smoking a pack of cigarettes a day.

Making the best of your time

The most common excuse people give for not exercising is lack of time. But many people do have spare time—much more than they think or realize. Unfortunately, most of it is used sitting down—with a bag of chips and over-sized bottles of soft drinks—in front of the television watching endless hours of sports, sit-coms and movies. To add to the problem, instead of energizing us as exercise

Timesaving devices may save us minutes, but they can literally take years off our lives ...

Doing it yourself

Timesaving devices may save us minutes, but they can literally take years off our lives by stealing opportunities to keep our bodies strong and fit. Use a little muscle instead of a machine with these heart-healthy exchanges.

INSTEAD OF ...	GET ACTIVE BY ...
Paying a cleaner to clean your home once a week	Doing a few hours of your own vacuuming and dusting and have a cleaner come once every two weeks
Driving to the car wash	Washing and waxing your own car
Internet or catalogue shopping	Walking around your favourite shopping area—yes, shopping on foot does qualify as exercise
Having a burglar alarm installed	Getting a dog and walking it each day
Ignoring the garden, or employing a gardener	Mowing the lawn or trimming the bushes for 1 hour each week
Driving to the corner store	Walking or riding your bike
Using the dishwasher	Hand washing dishes once or twice a week
Having groceries delivered	Buying and carrying your own groceries home

would, watching television leaves us even more lifeless. Of course, any figure that is an average conceals wide extremes. Those people who are putting in a long week, doing high-pressured jobs, commuting long hours and juggling the responsibilities of bringing up children, are counterbalanced by an increasingly large group of retired people, and those who are unemployed or are disabled.

Studies show that a vast majority of women workers say they never have enough time to get things done, and more than half of the adult population claims to be suffering from stress. Many of those claiming stress are also likely to be sitting for a good part of their time, which is not helping. Even retired or unemployed people appear to use their free time in sedentary ways, rather than engaging in physical activity of some sort.

The average North American spends more than 20 hours a week watching television; most of us watch it every day and

The average Canadian spends more than 20 hours a week watching television.

too many of us consider television the most popular leisure activity.

Years ago leisure activities included swimming, walking, running and gardening. Most have fallen out of favour and have been replaced with mostly sedentary activities that are taking a toll on our waistlines and hearts.

A study of 3,000 people by a sports dietitian revealed that 41 per cent took part in no sport at all, and another 22 per cent did less than an hour a week. More than half the group surveyed spent most of their day sitting down. While nearly 60 per cent said they had no time for exercise, all managed to find time to watch television and videos, and play computer games.

The link to obesity

A direct link between general activity level and weight was shown by Dr. James Levine, who with a team from the Mayo Clinic studied the way we burn up calories in the course of a normal day. Obese people, on average, sit for 150 minutes more each day—using up 350 fewer calories—the equivalent of about 15 kg (33 lb) over a year, given the same food intake.

The researchers found that even washing dishes or walking about can boost the non-exercise activity thermogenesis (NEAT)—the rate at which the body burns up calories. Thin people are more active, sit less and have a higher NEAT than obese people. Even pacing around when you're on the phone, instead of sitting down, can boost NEAT. Getting a cordless phone, or using your cell phone, means you can walk or even climb stairs, while chatting, to increase your NEAT.

Exercise simply means moving

When you think of exercise, you probably think of structured workouts such as aerobics or Pilates. You can reap similar rewards with this simple approach to fitness—don't sit when you can stand, and don't stand when you can walk. Exercise that fits into your lifestyle can be just as effective as formal exercise routines.

Taking the stairs rather than the elevator or escalator, dancing, gardening, taking the dog for a long walk and playing active games with children or your grandchildren can be just as good for you as more vigorous exercise—or perhaps even better, as sudden bursts of exercise by unfit people can have harmful effects on the heart and blood vessels.

Only trained athletes should regularly push their bodies to the limit. The rest of us are better off increasing activity in everyday life. Again, small-time investments yield big payoffs. The key is finding active opportunities throughout the day, every day. Once you start looking, you'll be surprised by how many minutes in motion you can accumulate.

Fitting in fitness

Through the rest of this section, we provide ideas and programs for conquering sitting disease. First, you will be walking, then stretching, then strengthening. All fit in perfectly with the 30-Minutes-a-Day Plan; and at no point will you need to try and fit in an hour of extra activity.

Before we get into more rigorous exercise suggestions, though, you need to be in the right frame of mind. You have to want to change if you are to succeed. Once the mental focus is achieved, adopting a daily style in which you always choose the more active alternative will come easily. As you go about your day, try to stand more, walk more and get outside more.

To get you going, here are some helpful tips that can increase your daily exercise time by 30 to 45 minutes while barely changing your routine.

■ Take at least two flights a day

Research shows that taking just two flights of stairs a day can add up to a 2.5 kg (6 lb) weight loss over a year. Regular stair climbing also improves bone density, aerobic fitness and levels of good cholesterol.

Always take the stairs at work and while shopping. If you have stairs at home, make one trip up and down before and after work to be sure you get in at least two flights a day.

■ Make a meal of it

Cooking dinner burns more than twice as many calories as phoning for a pizza (and even more if you count the food shopping time as well). And the food's often better, too. Prepare and cook dinner at least one night a week, and preferably more.

■ Stand up to meetings

Instead of sitting for long periods of time in meetings, suggest regular breaks. Stand up, stretch and walk in the hall. Stay standing until the meeting resumes.

■ Be an active spectator

Your children's or grandchildren's sports practices and games are perfect opportunities for extra movement. You can pace the sidelines. You can walk around the field. The added activity will really give you something to cheer about.

■ Take the farthest parking spot

If you drive to work or church, park as far from the parking lot as possible, to get the longest walk. Do the same when you go shopping, visit restaurants or park anywhere else.

■ Computer calisthenics at your desk

Once an hour you should straighten and bend each leg 10 times, stand up and rise up and down on your toes 10 times, and stretch your arms to the ceiling.

■ Start a walking bus

Get your day off to an active start and help your children, grandchildren or even the neighbours' children to fend off future heart disease by launching a "walking school bus." Talk to the school and parents and get their agreement for you to meet the children in the morning and walk them to school, following a set route. Then meet them after school and walk home. If the school is too far away, pick a central location, such as a park, where parents can take their children, and use that as the pickup and drop-off point for your trips. The children will benefit, too.

■ Be ready to go

Opportunities for extra activity may appear at short notice. Meetings get cancelled. Children's events run late. Clients get stuck in traffic. Put on your walking shoes and go for a walk.

■ Think on your feet

Stand up whenever you need to write a list or jot down notes. It means that you'll get up and stretch your legs a few times a day.

■ Dial M for "move it"

When the phone rings, stand up and don't sit until the conversation is over. Walk around your house—or garden—to add extra steps.

■ Turn TV break time into active time

Fit in chores during the commercial breaks in your favourite television programs. Getting up to load the washing machine with laundry,

Regular stair climbing also improves bone density, aerobic fitness and levels of good cholesterol.

empty garbage cans or gather up the dirty dishes can add up to 14 to 24 minutes of activity in an hour, and you'll save hundreds of calories by not snacking instead.

■ Keep your hands busy

People who knit or do needlework in front of the television burn energy and have to keep their hands clean—so they don't nibble.

For more information, go to Health Canada (www.hc-sc.gc.ca). The site provides an excellent guide for physical activity in its Healthy Living section. It includes suggestions on how to increase your level of physical activity and a list of resources available to you to help combat the unwanted effects of inactivity.

Walking can carry your healthy, beating heart well into your nineties and beyond.

Take your heart for a walk

Putting one foot in front of the other is a very basic skill but one that can help to keep your heart strong and healthy well into your nineties and even beyond. For mobility is the key to a central factor in heart health—making sure that you burn more energy than you take in.

Research has shown that the difference in the balance of energy intake and energy used between obese people and thin people can be very small—only one part in a thousand. A moderately obese person may eat only 0.1 per cent too much and a morbidly obese person only 0.2 or 0.3 per cent more than they burn up. But over the years these small gains add up. Relatively small increases in activity levels, such as a 30-minute walk every day or casual, light housework, can make all the difference between succumbing to "middle-age spread" and staying trim and alert.

Fatter people typically gain about 9 kg (20 lb) over 20 years as they age—but with exercise there's no reason why they should. Walking is free, simple and convenient. Anyone can do it almost anywhere. Unfortunately, fewer and fewer of us are doing it and, as a result, obesity is increasing in Canada.

The Heart and Stroke Foundation of Canada reports that close to 60 per cent of all Canadian adults and 26 per cent of all Canadian children and adolescents are overweight or obese. And research shows that more Canadian children are overweight and obese than they were in the past. About 14 per cent of girls and 18 per cent of boys were obese in 1981. Ten years later 24 per cent of girls and 26 per cent of boys were considered overweight or obese. Unless individuals and society change course, those numbers will continue to rise.

Step it up

Ask how much men and women think they walk and you're likely to get very inaccurate answers. People invariably overestimate how much they walk and underestimate how much they eat.

One way to know for sure is to count your steps—literally. Studies show that the number of steps you take each day has a direct impact on your overall health. When it comes to weight control, more steps are definitely better.

Researchers recently weighed and measured 80 women between the ages of 40 and 66, then asked them to wear pedometers for a week as they followed their typical work and leisure routines.

The investigators found a direct connection between the number of steps taken in a day and the amount of fat stored. On average, those who took the most steps (10,000 or more a day) had only 26 per cent

body fat and healthy body mass indexes (BMIs)—the most popular tool today for tracking the healthiness of your weight.

Those who spent more time sitting down than on their feet (stepping out 6,000 or fewer times a day) had an average of 44 per cent body fat—well into the obese category—and BMI measurements that clearly put them at high risk of heart disease.

Most sedentary people take only about 3,000 steps from the time they get up in the morning to when they go to bed. Although there's no magic number that's right for everyone—and certainly very elderly people may need to take fewer steps than those in their younger years—experts generally suggest about 10,000 steps for healthy living.

Studies from Harvard and the Honolulu Heart Program clearly illustrate you can get big benefits from even modest step increases. Research shows that for an average person, building up the number of steps taken each day—whether by purposeful "fitness" walking or just pacing while talking on the phone—can reduce the risk of diseases such as cancer, diabetes, osteoporosis and even heart disease.

What's more, scientists at James Cook University in Australia found that exercise has a positive impact on brain hormones involved in mood and depression. This endorses similar international findings that exercise reduces depression, stress and anxiety, and can enhance self-esteem; it also improves the quality of sleep.

Tracking your progress

The easiest and most effective way to find out how much walking you do in a day is to use a simple pedometer—sometimes called a step counter. These devices strap onto your waistband and keep count every time you put one foot in front of the other. They sell for as little as $10 in Canada, and some doctors have already prescribed them for

Walk this way

Walking feels easier when you do it properly. Here's what a good walking style should look like.

SHOULDERS Keep them relaxed, down and slightly back. If you feel them hunching up toward your ears, take a deep breath and drop them down again.

ARMS Bend your arms and keep your elbows close to your body. Swing your arms from the shoulders, raising them toward your chest so that they are in line with your hips.

BACK Stand up straight, not hunched forward or arched backward.

KNEES Don't lock them. Keep them loose and pointing in the direction in which you're going.

HEAD Imagine that a string is attached to the top of your head, pulling your crown straight toward the sky. Your chin will naturally lift so your ears are directly in line with your shoulders.

CHEST Yoga practitioners often refer to the area on the front of your breastbone as your "heart light." When you walk, keep this area lifted and pointing forward.

ABDOMINALS Pull your belly button toward your spine as though you were zipping up a snug pair of pants. Keep your abdominals firm as you walk.

FEET As you take each step, plant your heel, roll onto the ball of your foot and push off with your toes. Avoid rolling your foot inward or outward. Although you can safely walk short distances in casual fashion shoes, wear good walking shoes whenever possible to protect your feet and joints. Your shoes should be designed for walking (or jogging, if walking shoes aren't available) and should feel great from the moment you buy them. For proper fit, be sure there's one finger-width between the end of your longest toe and the front of the inside of the shoe.

patients in areas where there is a high risk of heart disease.

If you are not a gadget lover, it's not a problem. There are many ways to monitor your daily walking. For instance, there are about 1,320 steps in every kilometre, so if you know it's half a kilometre from your house to the closest mailbox, that's an easy way to keep track. Here are some other guidelines.

Faster on foot

You can clock up your steps just walking around the town or city where you live or work. With traffic jams and parking problems that clog so many areas, you may find that running errands and going to lunch on foot is actually faster—and much better for your health—than taking a bus, your car or a taxi.

Watch the clock

Keep track of how many minutes you spend walking and you'll know whether you've accumulated enough steps for the day. As a rule of thumb, you take about 100 steps per minute during everyday walking. The faster you walk, the more steps you squeeze into every second.

Walk as if you were on your way to an appointment, and you'll clock up 120 steps every 60 seconds. Pick up the pace as though you were heading to the bus stop, and you're up to 135 steps a minute. Head out for a power walk—at a pace so brisk that if you went any faster, you'd be jogging—and you'll accumulate 150 steps each minute.

To determine how many steps you take with your typical stride, walk as you normally do and count your steps for 60 seconds. Repeat this exercise three times and calculate the average.

Move to the music

Here's a secret to keep you moving steadily and rhythmically: most popular music pumps out a predictable number of beats per minute that nicely match a healthy walking pace. So plug in your headset (provided you are in a safe, traffic-free environment or on a treadmill) and stride to the beat of your favourite tunes. Some examples are:

- "Kiss" by Prince: 111 bpm (beats per minute)
- "Express Yourself" by Madonna: 115 bpm
- "YMCA" by the Village People: 126 bpm
- "Achy Breaky Heart" by Billy Ray Cyrus: 124 bpm

Include non-walking time

If you're already actively swimming or cycling, that counts, too. Here are a few "step equivalents" for popular recreational pastimes.

- 1 minute of cycling = 150 steps
- 1 minute of swimming = 96 steps
- 1 minute of yoga = 50 steps

It's worth it

Most of your steps will be woven into the natural fabric of your day, as illustrated in the previous chapter, but you should also devote 10 to 15 minutes daily to taking your heart for a purposeful, extended walk. By carving out a small chunk of time each day, you're sure to get the minimum dose of weekly walking that's known to protect your heart. You'll also automatically take about a fifth of your recommended daily steps.

If you are still not convinced of the return from such a short exercise investment, consider this groundbreaking study from the Harvard School of Public Health.

When researchers there examined the activity levels of 7,307 men (average age 66), they found that those who managed short daily bouts of walking and stair climbing not only burned as many calories as those who spent more time on recreational sports or leisure activities, but also had similar reductions in heart disease risk. Small steps, literally, add up to big gains.

Get more out of every step

People who start walking start to love walking. Its appeal is not only its simplicity but also its versatility—you can strip it down or enhance it to fit the occasion. Here are some tips to burn more fat, get rid of more stress, make more muscle and have more fun with every step.

Try Nordic walking

Originating in Finland where it began as a summer training exercise for serious cross country skiers, Nordic walking—striding with special rubber-tipped aluminum walking poles—is a way to combine the calorie burn of cardiovascular exercise with the body sculpting of strength training. In Finland, some 50,000 people regularly enjoy Nordic walking.

As each arm swings back, the tip of the pole lands creating resistance that you must push against to propel yourself forward. Instead of flexing each muscle a few times in the gym, you activate every muscle for longer, which improves muscular endurance and burns fat. It is said to use 90 per cent of your muscles and, because it engages your upper body muscles as well, it burns at least 40 per cent more calories than ordinary walking. You can burn about 500 calories an hour while strengthening your shoulders, triceps, chest, back, abdominals, gluteals, thighs and calves.

Even better, the poles help to propel you, so walking feels easier. And the bonus for older people is that the arm muscles take part of the strain, so the load on the knees, ankles and hips is reduced by about a quarter, making exercising much easier.

Walking tip

If you want to increase your pace, take short strides. One of the most common walking mistakes that people make is lengthening their strides to walk faster. When you do this, your front foot actually acts like a brake, jarring your joints and ultimately slowing you down. Instead, take short, quick strides. Your feet will roll forward more easily, and you'll move at greater speed without the stress.

Integrate exercises

For a change of pace, integrate your favourite strength-training moves into your walk (see "Building strength," page 163). Get moving for 2 minutes, then do 20 seconds of push-ups against a tree. Walk another 2 minutes, then do 20 seconds of walking lunges. This mix-and-match training raises your heart rate and burns more calories.

Achieve active intimacy

Take your daily walk with a partner. A study found that adults who do this are more likely to exercise regularly and less likely to give up than those who do it alone.

Meditate while you move

Taking a heart-healthy mental rest can be easier and more effective when done while walking. The exertion will burn off stress hormones, and the repetitive movement will keep your mind focused and away from distracting thoughts and worries.

Start by walking a familiar route so you won't be distracted by your surroundings. Concentrate on feeling each foot touch the ground and focus on breathing rhythmically with your footsteps. As thoughts come to mind, allow them to pass through. You can also use this time to think about the good things in your life.

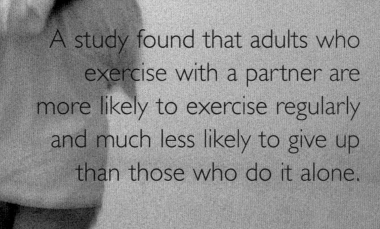

A study found that adults who exercise with a partner are more likely to exercise regularly and much less likely to give up than those who do it alone.

Working out your walking needs

How much time should you spend walking each day? Here are some helpful figures. We've already noted that very sedentary people walk about 3,000 steps in a day. Assuming that this is your base level as well, here's how much extra walking you need to do each day—measured for different paces—to reach specific step targets.

	EXTRA WALKING TIME NEEDED TO REACH:		
PACE	5,000 steps	7,000 steps	10,000 steps
Slow (80 steps per minute)	25 minutes	50 minutes	87 minutes
Normal (100 steps per minute)	20 minutes	40 minutes	70 minutes
Quick (120 steps per minute)	17 minutes	33 minutes	58 minutes
Fast (140 steps per minute)	14 minutes	29 minutes	50 minutes

IMPORTANT Your goal should be to get the majority of these extra steps during everyday activities—shopping, commuting and running errands. If you spend an extra 45 minutes a day on your feet as part of your daily routine and take a brisk, 15-minute walk for pleasure after lunch or dinner, you'll easily get to 10,000 steps.

Picking up the pace

The hardest part of rolling a boulder down a hill is fighting the powerful forces of gravity and inertia to get it started. But once you get it going, it gains momentum and becomes an almost unstoppable force.

Exercise is a lot like that: the hardest part is leaving your armchair and moving around. But once you start, your energy goes up, your weight comes down and you find yourself wanting to do even more—and when it comes to battling sitting disease and its ravaging effects, more is definitely better.

Although every little move you make helps to nurture a healthier heart, you can build even more robust cardiovascular strength by walking to work or to the store instead of taking the bus, for instance. Exercise doesn't have to be hugely vigorous to be beneficial.

One study was designed to discover what level of leisure-time activity would protect against premature cardiovascular death. Researchers followed 2,000 men, aged between 49 and 64 for more than 11 years. At the start, none showed any evidence of heart disease. But after 11 years, not surprisingly, a clear link could be established between total amount of physical activity undertaken and protection against premature death.

All gain, no pain

You don't have to (and, in fact, you shouldn't) heave, gasp and suffer pain to reap these rewards. Those new to exercise can raise their heart rates into the vigorous zone with little more than brisk walking.

Do you need a doctor's approval?

Most people don't need to see a doctor before they start exercising, but for those with existing conditions, it's wise to get your doctor's approval before participating in energetic exercise. To find out if you need a checkup, review this checklist. If one or more of the statements apply to you, talk to your doctor before starting a new program.

■ You have heart trouble or a heart murmur, or you have had a heart attack.
■ You frequently have pain or pressure in the left or mid-chest area or the left neck, shoulder or arm that occurs as you exercise but goes when you rest.
■ You get breathless during only mild exertion.
■ Your blood pressure is high and/or isn't under control, or you don't know whether your blood pressure is normal.
■ You have bone or joint problems, such as arthritis.
■ You are over the age of 60 and not used to vigorous exercise.
■ Your father, mother, brother or sister had a heart attack before age 50.
■ You have a medical condition not mentioned here that may need special attention in an exercise program.

When University of Massachusetts researchers asked 84 overweight men and women to walk a mile at a pace that was "brisk but comfortable," the vast majority of the volunteers immediately stepped up their pace to an average 3.2 mph, which translates into "hard" to "very hard" intensity (70 to 100 per cent of their maximum heart rates). The best part of it was that they found it easier than they expected. They anticipated having to suffer when, really, they just had to go from a slow stroll to a brisk walk.

To be able to tell if you are working hard enough, give yourself the talk test. If you're able to talk to a companion or on your cell phone while you walk, your exercise level is easy. If you can only speak, phrase by phrase, with little pauses for breath in between, you're right on target. If you can barely speak without gasping for air, you're working too hard. Try to keep in the middle of this range.

Don't feel guilty about not going to a gym and keeping up an exhausting pace. There is no reason why we should not aim to increase the physical activities that are pleasurable and fit in with our lifestyles and daily life.

Try the following:
- Take the stairs and walk up escalators
- Walk to the next bus stop
- Get a pedometer
- Enlist support from a friend
- Leave your car at home for short trips
- Take a walk at lunchtime
- Play active games with children
- Walk the children to school
- Buy a bicycle and use it
- Try something new like dancing or gardening

You don't have to heave and gasp and hurt to reap the rewards of exercise.

11 Ways to turn it up

Here are several small steps that can infuse heart-healthy intensity into your everyday work and play. If you're new to physical activity, start carefully—be sure you're comfortable with the walking and general movement advice in the earlier chapters before trying to do more. Then introduce small advances, easing up when you feel you need a break.

Avoid drinks containing caffeine before vigorous activity, especially if you have high blood pressure as caffeine further increases heart rate and blood pressure. Don't exercise after a big meal or when you have been drinking alcohol. Finally, be keen, but don't overdo it. You want to feel good enough tomorrow to do it again.

1 Sneak in surges

The next time you're out walking, and you're warmed up, step up the pace for a minute or two. Slow down to take a breather, then repeat. You'll not only burn more calories, but you'll also condition your body to feel comfortable at a faster pace so you'll be able to move more briskly every time you walk.

2 Power clean

Give your home a regular, energetic cleaning. Alternate between upstairs and downstairs chores (instead of doing one floor at a time) to make use of the stairs—they're your home's best calorie burner. But be careful going downstairs, especially if you have problems with balance. It's very easy to fall, particularly when carrying a vacuum cleaner.

3 Step up

Whenever you see a set of stairs, use them. If there's time (and you're really enthusiastic), go back down and climb them again. If flexibility and balance aren't an issue, take two steps at a time. It's an easy way to get a burst of exercise intensity every day.

4 Head for the hills

Walking or riding a bike uphill means working harder against gravity—an added challenge for your muscles, heart and lungs. Tackle some slopes (start with gentle ones) once or twice a week.

When walking uphill, lean forward slightly to engage your powerful gluteal muscles. Walking downhill can be harder on your knees, so slow your pace, keep your knees slightly bent and take shorter steps.

5 Dance, dance, dance

Whether it's country dancing or ballroom, dancing burns 480 calories an hour, uses your muscles in new ways—and puts joy in your heart. Some cardiologists say their patients who dance are the healthiest of them all. Try to go twice a month.

6 Make a splash

Water is 800 times denser than air, so it provides instant intensity. Head for the pool, wade into the water about chest deep and try these moves.

Side kicks Bend your right knee and then, without lowering it, kick out to the side, leaning toward the left as you kick. Lower your leg and repeat. Do 15 to 25 repetitions, then switch legs.

High steps March quickly across the pool, raising your knees as high as possible as you step. Then march back.

Zigzag run Pump your arms and legs and jog gently or run in a zigzag pattern across the pool and back. For the best results, keep your chest high and try not to bend forward.

7 Try some child's play

Children are natural stop-and-go exercisers as they run and run, stop to catch a breath and then run some more. Play Frisbee, fly a kite, kick a soccer ball around or toss some horseshoes. You'll raise your heart rate and build priceless family bonds.

8 Cultivate fast friends

Plan a few walks a week with someone who is just a little fitter and faster than you. You'll push beyond your comfort zone and get fitter, faster yourself. Exercising with a friend makes time fly, and you're more likely to stick to the routine if you do it with someone else.

9 Pre-program it

If you use a treadmill or other aerobic exercise equipment, choose the "interval" program to automatically add inclines, increased resistance and higher-speed bursts to your workout. Work up gradually and watch your strength and stamina improve.

10 Seek tougher terrain

Walking trails, soft sand and grassy fields all make you use more muscles and burn more calories than you would going at the same pace on the road. They're often in prettier places, too—so get off the beaten path whenever possible. But make sure, you're not trespassing.

11 Get in the game

Resolve to take up one active hobby this year. Sporting hobbies such as tennis, cycling and even golf include short bursts of heart-pumping effort. And they're fun, so time really flies. Below are some to choose from.

ACTIVITY	CALORIES BURNED PER HOUR*	SPECIAL BENEFITS
Bicycling	544	You feel like a child again
Gardening	340	Fresh, healthy vegetables
Golfing (walking with clubs)	374	Social contact; improves flexibility
Hiking	408	A chance to commune with nature
Ice skating/roller blading	408	Great family fun
Kayaking/canoeing	340	Builds upper body strength
Scuba diving	476	Scenic and serene
Swimming	544	Low-impact; eases joint pain
Tennis	476	Builds bones
Volleyball (casual)	204	Improves hand-eye coordination

*Based on a 67 kg (150 lb) person. Lighter people burn less; heavier people burn more.

The restorative power of stretching

As toddlers, most of us were so flexible that we could easily put our toes in our mouths but, as adults, many of us are so stiff that it hurts merely to clip our toenails. The cause of this loss of flexibility over the years can often be attributed simply to sitting disease.

The average sedentary person will lose a quarter to a third of his or her range of motion and possibly much more during adult life, which can dramatically curtail activity levels and contribute to a weakened heart. Because flexibility disappears slowly over the years, we may barely notice its departure.

"If you spend your day sitting on a sofa, sitting in a car and sitting at a desk, you can easily lose as much as 75 per cent of your normal range of movement by the time you're 60," says specialist sports physiotherapist

Claire Small. "Then it's a vicious circle. It's hard to move, so you don't try, and become stiffer and more sedentary. The less active your daily life, the more important it is to stretch."

The amazing thing about the human body is that when muscles and joints are used in the correct way, they continue to work well for longer. When we're active, our muscles, bones and joints get stronger, repair themselves and adapt; if we lead sedentary lives, our moving parts slowly lose these vital abilities. Of course, over-use must be avoided as it can have equally destructive effects.

As well as making your muscles more supple so that you can enjoy a more active life, stretching also helps to control high blood pressure and insulin resistance by lowering stress. Your muscles are equipped with stretch receptors that are in constant communication with your brain about your overall level of tension. When your muscles are chronically tight, your brain gets the message that you're under stress. Stretching helps muscles to relax, which sends a message to the brain that all is well.

Open your muscles

The body's tissues change as we age. Just as our skin thins and gets drier with time, so do our muscles and connective tissues. With less fluid keeping them plump and supple, muscles lose their elasticity and grow shorter and tighter. Short, rigid muscles act like tourniquets, constricting circulation so blood vessels can't deliver nutrients and carry out waste as well as they should. As waste builds up, hard knots (calcifications) form, which leave us feeling stiff and uncomfortable.

The result is that we literally get stuck in the hunched-over positions most of us assume for hours each day as we read, type, drive, eat, cook and clean.

"Poor posture is rampant and the main culprit is inflexibility," says Claire Small. "Many people dismiss bad posture as just an aesthetic problem, but hunching and slumping do more than look bad. They cause a whole series of problems, such as muscle imbalances, headaches, back pain and disc degeneration."

Poor posture even affects your breathing, making it shallower than it should be because your lungs can't fully expand when your chest is collapsed inward. Hunching tends to make people feel physically and emotionally bad.

When you progressively stretch your muscles through their full range of movement, you open the channels, promote circulation and encourage efficient nutrient transport and swift waste removal from those

Stay active without injury

Arrive early at a hockey or soccer game, and you will see the athletes twisting, bending, reaching for the sky, and dropping toward their toes. For active people, stretching has long been the hallmark of injury prevention.

Although recent U.S. studies suggest that stretching before exercise offers no protection against acute injuries such as sprains, stretching is still essential for general flexibility and can help you to avoid painful chronic conditions, such as Achilles tendinitis, that can arise from having chronically tight muscles and connective tissue. It can also improve your performance. When you regularly stretch your muscles, you increase your range of motion, which allows you to produce more power and makes you more balanced and agile when you work and play.

Finally, studies show that stretching after exercise is like wringing the lactic acid and accumulated metabolic waste out of your muscles. The result: less post-exercise muscle soreness, so you'll feel ready to go the next day. The stretches here will help to keep you walking, biking and playing tennis without pain.

tissues. Stretching will also increase the synovial fluid (the body's natural oil that lubricates your joints) in your hinges and sockets, which helps to keep your joints healthy and moving smoothly. When your muscles, tendons and ligaments are supple, your posture improves, and everything from picking socks off the floor to driving golf balls feels more effortless.

No matter how long you've been stationary, stretching can help to restore your mobility. In a small study at the University of California, researchers found that men and women who practised yoga twice a week became less hunched and improved their spinal flexibility—

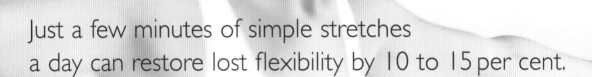

Just a few minutes of simple stretches
a day can restore lost flexibility by 10 to 15 per cent.

Are you supple?

People in their fifties shouldn't be expected to bend like contortionists, but neither should they be as stiff as a guard of honour.

Here are reasonable estimates of how supple you should be, given a healthy, moderately active lifestyle.

■ You should be able to sit on the edge of a chair (one leg extended, one bent) and bend over to tie a shoelace on the foot of the extended leg.

■ You should be able to scratch an itchy bite between your shoulder blades by reaching either behind your head or up from your waist.

■ You should be able to remove a well-fitting T-shirt by crossing your arms in front of your body, grasping the bottom hem, and pulling the shirt off in a smooth overhead movement.

■ You should be able to turn your head and look directly over either shoulder.

■ You should be able to reach behind you far enough with both arms to slip into a coat someone is holding out for you.

the ability to arch backward—by an astonishing 188 per cent. You don't have to spend hours twisting into acrobatic positions. Just a few minutes of simple daily stretches can restore lost flexibility by 10 to 15 per cent.

The perpetual stretch

Routines such as the one given here are valuable because they target all the major muscle groups and give you the maximum benefit in the minimum of time. But stretching is good at any time, anywhere. It boosts you out of afternoon doldrums, brings blood to your hands and wrists when you've been typing or writing too long, prepares you for walks, lifts your spirits and gets you on your feet (yet one more way to battle sitting disease). So while you should follow the 4-minute routine, we also advocate stretching all through your day and evening, too.

Take a look at some of the additional yoga-based stretches starting on page 234 and consider trying any others you may find in magazines and books. It is important to stretch safely and gently and to hold each position for at least 15 seconds if you want your muscles and joints to benefit.

Stretching is a lot like flossing: everyone agrees it's a good idea but few people actually take the time or make the effort to do it.

4 minutes to flexibility

Neglecting to stretch is one of the biggest mistakes that otherwise active people make.

Here's your chance to make up for neglecting your muscles. The following is a stretching sequence you can do practically anywhere in just 4 minutes. Although you can do these moves at any time of day, we suggest doing them after a bath or shower. Your muscles are most "stretchy" when they're nice and warm. Perform the sequence twice, flowing from move to move and holding each stretch for 15 seconds. Stretch only until you feel a slight "pull" or stretch in the muscle; you should feel tension relief, never pain. When you have finished, you'll be loose, supple and relaxed.

Sky Reach

MUSCLES AND JOINTS STRETCHED Back, shoulders, sides (obliques), abdominals and hands.

STAND straight with your feet about hip-width apart. Extend your arms overhead so that your fingers point straight at the ceiling. Rise on the balls of your feet and spread your fingers, stretching upward to make your body as long and tall as possible. Tilt your chin slightly to look at the ceiling. Hold, then return to the starting position.

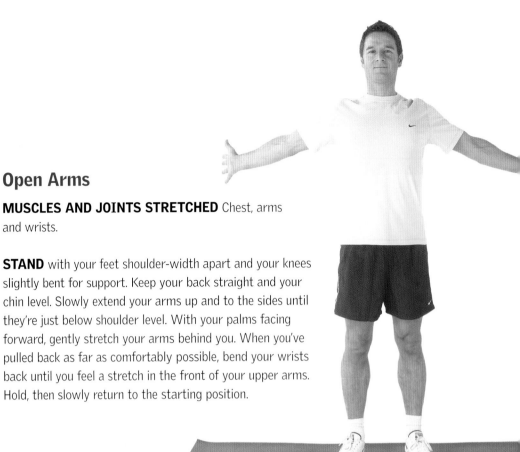

Open Arms

MUSCLES AND JOINTS STRETCHED Chest, arms and wrists.

STAND with your feet shoulder-width apart and your knees slightly bent for support. Keep your back straight and your chin level. Slowly extend your arms up and to the sides until they're just below shoulder level. With your palms facing forward, gently stretch your arms behind you. When you've pulled back as far as comfortably possible, bend your wrists back until you feel a stretch in the front of your upper arms. Hold, then slowly return to the starting position.

Wall Stretch

MUSCLES AND JOINTS STRETCHED Calves, hamstrings, back and shoulders.

STAND a metre away from a wall and place your hands on it, shoulder-width apart. Move your feet back until you're leaning into the wall and you feel a gentle stretch in your calves. Slowly press your hips back, keeping your back straight, and press your heels into the floor so that you feel a stretch in your back as well as your calves. Hold, then return to the starting position.

Triangles

MUSCLES AND JOINTS STRETCHED Sides (obliques), inner thighs, hamstrings and neck.

STAND with your feet wider than shoulder-width apart and point your right foot forward and your left foot to the side. Extend your arms straight out to the sides at shoulder level, then bend to the left, reaching for your left shin with your left hand. Extend your hand as far down your leg as comfortably possible while reaching toward the ceiling with your right hand. Turn your head slightly to look at the ceiling. Hold, then return to the starting position and repeat, stretching to the opposite side.

Sitback

MUSCLES AND JOINTS STRETCHED Hips, buttocks and thighs.

STAND straight and place your hands on a chair back or tabletop for support. Raise your right leg and place your right ankle on your lower left thigh, just above the knee. Bend your left leg, move back slightly, as if starting to sit, and gently press your right knee toward the floor, feeling the stretch in your right hip and the back of your thigh. Hold, then return to the starting position and repeat on the other side.

Measuring your exertion

Earlier, we urged you to count steps each day to track your level of activity. If you now want to up your exercise levels, there's a different measurement to use: the amount of time you spend with your heart beating at an accelerated rate.

Each of us has a maximum heart rate, above which we are over-exerting the heart and putting ourselves at risk. For most people, the maximum heart rate is 220 minus your age. So, if you are 60, your maximum heart rate is 160 beats per minute.

Doctors and fitness experts recommend that while exercising people reach and maintain roughly 60 to 65 per cent of their maximum heart rates. For vigorous exercise, getting up to 80 per cent of the maximum is acceptable, but only if you are really fit.

If you maintain the "breathing-hard-but-still-able-to-talk" exertion level, you are almost certainly in the target range of 60 to 70 per cent of maximum heart rate.

The recommended quantity of exercise for healthy living is keeping your heart rate at 60 per cent of your maximum rate for at least 30 minutes a day. For a 60-year-old, that would be 96 beats per minute. In comparison, the average person has a resting heart rate of about 70 beats per minute.

Measuring this can be done in two ways: with a heart-rate monitor or manually. Like pedometers, heart-rate monitors are becoming better known in fitness circles. Their cost runs from the not too expensive to the expensive, depending on the features, brand and style, but all are wonderfully easy to use. First, you put a strap around your chest right against your skin (once you've put your shirt on, nobody can see it). Next, you put a monitor on your wrist. Most look like wristwatches, and in fact, many include clocks; you can actually wear them all the time. But the monitor also receives signals from the chest strap, telling you your heart rate.

Most monitors are programmable. The most popular tool is the ability to program the target heart range you want to be in while exercising (say, 65 to 75 per cent of maximum). The monitor then beeps if you exceed 75 per cent or fall below 65 per cent.

If you don't want to use a monitor, it's quite simple to check your heart rate manually. Start by checking your resting heart rate, by counting your pulse for a minute. Then do the same again when you feel you have reached your maximum.

Checking your recovery time is a good measure of your improvement in fitness.

Building strength

Although we hear tales of 80- and 90-year-olds who perform amazing feats—running a marathon or swimming 15 kilometres at a time—most of us are content with getting a bit fitter and losing some weight. Finding your own level is most important and in this, as with so many things, common sense is called for.

If you are seriously obese or even just overweight, you should get your doctor's advice before engaging in any strenuous exercise. And once you start, if you feel giddy, nauseous, breathless or faint, or if you suffer a fall or muscular or joint strains, you should stop at once. Always start slowly and work up to a comfortable pace, then allow yourself to wind down afterwards.

Two important types of exercise that you should be aware of when thinking about heart health are "aerobic" and "strength training." Aerobic exercise increases the heart rate and circulation, and involves activities such as swimming, walking and cycling. As fitness increases, tennis, rowing or badminton can be added. On the other hand, strength training, or lifting weights, produces muscle tension and increases strength locally but does not immediately benefit the heart and circulation.

Some heart specialists say that people who already suffer from heart disease or hypertension should avoid strength training as it increases blood pressure and puts stress on the heart. But some of those same heart specialists recognize that strength training can prevent the loss of muscle mass that often accompanies aging and may stop the decline in metabolism that leads to "middle-age spread." In women, strength training can also increase bone density and help to stave off osteoporosis, which has an indirect heart benefit because activity levels are maintained.

Strong-arming heart disease

If you have ever moved furniture, you'll know that lifting something heavy makes your heart work harder, so it is obvious that using your muscles strengthens your heart.

Research from many countries shows that regular weight training can help fend off the major heart attackers by improving triglyceride counts, cholesterol levels, blood pressure and glucose metabolism and by reducing body fat. In a study of 44,000 men, researchers at Harvard found that those who lifted weights for 30 minutes or more a week reduced their risk of heart disease by 23 per cent.

Here's a summary of what else is known about the benefits of strength training.

■ Stopping metabolism meltdown

Unless you take steps to boost your metabolism—your body's calorie-burning ability—you can lose a third to half of your lean body mass and replace it with twice as much body fat by the time you're 65. That's a double blow to heart health as muscle tissue helps you to burn off blood sugar, while excess fat raises your heart disease risk.

This muscle loss happens so gradually that it often goes practically unnoticed for decades. It starts around your 35th birthday, when levels of human growth hormone begin to fall. At the same time, family and work demands may increase, leaving you with less time for physical fun than in the past. The combination means you can lose about 200 g (8 oz) of muscle a year. Not much, until you consider that each day muscle tissue burns about 15 times as many calories as fat does, even when you're not exercising. As your muscle lessens, so does your metabolism. The result is that you gain fat.

Strength training is the best long-term method for increasing resting energy expenditure—that is the number of calories you burn simply by existing. If you work every major muscle group twice a week, you can replace 5 to 10 years' worth of lost muscle in just a few months.

In a study of 15 sedentary older adults, the volunteers performed two sets of 10 to 12 strength-training exercises, three days a week for six months. By the study's end, they boosted their metabolism by 7 per cent, or 88 calories a day—enough to burn off more than 4 kg (9 lb) excess weight in a year. And that was without doing anything else. In other words, they lost weight independently of what they did or ate, solely because they had more muscle on their bodies (and the daily calorie figure doesn't include the calories burned while doing the exercise).

In a related study, women who followed a strength-training program for six months lost significant amounts of abdominal fat, the dangerous kind of fat that will likely take its toll on your health, including increasing your chances of developing heart disease and diabetes.

■ Improving cardiovascular fitness

When your muscles get stronger, they can perform better with less oxygen. That means your heart doesn't have to work so hard when you're doing everyday activities such as running up a flight of stairs or chasing tennis balls on the court. When a group of 46 adults lifted weights three times a week for six

Muscle making

All this talk of sets and repetitions can sound intimidating to someone who's never routinely lifted anything heavier than a shopping bag but it's really simple. Here's a guide to get you started.

REPETITIONS (reps) This term refers to the number of times you lift a weight or perform an exercise. Squatting up and down once is considered 1 repetition. Squatting 10 times is 10 repetitions.

SETS This is the number of times you perform groups of repetitions. When we tell you to do 2 sets of 10 to 12 reps, we mean that you should do 10 to 12 consecutive repetitions, take a 30-second break, and do a second set of 10 to 12 repetitions.

WEIGHT SELECTION As a general rule, the weight you lift should be heavy enough to make the final 2 or 3 repetitions feel tough. If you can do 15 reps without a problem, pick a heavier weight. If you struggle to manage 6, go lighter. If an exercise is new to you, practise the movements without weights before your first workout.

SPEED Take your time. Each repetition should take about 6 seconds, so slowly count 1–2–3 as you lift, pause a moment and count 1–2–3 as you lower. By doing this, you'll be sure to use your muscles, not momentum, to do the work, and you'll get better results from your efforts.

BREATHING It may sound silly to remind someone to do something so automatic but many people hold their breath while they lift, which could be dangerous. For the best results, exhale as you push the weight against gravity and inhale as you move with gravity.

Finding your own level is most important
and in this, as with so many things,
common sense is called for.

months, they not only got a lot stronger, they also improved their fitness by about 25 per cent. This study, undertaken at the University of Florida, was the first to demonstrate that strength training builds aerobic fitness as well as strength.

The finding was endorsed by a European study which introduced weight training into a rehabilitation program for elderly people with chronic lung disease. After just seven weeks they were able to lift almost twice the weight they could at the start, and had improved their walking distances.

■ Fighting free radicals

Lifting weights enhances your body's defence system against free radicals—natural by-products of metabolism that have been linked to illnesses such as heart disease.

In a study of free radical damage, researchers at the University of Florida asked 62 men and women to lift weights three times a week for six months.

At the end of the study, the weightlifters showed no evidence of damage from these harmful elements, compared with a 13 per

cent increase in dangerous free radical activity among a similar group of adults who didn't lift weights.

■ Building heart power

Strength training conditions your heart to work better when you have to lift and carry heavy objects, so your blood pressure and heart rate are lower during everyday chores.

Strong muscles also help to share the load, so there's less demand on your heart when you carry groceries or mow the lawn. If you find strength training a strain, try lighter weights and consult your doctor if you experience pain or other symptoms.

Time investment

Two sets of two strength-training exercises will take about 5 to 6 minutes to complete. Try doing them while you watch your favourite television program. (Keep the weights handy as a gentle reminder.) That way you invest no extra time for a lifetime of heart benefits.

■ Finding an alternative

There are other routes. "Weightlifting is not the only way to gain muscle strength," says sports physiotherapist Claire Small. "Exercises like Pilates also work the major muscle groups and the core." ("Core" refers to the abdomen, lower back and hip).

Pilates classes are held across the country, and you can choose a class that suits your needs. Or if you prefer, you can tackle Pilates at home with a DVD or video exercise. Before starting any program of new exercise, it is wise to consult your doctor.

Two exercises a day

Boredom and lack of time are the two most common reasons for not following a regular exercise program. The solution to both is to keep the exercises short, but effective.

With a few pieces of inexpensive equipment, such as the balance ball

mentioned on page 167, you can build strong muscles and a healthy heart in as little as 5 minutes a day, without having to leave the house and go out to a gym.

Spread out your routine so that you perform two quick exercises a day. As you'll see in the following program, you still work all your major muscle groups twice a week but the daily time commitment is minimal.

Consider this an important part of your 30-Minutes-a-Day commitment: 5 minutes each morning or evening to do strength exercises. To get you going, we've created the Healthy Heart Strength Plan, a week's worth of exercises for your whole body. It's easy, it's fast, and it has been proved to work.

What you'll need Two sets of dumbbells—a lighter set for arm exercises and a heavier one for leg exercises. Talk to the salesperson at the sporting goods store about what weight is appropriate for you, but if you want to be absolutely sure about the choice, it is always worth talking to a physiotherapist or trainer to decide what is best for you. Make sure that the dumbbells you choose can be held in your hands firmly and comfortably. You'll also need a balance ball, a large, inflated exercise ball that can be purchased separately or as

Build strong muscles
and a healthy heart in as little as 5 minutes a day.

part of an exercise kit. (see "Get on the ball," below). Not only can you use a balance ball as a substitute for a weight bench, you can also do dozens of exercises using just it and your body weight to strengthen and tone every major muscle, especially your "core"— the abdomen, back and hips.

Both dumbbells and balance balls can be purchased at any major sporting goods store, where you'll find numerous brands.

What to do Follow the program starting on page 168, performing two sets of 10 to 12 repetitions of each exercise. Rest for 30 seconds between sets. If you are new to training, see the "Muscle making" guide on page 164 for more advice on getting started.

Bonus You'll find that these moves become easier in a month or two as your body adapts to the workload. Studies show that strength training is most effective when you "surprise" your muscles with new challenges every eight to 12 weeks. We've taken the guesswork out of changes by providing two more complete routines in "The 30-Minutes-a-Day Plan Workbook" on page 226. Simply rotate through the three routines to keep your muscles (and your mind) from getting bored. And add a little music to the routine.

Get on the ball

Balance balls are excellent, versatile training tools. When you perform strength-training exercises on one of these inflated exercise balls, all your muscles, especially those in your core, kick in to help you to maintain form and balance, so you get more benefit from each move. They also improve your balance and coordination—something most people need as they get older. But the balls can seem somewhat odd and unstable at first, even for people who exercise regularly. The following tips will help you to start with confidence.

BUY THE RIGHT SIZE Using a ball that's too big or too small will make these moves more difficult, or even dangerous if the ball is much too large. As a rule of thumb, when you sit on the top of the ball, your legs should be bent at 90 degrees when your feet are flat on the floor. Most balls include size charts on their packages. Ask a salesperson or a personal trainer if you are not sure which size to choose.

HAVE A SEAT Practise getting comfortable on the ball by simply sitting on it. Place it near a wall, put your hand on the wall for support, and have a seat. For better balance, place your feet wide apart for a more stable foundation. As you find your centre of gravity and feel more stable, take your hand off the wall and practise sitting while raising your arms to the sides, then overhead.

CHEAT A LITTLE If balance is a problem when you start out, simply prop the ball against a wall and sit on it with your back to the wall. It will be less able to roll around beneath you while you build your balance and confidence.

KEEP IT PROPERLY INFLATED The ball is hard to use if it's too soft. It should be firm enough not to be easily squeezed between your hands, but soft enough to give a little when you sit on it.

IMPORTANT NOTE Stability balls are designed to hold hundreds of kilos of pressure without popping, so use only these specially designed exercise balls. Don't substitute beach balls, department store children's toys or other non-exercise-specific balls for these moves.

Monday Back and biceps

Your back is made up of multiple layers of muscles that help you to lift, pull and hold your body upright. Your biceps are the muscles in the front of your upper arms that you use to pick up bags and small children. These exercises target those two muscle groups.

Curl and press

SIT on the balance ball or a chair with your feet flat on the floor about shoulder-width apart. Hold a dumbbell in each hand with your arms at your sides, palms facing out.

KEEPING your upper body stable, bend your elbows and curl weights toward your shoulders.

IMMEDIATELY turn your wrists so your palms face out in front of you and press the weights straight overhead. Pause, then slowly reverse the move, lowering the weights to your shoulders, rotating your palms, and lowering the weights to your sides.

KEEP your shoulders down as you curl and lift; don't let them hunch up toward your ears.

Back fly

SIT ON the edge of the balance ball or a chair with your feet together and flat on the floor. **HOLD** a dumbbell in each hand. Keeping your back flat, bend forward at the waist and lower your chest to about 7–10 cm (3–4 in.) above your knees, letting your arms hang down on either side of your legs with your hands by your feet. **SQUEEZE** your shoulder blades and raise the weights out to the sides until your arms are outstretched parallel with the floor. Pause, then slowly return to the starting position.

The healthy heart strength plan

Tuesday Chest and triceps

Your chest is composed of fan-shaped muscles that span from shoulders to sternum and help you to push shopping carts and hug loved ones. Your triceps are also "pushing" muscles, located on the backs of your upper arms—notoriously weak and saggy spots.

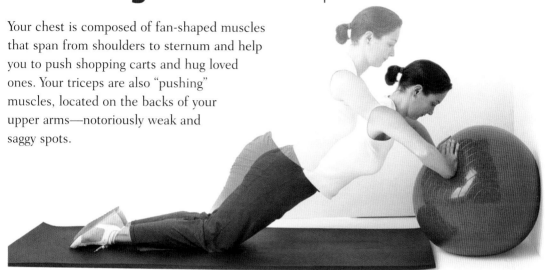

Balance ball push-ups

PLACE the balance ball against a wall, then kneel in front of it so it's between you and the wall.
PLACE your hands on the ball so they're directly below your shoulders. Walk back on your knees until your body forms a straight line from your head to your knees. You should be leaning forward into the ball.
KEEPING your torso straight and your abdominal muscles contracted (concentrate on pulling your belly button to your spine), bend your elbows and lower your chest toward the ball.
STOP when your elbows are in line with your shoulders. Pause, then return to the starting position.

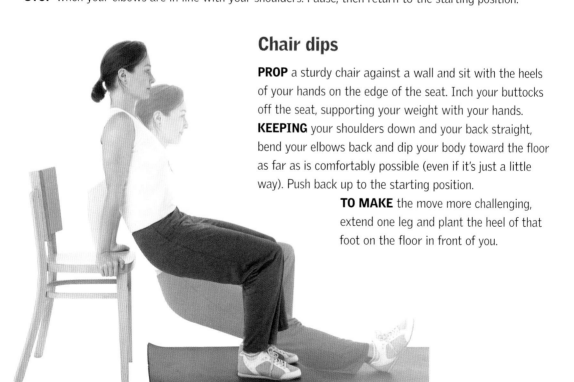

Chair dips

PROP a sturdy chair against a wall and sit with the heels of your hands on the edge of the seat. Inch your buttocks off the seat, supporting your weight with your hands.
KEEPING your shoulders down and your back straight, bend your elbows back and dip your body toward the floor as far as is comfortably possible (even if it's just a little way). Push back up to the starting position.
TO MAKE the move more challenging, extend one leg and plant the heel of that foot on the floor in front of you.

Wednesday Legs and core

The muscles in your thighs, calves and buttocks account for about half your muscle mass. Core (abdominal, lower back and hip) strength is vital to good health. Researchers who followed a group of adults for 13 years found that those who could perform the most sit-ups were significantly less likely to die prematurely than those who could perform the least.

Balance ball squat

STAND with the balance ball between your back and the wall so the ball supports you from your hips to your shoulders. Move your feet forward so they're slightly in front of your body.
LOOKING straight ahead and keeping your torso erect, bend your knees and squat down, rolling along the ball until your thighs are parallel with the floor. Hold for 2 seconds, then return to the starting position. You can make the move more challenging by holding dumbbells at your sides.

Hover

LIE face down on the floor with your upper body propped on your forearms. Your elbows should be slightly behind your shoulders and your palms flat on the floor.
RAISE your body so that your torso, hips and legs are off the floor and your body is in a straight line, supported on your forearms and toes. Don't let your back arch or droop, and hold for 10 to 20 seconds. Perform just one repetition per set.

The healthy heart strength plan

Back and biceps **Thursday**

A return to the muscles exercised on Monday, but with two different exercises.

Arm lifts

SIT on the balance ball or a chair with your feet flat on the floor and a shoulder-width apart. Hold a dumbbell in each hand, letting your arms hang naturally at your sides, palms facing in.
SLOWLY LIFT the dumbbells toward your collarbone, turning your wrists toward your body as you lift, so that your palms end up facing you. Pause, then slowly return to the starting position.

Bent-over row

STAND with your feet a shoulder-width apart, your back straight and your knees slightly bent for support. Hold a dumbbell in each hand. Keeping your back straight, bend 90 degrees from the waist and let your arms hang toward the floor, palms facing your legs.
SQUEEZE your shoulder blades together and bend your elbows, raising the dumbbells on either side of your torso. Pause, then slowly return to the starting position.

Friday Chest and triceps

Back to the muscles exercised on Tuesday, with
some fresh strengthening moves.

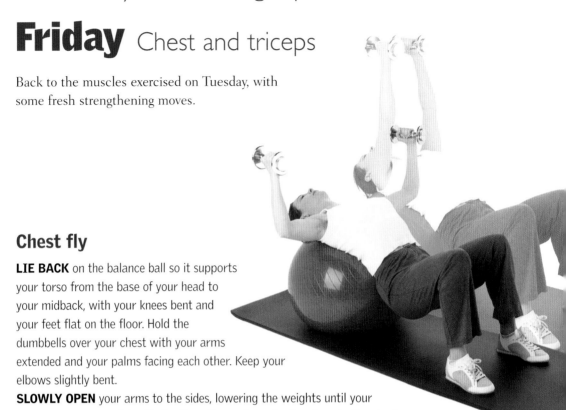

Chest fly

LIE BACK on the balance ball so it supports
your torso from the base of your head to
your midback, with your knees bent and
your feet flat on the floor. Hold the
dumbbells over your chest with your arms
extended and your palms facing each other. Keep your
elbows slightly bent.

SLOWLY OPEN your arms to the sides, lowering the weights until your
upper arms are parallel with the floor. Pause, then slowly return to the starting
position. Keep your shoulders down and back throughout the move.

Triceps pressback

SIT ON the balance ball with your knees bent
and your feet flat on the floor. Hold the dumbbells
in front of you with your arms bent at 90-degree
angles and your elbows at your sides. Keeping
your back straight, bend slightly from the hips.

STRAIGHTEN your arms and extend the weights
behind your back, turning your palms toward the
ceiling once your arms are fully extended. Pause,
then return to the starting position.

The healthy heart strength plan

Saturday
Legs and core

A return to the muscles exercised on Wednesday, but with interesting variations.

Balance ball leg curls

LIE ON your back on the floor, extend your legs, and place your heels on top of the balance ball. Rest your arms on the floor by your sides, palms down.
PRESS your heels into the ball and lift your buttocks up a little from the floor.
BEND your knees, using your heels to pull the ball toward your buttocks so your feet end up flat on the ball. Pause, then return to the starting position.

Side plank

LIE ON your left side with your knees bent. Bend your left arm so your forearm is extended in front of you perpendicular to your body, then lift your torso off the floor. Your upper body should form a straight line from your hips to your shoulders.
PLACE your right hand on your hip and hold for 5 to 15 seconds. Return to the starting position, then repeat on other side. Work up to holding on each side for 30 to 60 seconds. Perform just one rep per set.

Sunday Rest day!

Research has shown conclusively that your emotions and attitudes have a direct influence on the health of your heart. Surely that's a good reason to enjoy life more.

Nurturing a happy heart

How to be kind to your heart

Imagine you had a dog. You would probably look after him by feeding him healthy, nutritious food, giving him plenty of exercise and providing him with a warm, comfortable place to sleep. But those are just the bare necessities. Like most dog lovers, you'd also dote on him, play with him, cuddle him if he seemed anxious and provide lots of happiness and fun in the interest of a long, healthy life.

Shouldn't you treat your heart as well as you'd treat a dog? The analogy is less of an imaginary leap than you might think. As with any pet, whether your heart thrives or becomes ill largely depends on your care, love, nurturing and kindness.

In the long run, being kind to your heart is better than any medicine money can buy. In the Lifestyle Heart Trial, a group of researchers in California observed nearly 50 men and women with moderate to severe coronary disease for five years. Half of the group did not take any medicines but instead made lifestyle changes that included healthy eating, exercise, support group meetings, stress management and giving up smoking. The other half followed the more routine medical regimen that focuses on medicines and subtle lifestyle changes.

At the end of the study, the "lifestyle" group's arteries were about 8 per cent clearer, while in those having routine treatment, arterial clogging had increased by almost 28 per cent—despite medication.

Furthermore, the volunteers in the "routine" group had twice as many cardiac events (such as arrhythmias or heart attacks) as the "lifestyle" group.

Lifestyle measures are responsible for much of the significant decline in mortality rates from coronary heart disease observed in recent years.

Research has confirmed the healing power of a positive attitude and a good laugh.

6 steps to a happy heart

It is interesting how many people shun emotional health advice. They believe that heart health requires more serious steps: medicine, supplements, rigorous diets, formal exercise regimens. But this isn't the whole picture. Research has confirmed the healing power of a positive attitude and a good laugh. A sense of spirituality can help as well. This is not alternative medicine or the wishful thinking of eternal youth-seeking baby boomers. Happiness does matter. The following six steps are essential to the 30-Minutes-a-Day Plan.

1 Your soul

Belief, whether in a higher being, the power of nature, or even yourself, is both grounding and healthy. A big part of this is optimism. People who use words such as "joy" and "hope" to describe their attitudes toward life outlive their more pessimistic counterparts by a decade. No matter what your situation, the power to do away with anger and embrace the good things in life lies in your hands.

2 Enjoy life

Some time between leaving our parents' homes and signing up to a 25-year mortgage agreement of our own, we stop having as much fun as we used to. We all have serious adult responsibilities, but we also have a responsibility to our hearts to let go and have some childlike fun. Studies show that people whose lives are filled with laughter are much less likely to have heart disease.

3 Practise relaxing rituals

As life gets more rushed, stress rises and heart disease follows. You can't change the world, but you can change your response to it. Daily rituals such as meditation, yoga, quiet time, bedtime relaxation and even just walking a dog can quell stress and reduce your risk of heart disease.

4 Drink a glass a day

Those who enjoy a glass of wine with dinner may lower their heart disease risk, according to some health experts. Limit your alcohol to a weekly maximum of 14 drinks for men and nine for women. Interestingly, wine, especially red wine, seems to have a more beneficial effect than other alcoholic drinks.

5 Create a safe haven

They say that home is where the heart is, so make yours a refuge for your heart. Create a soothing ambiance with fresh flowers and plants, music, a relaxing bedroom and some quiet space where you can go when you need to think. Spending most of your time relaxed instead of stressed can halve your heart disease risk.

6 Share yourself

Hearts are happiest and healthiest when they're in the company of others. Don't be so busy that you can't make time for loved ones—whether they are your family or your friends, or both.

Soothe your soul

If you want to add seven years to your life, then consider making more time for your "spiritual" side. Over the years, scientists around the world have conducted more than 1,200 studies around the world, all of which suggest a positive relationship between spirituality and long life. Nurturing your spiritual health and sense of purpose is associated with an increase in longevity.

This does not necessarily mean attending religious services; it could involve anything that boosts your spiritual self, like doing something to help other people or supporting a cause in which you strongly believe.

Some scientists recognize the physiological benefits of prayer and a spiritual belief. Studies show that attending a religious service can slow down heart rate, alleviate stress and promote a general sense of well-being.

In one U.S. study, people undergoing open-heart surgery who said they gained strength and comfort from their religion were three times more likely to survive than those with no spiritual beliefs. Even skeptics accept that faith probably exercises a powerful placebo effect. Put simply, people often get better because they believe they will. Of course, it would be unrealistic to suggest that you must "find religion" to save your heart.

But even if you're not interested in formal religious services, nurturing your spiritual side through activities such as voluntary work, spending time out in the open countryside or meditation has clear benefits.

People who tend to their inner selves are less likely to drink too much, smoke or be lonely.

The power of prayer?

Praying for the sick or dying is a common practice among people of all faiths. Praying for yourself or knowing that others are praying for you can help to improve your ability to cope with and reduce your anxiety about whatever is worrying you. Many people believe that positive thinking or prayer boosts immunity and improves the overall function of our body systems, and scientists remain intrigued by the potential power of prayer.

Discover your soul

You may have no formal religious faith, or you may be Christian, Jewish, Muslim or Hindu, or you are not quite sure what to believe. Whatever your standpoint, there are many ways to celebrate your spiritual side. The most obvious is to attend religious services, but there are plenty of other ways.

■ **Meditate** Meditation eases anxiety and lowers blood pressure. It's also a tool used in most religions to bring you closer to a higher spiritual level. According to the British Heart Foundation, transcendental meditation has been found to be effective in slowing both breathing and pulse rate, leading to deep relaxation. Recent studies have produced positive results in terms of the effects of transcendental meditation on blood pressure levels.

Most people believe that you need to sit still to meditate but it can be just as effective on the move: exercise lowers stress hormones and supplies the body with fresh oxygen. During your daily walk, take a few minutes to calm and clear your mind simply by focusing on your footsteps and the sensation of air moving in and out of your lungs.

■ **Help others** Helping a good cause, whether by giving money or volunteering your time, deepens your connection to humanity and promotes a feeling of greater purpose. If you have time, offer help in delivering food to the elderly, manning a charity store, walking dogs at a local animal shelter or teaching someone to read. Your local paper may have listings of volunteers needed.

Or every so often, take a good look at the clothes or shoes in your closet, the blankets and sheets in the linen closet and any surplus canned or bottled foods from your kitchen cupboard and give them to a local homeless charity.

Other feel-good activities include writing letters to old friends and being kind to others, whether opening doors for someone carrying heavy bags or giving up a parking space to a mother with a carload of children—or simply saying "well done" to family, friends or work colleagues.

■ **Go for a walk** Few people can walk by a river or on the common, or even sit in a park, without feeling the beauty and power of a larger force around them. Make a point of getting outside once a day, if only to sit under a tree in your garden.

■ **Say it out loud** If you use meditative phrases or prayers, it seems that saying them out loud may increase their effect. An Italian study of men and women reciting either a yoga mantra or the "Ave Maria" found that both appeared to slow breathing rhythms to six breaths a minute (the normal rate is between 16 to 20 breaths per minute).

Stock your spiritual pantry

Since the beginning of time, places of worship have used music, incense and candles to help set the spiritual stage. You can use the same tricks at home.

■ Candles: nothing soothes the soul like a flickering flame.

■ CDs: whether violin concertos or arias, funk or folk, music opens your heart, alters your brain waves and connects you to your spiritual self.

■ Symbols or statues: for some people, a crucifix, Buddha figure or other religious symbol is a powerful reminder that they are not alone.

■ Flowers, plants or both: living things evoke the beauty and simplicity of the natural world.

■ Incense: the rising smoke from burning incense once symbolized prayers rising up to God; the scent is also soothing. If you don't fancy smoke, use a scented light ring filled with a soothing essential oil instead.

Nurturing your spiritual health and sense of purpose is associated with an increase in longevity.

When chanting, they also appeared to synchronize their breathing rate with cardiovascular rhythms—which calms the central nervous system and induces a feeling of well-being. Interestingly, these effects weren't present when the words were not recited aloud.

■ **Appreciate the good things** Once a day, whether first thing in the morning, before dinner or at bedtime, give mental thanks for all the good things and lovely people in your life. Actively expressing appreciation for essentials such as food, your home or even your job can be a positive reminder of how lucky you are.

At the same time, mentally send good wishes and positive energy to others, especially those who you know are in need of some special luck at that particular time.

■ **Express yourself** There are lots of ways to get in touch with your creative self. You could keep a diary, try your hand at painting or pottery, try gardening or learn furniture restoration.

Being creative helps many people to nourish their spiritual side. Whichever way you choose, expressing yourself artistically is a great way to soothe and feed your soul.

Enjoying life

When was the last time you felt lighthearted—or were heartbroken? All of our heartfelt emotions—from love to loneliness, happiness to hate—affect not only the way we see the world but also how long we spend living in it.

In a 15-year study of 678 nuns living and teaching in the United States, researchers found that those who most often used positive words such as "happy," "joy," "love" and "glad" when describing their lives in letters and diaries lived as much as 10 years longer than those who expressed fewer positive emotions.

The researchers concluded that good feelings can act as a biological shield against daily stresses that otherwise take their toll in the form of high blood pressure, heart disease and more. And a Dutch study of almost 1,000 people aged 65 to 85 at the outset found that 10 years later the optimists among them had a 55 per cent lower risk of death from all causes and a 23 per cent lower risk of cardiovascular death, than the pessimists.

The Dutch researchers suggest that the optimists' better survival rates may be due to more positive behaviour, such as not smoking, staying slim and taking exercise, and also to having better coping strategies.

Happiness helps you to live longer even if you already have heart disease. For 11 years, U.S. researchers monitored the emotions and overall health of 866 men and women (with

> Happiness helps you to live longer even if you already have heart disease.

an average age of 60) after cardiac cathet-
erization. Those who most frequently ticked
phrases like "ability to laugh easily" or
"lightheartedness" on questionnaires about
themselves and their moods were 20 per cent
less likely to die prematurely of any cause,
including heart disease, than those whose
responses were less positive.

"Type A" anger

Just as all those happy feelings can act as
powerful life extenders, negative emotions
can have the opposite effect. Anger,
impatience and hostility significantly raise
your risk of heart disease. Research suggests
a possible link between levels of triglycerides
in the blood and personality type.

In the Edinburgh Artery Study, a random
group of 1,592 men and women aged
between 55 and 74 years underwent
personality tests and had their blood lipid
concentrations measured. Those with higher
triglycerides, especially men, were more
likely to behave in a hostile and domineering
way. An angry personality was associated with
a higher risk of peripheral arterial disease and
claudication, symptoms of vascular disease in
the legs.

A seven-year U.S. study of 1,300 men
found that those who reported the most
intense levels of anger were three times more
likely to have chest pain or heart attacks—or
both—than those with the least anger.

What makes hostility so harmful? Think
about what happens when you get really
furious. Your face flushes; your hands shake;
you clench up. Internally, the effects are
equally profound. As you shake your fist at
that idiotic driver, the arteries supplying
blood to your heart constrict. Your blood
becomes stickier and thus more likely to clot.
Your blood sugar rises sharply. Surging
adrenalin sends your heart rate soaring.

Repeat this cycle over and over again—with a
wretched boss, irritating neighbours, those
noisy children next door—and the physical
wear and tear leads to higher homocysteine
levels, raised cholesterol, high blood pressure
and ultimately heart disease.

Likewise, spending each day feeling
miserable damages your heart, too.
Researchers have suggested that not only
does depression increase the risk of vascular
diseases but, interestingly, the relationship
operates in the other direction—vascular
diseases may increase the risk of depression.
And British researchers have shown that
treatment with antidepressants reduces the
risk. (See "Are you depressed?" page 184.)

Choosing happiness

Why are so many of us so sad and angry?
There's no question that we're born with
certain innate personality characteristics, but
experts say that much of how we respond to
the world around us is learned.

Most of us face the same dismal
headlines, monthly mortgage payments, daily
traffic jams and a stream of bills through the
mailbox. Some of us have accepted that that's
life and we sail through it with a shrug.
Others take such everyday affronts personally
and get angry about all the injustices of
modern life. Whichever path you take is
simply a matter of personal choice. Nothing
can make you angry—except yourself.

You obviously cannot undergo a
personality transplant in order to protect your
heart. You are who you are. Instead, when
you're confronted with a challenging
situation, try pausing before you react in your
usual way. Look at your choices and choose a
more positive response. Life is so much
better when we smile than when we frown—
and it's easier than you might think to walk
away from anger. Here are some ways to

A special kind of meditation

Try the "loving-kindness" meditation, which you can do anywhere:

■ Take a break from what you're doing and focus on your heart.

■ Think about a time when you felt really happy, loving and appreciative.

■ Breathe deeply and feel your heart lighten as you focus on those feelings.

This meditation can smooth out your heart rhythm in just 60 seconds.

increase everyday happiness and improve your heart's health.

■ **Let it out** A nine-year study of 2,500 men showed that those who bottled up their anger were up to 75 per cent more likely to develop coronary artery disease than those who vented their frustration. The next time you're angry, find a friend and let off some steam (but don't create an enemy).

■ **Count to 10** When you count, your brain activity shifts to the frontal cortex, the area of rational thought—and away from the emotionally charged limbic system where there's little control over emotions. That's why you feel more able to cope after counting. You can increase the effectiveness by breathing deeply at the same time.

■ **Feel love** This simple advice is not as trite as it seems: studies show that feelings of love actually make your heart beat more smoothly

and regularly. And conversely, one British study in the late 1980s showed that an unhappy love life increased the risk of heart disease in women. Try doing something each day that makes you feel a warm, loving glow. Choose some happy photos of your children, download them onto your computer and use them as a screensaver or click on them when you need a smile. Give your partner lots of hugs. Listen to some love songs.

■ **Give the benefit of the doubt** As soon as you start feeling cross with a shop assistant, for example, stop and take a mental step back. Is the shop's ridiculous refund policy really the cashier's fault? Is it fair to expect a schoolboy doing a summer job at the grocery store to know where the pesto sauce is kept? Lashing out rarely results in getting what you want, and it's often unfair. Worse still, it transfers your anger to a second

When was the last time you had fun? If no recent events spring to mind, it's time to write some fun into your calendar.

Are you depressed?

Many Canadians are overweight and some fall into the category of being obese, a well-defined medical condition that needs to be treated by a doctor. Likewise, virtually all of us have the blues now and then, but depression is a serious medical condition that requires medical treatment. Left untreated, depression sets up a vicious cycle of not exercising, increasing worries, weight gain and fatigue that exacts a high toll on your heart. These are signs of depression.

- Waking in the early hours and being unable to get back to sleep
- Problems sleeping or sleeping excessively
- Loss of energy or fatigue: "tired all the time"
- Loss of appetite
- Inability to concentrate or make decisions
- Being in a sad mood most days
- Feelings of worthlessness or guilt
- Weight loss or gain
- Lack of interest in pleasurable activities or sexual activity, or both
- Thoughts of death or suicide

If you think you may be depressed, see your doctor. Depression isn't merely a mental state; it's usually linked to chemical imbalances that can be treated with medication and lifestyle adjustments.

person. Feeling empathy calms anger quickly (and often gets better results).

■ **Don't try and do it all** Anger, frustration and impatience peak when we try to do too many things at once. Look at your list of things to do each day and cross out the least important. This will help you to get into the habit of focusing on what's most important, and stop worrying about the trivial stuff.

■ **Forgive** One study showed that men with coronary artery disease who were prepared to forgive and forget had improved blood flow to their hearts. Harbouring a grudge increases adrenalin levels while destroying the feel-good hormone serotonin. Forgiveness releases bottled-up anger and creates a healthier hormone balance.

That does not mean excusing bad behaviour. It means that you decide not to let that incident or person have control over your life or power to hurt you. It may take time but just by trying to do it, you're halfway there. Try choosing one event you're still upset about and make a decision to let it go.

■ **Forgive yourself, too** We are often our own harshest critics. While you're trying hard to forgive others, remember to go easy on yourself as well. You know you can't change the past, but you can improve the present—and that means being kind to yourself.

■ **Have fun** When was the last time you had fun? If no recent events spring to mind, it's time to write some fun into your calendar. It doesn't have to be elaborate, just something you look forward to. Once a week, organize a game of golf, rent a comedy film or take your children or grandchildren to the park. You'll feel less bogged down in daily life if you reward yourself regularly with fun times.

■ **Give and take control** We can't control world events, corporate downsizings, bad weather or the stupid behaviour of other people but many of us take such happenings personally. Learn to let them go without anger or guilt. Put things that are out of your control in the hands of a "higher power," whether that means fate or your God, then take control of what you can. You can't make rude people polite, for example, but you can choose to avoid them in future.

Defeating stress

Stress. The word alone is enough to conjure up clammy palms, a sweaty brow and the spectre of blood pressure pills—but in the right dose, stress can be good. Think about it. A violin string without stress is dull and lifeless, yielding no resonance or melody to the touch. If wound too tight, it snaps. With just the right amount of stress, the string sings, creating energetic, harmonious music.

That's how life is, too. A little bit of self-created tension generates the mental and physical energy you need to accomplish goals and meet dreams. If there's too much, however (and most of us are swimming in it), your heartstrings do their own "snapping."

Research shows that excess stress leads to numerous symptoms, including insulin resistance, increased abdominal fat, elevated blood pressure and reduced "heart rate variability"; this impairs your heart's ability to react properly, increasing the risk of sudden death or fatal rhythm disturbances. Your goal is to make small changes in your lifestyle to maintain healthy

tension while reducing excess stress so your life (and heart) keep humming along happily and productively.

Nagging worries

You're driving along a two-lane highway and someone cuts in front of you. You slam on the brakes; your passengers gasp; your heartbeat surges. This type of event is called acute stress, and refers to unexpected, one-off bursts of fear or excitement that trigger the "fight or flight" reflex in which your body tenses in response to danger.

Drivers do not need to worry, though—the odd episode of acute stress isn't what doctors are worried about. Instead, it's what is known as chronic stress—anxiety that lingers for days, months or years. It's having

Your goal is to make small changes in your lifestyle to maintain healthy tension ...

perpetual money troubles, or being in a destructive relationship, or always fearing the loss of your job, or driving in stop-start commuter traffic every day.

The problem is, more and more of us are encountering chronic stress. In our text-messaging, emailing, multi-tasking chaotic world, we're forever rushing to get more done and becoming anxious about anything from the threat of redundancy to terrorist attacks. Our hearts pay the price.

For one thing, chronic stress makes us impatient, and impatience sends blood pressure skyward. In a study of 3,142 men and women who were followed for 15 years, researchers at Northwestern University found that people who said they usually felt pressed for time, ate too quickly, and got upset when they had to wait were twice as likely to develop hypertension as those who walked through life more relaxed.

Constant worrying can be even worse. In the Brigham and Women's Hospital study of 37,000 nurses, researchers found that those who fretted the most about losing their jobs faced an almost twofold risk of having heart attacks compared with those who worried the least. Chronic mental stress affects the endothelium, the protective barrier that lines your blood vessels, paving the way for a series of inflammatory reactions that lead to fat and cholesterol buildup in the coronary arteries and ultimately—as the study above indicates—a heart attack.

In addition, constant stress may also increase your chances of smoking, drinking, consuming too much alcohol, getting fat and having high blood pressure—all of which, directly or indirectly, adversely affect your heart health. And those conditions help maintain the stress that helped create them. What's more, for people who already have some symptoms of coronary heart disease, stress can make their condition worse.

Do away with stress

Stress reduction is big business—we buy self-help books, massages, scented candles or Caribbean cruises—all in the name of relaxation. But in reality, you don't have to spend a penny to soothe stress, nor do you need a lot of time. First, eat well and exercise to bolster your immunity and burn off built-up stress: a healthy weight and general overall fitness make you much better equipped to deal with daily stress. Then practise a few of these mental tricks to stay cool, calm and collected in the face of even the most hectic day.

■ **Focus and finish** Canadians are obsessed with multi-tasking. Why just talk to a friend on the phone when you can also eat a sandwich and make a shopping list? When you split your attention nothing has your full focus, leaving you frazzled and dissatisfied—and likely someone you know.

Instead of trying to do ten things at once, try doing one at a time. Focus on and finish one job before moving to the next. With your full attention, each task will take less time (and may be more enjoyable), and you'll feel a greater sense of control and accomplishment.

■ **Take a news break** Boycott all news for one day a week. If something really important happens, you'll hear about it but you won't inflict on your body the daily stress triggered by reading about the crimes and catastrophes happening in every corner of the world.

■ **Have some quiet time** Some forward-thinking companies have "quiet rooms" where employees can escape the whir of printers, telephones, fax machines and pagers, if only for a few minutes. Make sure there is somewhere quiet at home, too, a place that you can go to gather your thoughts when everything gets too much. It's surprising how effectively just sitting there for 30 seconds can help to ease stress.

■ **Practise meditation** Classic meditation, which involves sitting silently for 10 to 20 minutes while repeating a word like "Om," is scientifically proven to reduce stress. But few Canadians actually do it. A more practical alternative is mindful meditation, which you can do while walking down the road or cleaning the car.

Simply focus on what's happening in the immediate present. For instance, when washing your car, think of nothing but how the cool water bubbles up in the bucket, how the hose sounds as it hits the hood of your car and how the water runs in sheets and beads in the sun. Sense how much calmer you feel when the job is done. Try practising mindful meditation once a day.

■ **Take time off** Vacation is a time to get away from the routine, from the job and from the stress of life. Yet surprisingly, four in ten employed Canadians don't actually use all of their vacation days. Even more shocking is that 76 per cent of those Canadians who don't use all of their vacation time have up to 14 days of vacation left at the end of the year. This is definitely not a good way to avoid stress and its harmful effects.

But time off actually makes you a more productive worker and helps your heart. Your co-workers and your family will appreciate it. Plan your vacations in advance so that (a) you'll take them; (b) everyone can plan for when you're gone; and (c) you always have something to look forward to.

■ **See yourself succeed** Before you embark on any stressful project, mentally rehearse it. As top athletes are sometimes told "when you visualize a task, you're mentally programming yourself to act it through; then when you start, it's second nature."

Have a laugh

In a study of 300 men and women, researchers at the University of Maryland found that people with heart disease were 40 percent less likely to laugh in a variety of situations than those of the same age without heart disease. Researchers believe that stress reduction plays a major role. Other researchers conclude that during laughter the heartbeat quickens and blood pressure rises; after laughter, heart rate and blood pressure drop to a point lower than their initial resting rate. Rent a good comedy or call a funny friend. Try to have a good laugh at least five times a day.

Laughing offers a sort of "internal aerobics"— it is possible for all 400 muscles of the body to move when we laugh. Laughter also releases endorphins—the body's "feel-good" hormones, lowers levels of the stress hormones adrenalin and cortisol and restores proper breathing patterns.

Laughing offers a sort of "internal aerobics"...

Meanwhile keep positive. Simply telling yourself "I can do this" will make you feel calmer and more confident than will thinking "Oh help! I can't."

■ **Keep a pet** Pet ownership helps people to stay healthy. Research in Australia and Germany shows that pet owners make fewer visits to their doctor each year, suffer fewer sleeping difficulties and are less likely to be taking medicine for a heart condition.

In another study, U.S. researchers tested 48 stockbrokers already taking medication for high blood pressure in stressful situations, such as trying to calm a client who had lost $86,000 because of bad advice. Those who had pets had their systolic blood pressure rise from 120 to 126; those without a fluffy friend saw their systolic reading skyrocket from 120 to 148. Nothing calms like unconditional love.

■ **Breathe deeply** In a stressful situation, stop and take four or five deep breaths, inhaling so that your stomach rises. A team of European researchers has shown that deep breathing counteracts the physical effects of stress.

When volunteers had to perform a mental math task, blood pressure increased and heart rate variability (HRV) decreased, whereas when they engaged in a paced breathing exercise blood pressure decreased and HRV increased (HRV is an important indicator of heart health: reduced HRV is associated with increased heart attack risk). It is almost impossible not to calm down when you breathe slowly and deeply.

■ **Listen to music** In one Hong Kong study, patients who listened to their choice of music during minor surgery under local anaesthetic were found to have lower anxiety levels, lower heart rates and lower blood pressure than those who did not listen to music.

German researchers also found that levels of the stress hormone cortisol, which would normally rise during a procedure known as cerebral angiography, remained stable and blood pressure remained lower when the patients listened to music.

■ **Massage it away** Stress makes your muscles tense, which reduces circulation and thus the flow of oxygen and nutrients to the heart. Massage counteracts this by loosening those muscles. For a simple self-massage, hold a tennis ball in the palm of your hand and roll it in a circular motion anywhere you feel tension—around your neck and shoulders, along your thighs and calves, even over the soles of your feet.

■ **Don't get upset** Stress is your reaction to external events, not the events themselves. You may not be able to control what is happening, but you can control your reaction. The next time something makes you angry or tense, pause and ask yourself, "Is this worth getting upset about? Will feeling stressed make anything better?" Often, the answer to both questions is no. This can go a long way toward reducing stressful reactions.

■ **Get enough sleep** Tiredness makes us less able to cope with stressful situations. When you are well rested, you are more resilient and better able to handle daily life. Aim for 8 hours a night.

■ **Shed a few tears** Have you ever noticed how much better you feel after a good cry? That's because tears flush out harmful chemicals produced during stress and release pent-up negative energy. If all else fails, let the tears flow. You'll probably feel much better afterwards.

Alcohol

We all have different alcohol habits. Some of us like wine with dinner; others enjoy a cold beer watching a hockey game. Some choose not to drink at all; others drink too much. People have been indulging in fermented beverages for 10,000 years and have been debating their health benefits (and harmful effects) for nearly as long.

The fact is that alcohol can be both medicinal and poisonous. The distinction between its Jekyll-and-Hyde natures lies in the dose. Taken in moderation—that's no more than one or two drinks a day—alcohol may provide some benefit. Studies show that not only do moderate drinkers enjoy longer lives than either heavy drinkers and teetotallers, they also have better heart health.

Years of research, collectively involving more than 750,000 men and women, have shown that moderate drinking lowers the risk of heart disease, heart attack, and/or cardio-vascular-related death. Sensible drinkers also tend to have healthy lifestyle habits. They are more likely than non-drinkers or heavy drinkers to maintain a healthy weight, get 7 to 8 hours of sleep a night and exercise regularly, according to surveys. They also report enjoying rewarding, relaxed social lives. In short, they have happy hearts—emotionally and physically.

The opposite can be said of those who drink too much. Ethanol, the active ingredient in alcoholic drinks, impairs cognitive function and wreaks havoc on all the body's organs when consumed in excess. Heavy drinking can contribute to or directly cause high blood pressure, obesity, cardio-myopathy (severe weakness of the heart muscle), heart failure, cardiac arrhythmia

... one or two glasses of wine a day may help to protect against heart attacks ...

ASA and alcohol?

If you take ASA for heart protection, check with your doctor that it's OK for you to drink. The dose of ASA taken as a preventative is very low, so the likelihood of a glass of wine a day causing adverse effects is slim. You should not stop taking ASA without consulting your doctor.

(irregular heartbeat) and sudden cardiac death. Other risks include alcoholism, and car crashes.

Because the risks of drinking to excess can far outweigh the benefits of moderate drinking, if you do drink, then limit yourself to a glass of wine a day with dinner. Most heart specialists agree that one or two glasses of wine a day may help to protect against heart attacks in men over 40 years old and in post-menopausal women. But they would also stress that larger amounts of alcohol can raise blood pressure and contribute to weight gain and other serious medical and social problems. If you are already a moderate regular drinker, here are some ways to improve the benefits to your heart.

The great grape

While all drinks offer some heart benefits, wine seems to be the best. You may have heard of the "French paradox"—the ironic discovery that although many French people smoke cigarettes and eat a diet relatively high in saturated fats, they are far less likely to die from cardiovascular disease than Canadians.

Scientists used to attribute French heart health solely to their liking for red wine, but it seems more likely that their Mediterranean diet—high in fresh fruit and vegetables, olive oil, garlic and fish—is an important

influence, too. Other factors in French life, such as daily physical activity and a relaxed lifestyle, are also good for the heart, but there's no disputing the fact that wine contains substances that fight the heart attackers; studies also confirm that wine-drinking nations have lower rates of heart disease than those favouring beer or spirits.

Wine contains antioxidants known as polyphenols, including a flavonoid called quercetin and the compound resveratrol, both of which appear to help prevent the body's LDL cholesterol from oxidizing. This makes cholesterol less likely to stick to artery walls. Scientists are now investigating another group of compounds called saponins. These occur in waxy grape skins and appear to promote heart health by binding to cholesterol and preventing its absorption in the blood.

Think when you drink

If you choose to indulge, choose wisely. The following tips will help you to enjoy alcohol while also helping your heart.

■ **Enjoy full-bodied red wine** White wines are traditionally made without grape skins (or the mashed mixture containing the skins is removed early in the process), which is where most of the protective compounds are found.

■ **Get benefits without alcohol** You can get some of the benefits of grapes without the alcohol by drinking red grape juice, which contains many of the same active ingredients as wine.

■ **Drink with dinner** Some studies suggest that the powers of wine are most pronounced when you drink it with your main meal.

■ **Make the most of mealtimes** Take the time to enjoy a leisurely dining experience. Set an attractive table, turn on some music, and share your meal with family or friends. A glass of wine adds to eating pleasure.

...the relaxation response doesn't just happen in normal, hectic everyday life. You have to pursue it...

Yoga

Stand up. Really, stand up. Inhale deeply and reach for the sky, as high as you can. Next, slowly blow your breath out, sweeping your arms past your sides and bending toward the floor as you empty your lungs. Draw fresh air into your lungs and slowly roll back up to a standing position, arms by your sides. It feels good, doesn't it?

At one with your inner self

What you've just done was to sample the simple science of yoga—moving your body while clearing your mind.

Traditional Eastern medicine uses holistic systems such as yoga to treat your mind and body as one. Even the term "yoga" is a Sanskrit word for "union," implying the experience of oneness or union with your inner being. There are several types of yoga, with hatha yoga being one of the most popular. This combines physical exercises and postures (asanas) breathing techniques (pranayama) and meditation. Its goal is to achieve perfect physical and mental health,

Hooked?

Once you have sampled yoga, you may find yourself wanting a full course. Spending more time on it will help you to reap more benefits. If you are interested, turn to page 234 for a complete "sun salutation" workout—a series of 12 yoga postures performed in a single, graceful flow. The sun salutation builds strength as well as increasing flexibility and promoting a sense of calm. If that isn't enough, yoga information is easy to find. You can buy yoga books or magazines, or borrow videos or DVDs from the local library; most sports and fitness centres and gyms offer classes; and the Internet has a vast amount of information.

happiness and tranquility. Yoga's advocates include Madonna and Sting—along with teachers, mechanics, politicians, scientists, doctors, cooks . . . and thousands of people like you.

Some people use yoga only as a way to improve muscle tone and physique. But a decade or more of scientific evidence shows that this traditional—if trendy—mind-body medicine can relieve symptoms of chronic diseases such as cancer, arthritis—and heart disease. Studies in India have shown that regular yoga practice improves cardiac performance and heart rate variability in healthy volunteers, and even gives better blood sugar control in diabetic patients.

Disease reversal

Internationally renowned heart disease researcher Dr. Dean Ornish, of the Preventive Medicine Research Institute in California, may have been the first Western doctor to rank yoga alongside diet and exercise at the core of a heart-healthy lifestyle.

In 1990, Dr. Ornish tested 48 men and women with a history of coronary heart disease. He assigned 28 participants to a lifestyle regimen that included yoga, group counselling and an extremely low-fat vegetarian diet. The remainder received their normal care and maintained their usual lifestyle.

After a year, those in the test group had clearer, more supple arteries—indicating that their heart disease was actually in reverse—while the arteries of those in the control group continued to clog and harden.

Eight years later, Dr. Ornish published a follow-up study showing that 80 per cent of 194 men and women with heart disease were able to avoid bypass surgery by following a similar lifestyle intervention program that

Sweet dreams

You can do yoga anytime but we recommend it before bedtime as a way to soothe away the stresses of the day. The following four introductory yoga poses are good for increasing circulation around the heart and promoting relaxation. And you can actually do them in bed, in your pyjamas, before going to sleep. Hold each pose for at least 30 seconds.

Cobra pose

Lie face down with your feet together, your toes pointed behind you and your hands palms down just in front of your shoulders. Lift your chin and gently raise your head and chest so that your torso is supported on your forearms. Be sure to keep your shoulders down and back, not hunched up by your ears. Remember to breathe deeply throughout. People sometimes hold their breath during this move, which is not good if you have existing heart disease.

Prayer pose

Kneel with the tops of your feet on the floor or bed and your toes pointed behind you. Sit back onto your heels, then lower your chest to your thighs. Extend your arms and rest your palms and forehead on the floor or mattress (or as close as comfortably possible).

Corpse pose

Lie on your back with your arms at your sides and your palms facing up. Place your heels slightly apart and allow your feet to fall naturally to the sides. Starting with your feet, progressively contract (or flex) and then relax all of your muscles—in other words your toes, then your ankles, calves, knees, thighs and so on to the top of your head. When you have finished, relax, breathe deeply—and sleep.

Spinal twist

Lie on your back with your knees bent, your feet flat and your arms at your sides. Slowly lower your knees to the left while simultaneously extending your arms to the right as far as comfortably possible. Keep your shoulders in contact with the floor or bed. Repeat on the other side, holding each position for 15 seconds.

included yoga. Dr. Ornish firmly believes that the practice of yoga is beneficial.

Fight-or-flight deactivated

While there's no denying that diet is a powerful component of the "yoga lifestyle," the way that this flowing, serene exercise diffuses stress is probably the reason that yoga is so powerful in combating heart disease. We are all aware of the fight-or-flight response, which occurs when, at the slightest hint of threat, your body's defence mechanism sends a surge of adrenalin and cortisol into your bloodstream to mobilize fat from your body's stores to fuel your muscles—and your escape.

The problem is, in today's society, you're more likely to face an angry boss than a charging mammoth, so instead of fighting or fleeing, you're left stewing in that toxic self-defence cocktail. The result is raised blood pressure, higher cholesterol and an increased likelihood of blood clots.

On the plus side, however, just as your body is equipped with a hit-and-run reflex during times of perceived danger, it also has a pretty good peacetime plan, known as the relaxation response, which gives your weary nervous system some much needed rest.

But, like rare days spent wrapped up in a novel with your toes nestled in warm sand, the relaxation response doesn't just happen in normal, hectic everyday life. You have to pursue it—and yoga is one of the best paths you can take.

As you draw in deep abdominal breaths and release built-up tension by extending your limbs through their full range of motion, focusing your thoughts on each pose, you flick the switch that deactivates the fight-or-flight system and engages the relaxation response. Your heartbeat slows down and your blood pressure drops.

In time, if you practise regularly, you can even lower the "alert level" of your autonomic nervous system so that you move through life feeling more relaxed—all the time.

Like ordinary stretching, yoga also boosts circulation and improves blood supply to the heart. With better blood flow, your heart doesn't have to work as hard to deliver fresh nutrients and oxygen to your organs and muscles. By entering a relaxed state, you also increase your coronary blood flow by decreasing artery constriction.

As an extra benefit, regular yoga stretching lengthens muscles and connective tissues, improving your flexibility and range of motion so that you will be able to enjoy heart-healthy aerobic and strengthening activities with less muscle soreness or chronic aches and pains.

Germs and harmful chemicals are everywhere. Ignoring them is all too easy. But recognizing and combatting them is also quite straightforward, and will help to protect your heart—and your life.

Purging the poisons

Environmental pollution—especially in the air you breathe—can have a significant effect on the health of your heart.

Heal with clean living

Cleanliness is next to godliness, so the saying goes. That may or may not be the case—but what is known for certain is that cleanliness is next to healthiness. Like your car, lawn-mower or household appliances, your body works best when you keep it clean. Your heart, in particular, will benefit from a clean environment, free of bacteria and viruses,

smoke, dirt and general artery-clogging grime. Non-smokers live 10 to 15 years longer than those who light up day after day, according to a number of long-term studies.

Shielding yourself from flu viruses can cut your risk of heart disease by a fifth or more. And, surprisingly, brushing your teeth twice a day is now known to be important for the health of your heart. Another fact of life is that, much as we appreciate the end result, most of us do not particularly enjoy cleaning—and that goes for our lifestyles as much as our living rooms.

In a culture that regards eating rich foods, and smoking and drinking too much as grown-up entertainment, clean living gets a bad press for not being a bundle of laughs. But living a clean, heart-healthy life doesn't have to be boring.

Purge the poisons

Some of this advice—such as the case against cigarette smoking—you will have heard before, but some of the revelations linking everyday environmental offenders to heart disease will probably surprise you. Back in "Heart-healthy eating" (see page 66), we talk about how some additives, man-made fats and processed foods may be harmful for your heart.

In this section, we discuss the non-food toxins that affect it. You'll discover how the smallest steps, such as using mouthwash or having a yearly flu shot, can help to keep your heart healthy for years to come. Outlined in the following pages are a few simple steps for purging heart-damaging poisons.

■ **Ban tobacco** Tobacco is the worst of the pollutants that cause cardiovascular disease. And lighting up not only damages your own heart and arteries; every time you expose someone else to cigarette smoke, it accelerates hardening of their arteries, too.

Smokers have a 70 per cent greater chance of dying from heart disease than people who don't use tobacco. Overall, a smoker is two to three times more likely to have a heart attack than a non-smoker. Smokers who have high blood pressure are four times more likely than non-smokers with normal blood pressure to fall victim to a heart

attack. And smokers with high blood pressure and high blood cholesterol are a whopping eight times more likely to have a heart attack than non-smokers without high blood pressure and high blood cholesterol. The longer you smoke, the higher your risk; conversely, the sooner you quit, the faster your heart heals. Giving up is hard, but with nicotine replacement, modern drugs and willpower, it's certainly not impossible.

If you care about your heart, you must stop smoking. Your doctor will help, and if you use the strategies that follow, you can be free of smoke today—and you'll enjoy life more than ever.

■ **Scrub your hands** Using soap and water stops germs on your hands from getting into your eyes, nose or mouth, where they can multiply and pave the way for infection and heart-damaging inflammation.

Practising good personal hygiene fights more than colds; it can keep heart disease at bay as well.

■ **Have your flu shot** Being vaccinated against influenza can cut your risk of being hospitalized with heart disease-related problems and reduce your risk of having a heart attack if you're already in a high-risk category. Having the flu vaccine is strongly recommended for seniors and those with health conditions, such as diabetes.

■ **Keep your teeth clean** The way to your heart is through your mouth—not by way of your stomach but via your arteries. Believe it or not, bacteria from sticky dental plaque can seep through infected gums and cause problems in your circulatory system.

Having clean teeth and healthy gums will really give you something to smile about.

Smoking is especially hard on your heart. Smokers have a 70 per cent greater chance of dying from heart disease than non-smokers.

Tobacco

It is thought that the first peoples ever to have smoked tobacco were the Mayan civilizations of Central America in around 1000 B.C. In 1492, when Christopher Columbus sailed to the New World, members of his crew returned home with stories of Cuban peoples inhaling smoke from burning leaves, a ritual which they claimed reduced weariness, induced intoxication and lessened the effects of syphilis.

In 1586 the English scientist Thomas Hariot marvelled at the healing power of "holy" smoke—taken by means of clay pipes into the stomach and head, "from whence it purgeth . . . gross humours and opens all the pores and passages of the body."

But by 1858, fears about the effects of smoking on health were first being raised in *The Lancet*. Almost a century later, in 1950, evidence of a direct link between lung cancer and smoking was published.

We know a lot more now

After decades of warnings from most doctors and other health specialists, today we know that rather than healing, tobacco use—specifically, smoking cigarettes—shaves 10 to 15 years off users' lives. It's true: A 50-year study of 34,439 British doctors by a researcher who first connected cigarettes to lung cancer in the 1950s linked smoking to

25 diseases and a steep rise in mortality— shortening life expectancy by a decade. Among men born in the 1920s who became regular smokers, two-thirds died from their habits. Recent reports from a variety of experts are even graver. Based on data collected from 1995 to 1999, adult male smokers lost an average of 13.2 years of life and females an astonishing 14.5 years.

Smoking is especially hard on your heart. Smokers have a 70 per cent greater chance of dying from heart disease than nonsmokers. If you're under 40, you're five times more likely to have a heart attack if you smoke than if you don't, according to a Finnish study of 4,047 men and women.

Smoking cigarettes elevates your heart rate, raises your blood pressure, increases the clotting factors in your blood, depletes good HDL cholesterol, increases dangerous triglycerides and damages the linings of your blood vessels. That's not even considering its role in related vascular disease such as stroke and impotence, as well as lung diseases like chronic bronchitis and emphysema.

Every puff you take

Each inhalation from a cigarette introduces more than 4,000 chemicals into your bloodstream, of which 50 are known to cause cancer in the long term. Each puff also contains two potent poisons—nicotine and carbon monoxide; together they create a burden greater than most hearts can bear.

Nicotine is the reason most smokers light up. It creates a pleasant, relaxed feeling of euphoria. Ironically, it's also a highly toxic stimulant that would probably kill you if you actually absorbed all the nicotine in just two cigarettes. In fact, you absorb only a fraction of the chemical from each cigarette, but it's still enough to push your heart rate into

unhealthy territory. Nicotine is a potent vasoconstrictor—that is, it causes the blood vessels of the heart to narrow.

Carbon monoxide, the poisonous gas in car exhaust fumes, is also formed when tobacco burns. When you breathe it into your lungs, it replaces the oxygen in your red blood cells so your heart has to beat that much harder to get oxygen and nutrients from your blood. On top of that, the buildup of fat deposits caused by exposure to nicotine and carbon monoxide makes blood vessels and arteries narrower, further limiting blood supply to your heart.

In time, your blood vessels and arteries will become blocked, which can lead to permanent heart damage. In turn, the lack of oxygen for your overstressed heart puts you at risk of a heart attack. The longer you smoke and the more cigarettes you get through, the higher your risk.

Put out the fire

While most of the news surrounding tobacco use is grim, there is a silver lining. You can stop the harmful effects in their tracks and even eventually reverse the damage by quitting now. No matter how long you've smoked, your risk of a heart attack decreases just 24 hours after you give up.

After a year, your risk of tobacco-related heart disease is half that of a smoker's, and 15 years after you crush your last stub, your risk drops to the level of someone who has never smoked. Here's what you need to know in order to quit.

■ **It takes inspiration** You've just read all about how terrible tobacco is for you— information on the front and back of every pack of cigarettes. Most smokers know that smoking is bad for them but that doesn't always inspire them to give up.

Nicotine is very addictive. They need external motivation, perhaps quitting for people they love, such as their children or grandchildren.

Think about the happy events that you would miss if your life were cut short by 10 or 15 years. The birth of a grandchild? A grandchild's wedding? Consider everyone who is close to you—family and your best friends. Whom will you miss, or who will miss you most, if you die more than a decade prematurely? Give up for them.

■ **Your doctor can help** It may be perfectly legal, but tobacco is as addictive as illegal street drugs such as cocaine or heroin. It can take two or three tries, or more, to quit for good. Involving your doctor improves your chances. Studies have shown that about 70 per cent of smokers want to quit and that those who have the support of their health care providers are most successful. But don't count on your doctor to broach this sensitive subject. Only half of smokers who see physicians have ever been urged to quit, according to surveys. Take the initiative. Tell your doctor you want to quit and ask for help.

■ **Try nicotine replacement** People often find using nicotine replacement therapy (NRT) during the initial adjustment period helpful. Nicotine replacement products include gum, patches, lozenges, inhalers and nasal sprays, and are available both on prescription and over-the-counter. (See page 204 for more on NRT.)

■ **Switching to "lights" rarely works** Swapping to "lighter" cigarettes will not protect your health or help you to quit. People tend to puff harder, longer and more often on lights to get the desired nicotine hit. Smoking cigars or a pipe is a poor strategy, too: you still absorb nicotine into your bloodstream and probably still inhale at least some of every puff.

■ **But exercise does** Regular exercise can help you to stop smoking by burning off stress hormones—so you will feel less of an urge to smoke—and by producing feel-good brain chemicals that can help to reduce the uncomfortable effects of nicotine withdrawal. And if you start taking extra daily exercise you may well be able to avoid the dreaded 2–4 kg (5–10 lb) weight gain commonly associated with kicking the smoking habit.

■ **Avoid bad influences** Spending time with smokers not only makes it harder to quit because of the ever-present temptation, it also harms your heart to breathe the air they pollute.

Persistent exposure to cigarette smoke, either at home or on the job, nearly doubles your risk of having a heart attack even if you don't smoke, according to a landmark 10-year study of more than 32,000 women. Another recent analysis combining the results of 18 studies that involved more than half a million men and women showed that regular exposure to passive tobacco smoke raises risk of heart disease by 25 percent. If you socialize with smokers, do so in non-smoking establishments, where they can puff outdoors. If you live with a smoker, take the ashtray outside and keep it there. Establish a non-smoking house today.

Quit smoking for good

"Quitting smoking is easy. I've done it a thousand times." So said the American wit Mark Twain—and few truer words have been spoken. Nicotine is highly addictive and hard to kick.

Once you're hooked, cutting down or quitting can cause unpleasant withdrawal symptoms such as irritability, depression, anger, restlessness, headaches, fatigue, increased appetite, trouble concentrating and sleep disturbances. Here are some strategies to help you succeed.

My quit-smoking contract

I, _____, will quit smoking on _____ (date). From that day on I will be a non-smoker, free of the physical, mental, social and economic burdens of tobacco use.

I am giving up smoking for myself, but also for (list loved ones)_____
_____

When I feel the need to smoke, I will use the following strategies to overcome the craving:
_____
_____

If I need support, I will phone _____

After three months smoke-free, I will reward myself with _____

My six-month reward will be _____

My nine-month reward will be _____

I will celebrate one year of smoke-free living with _____

Signature: _____   Witness: _____

1 Set a date

Quitting smoking takes mental (and physical) preparation. Pick a "quit date" within the next month and circle it on your calendar. Between now and then, set the stage for your smoke-free life. This is an exciting time, so be enthusiastic.

Stock up on healthy or non-fattening foods to nibble, such as sugar-free chewing gum, baby carrots, pumpkin and sunflower seeds and fresh fruit.

The night before the big day, throw out all cigarettes, ashtrays, matches, lighters and other smoking paraphernalia. Remember, you are a non-smoker now; you don't need them.

2 Make an announcement

Tell your friends, family and work colleagues about the date you plan to quit. And try not to be embarrassed if you've made the announcement before. Remind them that it often takes repeated attempts for quitting to work and ask for their help in making this the last one.

3 Be prepared

People can become depressed when quitting smoking—especially the elderly, who can also become confused because memory and concentration may be temporarily impaired. As with weight gain, it helps to be prepared—in other words, plan how you might deal with such symptoms if they occur, and don't be afraid to seek help from your doctor, rather than lighting up again in desperation.

4 Establish support

Studies show that having a strong support network increases your chances of successfully quitting smoking. Many hospitals and health centres offer quitting programs. Go to Go Smokefree! in the Healthy Living section of the Health Canada website (www.hc-sc.gc.ca) to find helpful resources on how to quit. Think about joining a support group for the first three months—the time during which most relapses occur. For a support group near you, look online or in the Yellow Pages.

5 Create diversions

Smoking often occurs in stressful or social situations. It's something to do in a work break, when stuck in a traffic jam or during quiet evenings at home. Once you quit, you'll feel that something is missing during these times. Depending on where you are, fill the gap with another activity.

Sing along to a favourite CD in the car. Take short walks instead of smoking breaks. Do something with your hands, such as jigsaw puzzles as you wind down in the evening. You'll miss cigarettes less if you keep busy.

6 Consider nicotine replacement

Some smokers successfully quit cold turkey, but you can double your chances of success by using some form of nicotine replacement in the early days. Most forms of NRT can be bought over-the-counter, but it is also available by prescription. Nicotine replacement doesn't give you the same buzz as cigarettes, but it does reduce cravings. It isn't meant to replace smoking, rather to eliminate withdrawal symptoms.

Your odds of succeeding are increased slightly if you combine NRT with a prescription-only drug called bupropion. Originally intended as an antidepressant, it appears to interrupt the areas of the brain

associated with addiction and the enjoyable effects of nicotine. This lessens not only your wish to smoke but also the physical symptoms of nicotine withdrawal. [Note that nicotine products may cause headaches, nausea and dizziness. Side effects include nausea, agitation, anxiety, dry mouth and headaches; it can also worsen the sleep problems that many people suffer when they stop smoking.]

7 Avoid triggers

Identify your triggers—coffee and alcohol are common ones—and do your best to avoid situations where you might have reached for a cigarette automatically back in the days when you were a smoker. It may help to avoid alcohol altogether and drink mineral water or fruit juice during that vulnerable initial period of two to three months. Later on, you'll be able to enjoy a drink with more confidence—but remember that alcohol always lowers inhibitions, so you'll need to remain vigilant.

8 Take 10

When you feel the urge to light up—and you will—look at your watch and give yourself 10 minutes. During that time, take full, deep breaths as you would if you were drawing on a cigarette. Deep breathing will fill your lungs with clean, smoke-free air and trigger a relaxation response.

By the time 10 minutes is up, the acute urge to smoke will have passed, and you'll be better able to move past the craving.

9 If you have a relapse

Put out the cigarette and "keep on quitting." Leave the situation or setting where smoking resumed—and don't look back!

Air pollution

It's common sense, really, but only recently has research confirmed it: Air pollution causes heart disease.

This is a statement from the American Heart Association (AHA). In fact, the AHA says, air pollution is even worse for your heart than it is for your lungs. In a study that analyzed data from a survey of 500,000 adults, epidemiologists found that air pollution in U.S. cities causes twice as many deaths from heart disease as it does from lung cancer and other respiratory ailments. And in Canada, the Heart and Stroke Foundation has stated that smog can be as detrimental to your arteries as cigarette smoke.

Experts believe variations in levels of urban air pollution affect mortality rates. Certain pollutants are thought to have an inflammatory effect on the inner lining of arteries, which can trigger atherosclerosis. They may also cause inflammation of the lungs, which could aggravate lung problems.

High traffic hurts hearts

A German study has found that people caught in traffic are three times more likely to have a heart attack within the hour than those who are not stuck in a jam.

Researchers studied 691 people who had suffered heart attacks and concluded that 1 in 12 was linked to traffic. The researchers could not say for sure whether the attacks were due to traffic-related stress or exposure to high levels of air pollution—but because people using public transport were also affected, pollution seemed the more likely culprit. Women and people over the age of 60 were found to be particularly at risk.

Living near the traffic is not good, either. A study of 5,000 adults showed that people who resided near heavily trafficked roads were more likely to die from heart disease-related conditions than those who were farther from the exhaust-belching flow of cars and trucks.

The pollution risk comes from ozone and particulate matter—a very fine soot. Both are generated by cars, trucks, factories and

Air Quality Advice

If you or someone you know has heart-health problems, diabetes or asthma, air quality is particularly important during the hot summer months. Health Canada suggests the following:

■ Listen to the radio or watch television reports for air-quality and smog advisories. Plan your day based on this information.

■ Limit or reschedule physical outdoor activities on smog advisory days when air pollution is more harmful than usual.

■ Reduce exposure to vehicle exhaust by limiting physical activity near heavy traffic areas, especially at rush hour.

■ Stop idling your vehicle. This is the easiest way to help improve the air quality in your community.

coal-fired power stations. When you breathe in particulate matter, it irritates your airways and triggers an inflammatory response, which, like all inflammation, accelerates plaque buildup and narrowing of the arteries.

Even heart-healthy activities such as jogging or cycling can be harmful if done in areas where the air quality is poor. In a study of 45 women with a history of coronary artery disease, Finnish researchers found that when pollution levels were high, the volunteers—who participated in bi-weekly ECG-monitored exercise sessions over six months—had significantly higher levels of ischemia—that is, decreased blood flow to the heart.

Although air pollution hurts everyone, older adults and people with existing conditions such as heart disease and diabetes are at particularly high risk.

Where is it?

Unfortunately, pollution is pervasive. It's not just in the air we breathe but also in the water we drink and sometimes the food we eat. These other environmental offenders can also be hard on your heart. In a recent study of 2,125 men and women ages 40 and over, researchers at the Johns Hopkins Medical Institutions found that on average, those with peripheral artery disease had 14 per cent higher blood levels of lead and 16 per cent higher blood levels of cadmium. Both pollutants can be found in air, food, and water (cadmium is also present in cigarette smoke). Other studies have suggested that high blood levels of mercury from eating too much highly contaminated fish may elevate heart disease risk as well.

Limit your exposure to harmful chemicals: Use water filters either on the tap or in a special pitcher to eliminate contaminants in your drinking water.

Breathe better

There is not much you can do to change the air that you breathe when you go outside (except move to the country). However, there are a number of things that you can do to limit your heart's exposure to the damaging effects of dirty air.

■ **Avoid rush hour** Even if the air in your area tends to be clean, avoid exercising outside—including cycling or jogging—during rush hour when vehicle emissions are highest. Your best bet is to exercise very early in the morning and avoid main roads.

■ **Stay away from smokers** The good news is that provincial legislators have or are in the process of forcing bars, restaurants and other public places throughout the country to ban smoking. The bad news is that exposure to second-hand smoke from just a single cigarette each day speeds up the development of atherosclerosis. So be very selective about the establishments you frequent when out in public.

■ **Go green** Good insulation and new windows may save money on your heating bills, but they may affect your home's air quality. Get some houseplants, especially palms, spider plants and ivy varieties (see right), which act like air filters.

■ **Eat your antioxidants** Antioxidant nutrients, such as vitamins C and E and beta carotene, protect your heart and lungs from the ill effects of pollution-induced free radical damage. Eat lots of fresh fruits and vegetables.

■ **Use your nose** When exercising in less-than-perfect air conditions, try to breathe through your nose as it is equipped with fine hairs that help to filter the air before it reaches your lungs.

Gerbera

English ivy

Lady palm

Spider plant

Peace lily

Purifying plants

Houseplants are not only decorative; research suggests they may improve the air quality of our homes. The **5 plants** pictured here are among the most effective for combatting the effects of the three most harmful household pollutants: **benzene**, a common solvent found in inks, oils, paints, plastic and rubber; **formaldehyde** whose major sources are insulation, paper products and cleaning agents; and **trichloroethylene**—a carcinogen that attacks the liver—found in inks, paints, varnishes and adhesives.

Viruses and bacteria

If there were a safe, quick treatment that could help to decrease your risk of heart disease and stroke and reduce your risk of premature death, you'd go for it. One thing you can do is have a flu shot every year.

In a large U.S. survey, researchers studied more than 286,000 men and women over the age of 65 who received flu vaccinations during two flu seasons. They found that, compared with people who weren't vaccinated, those who had the shots were a fifth less likely to be hospitalized for heart disease or stroke, 30 per cent less likely to succumb to pneumonia and half as likely to die from any cause.

In an unrelated study, researchers studying more than 200 men and women with coronary heart disease found that those who had had flu vaccinations were 67 per cent less likely to have second heart attacks than those who hadn't been vaccinated that year.

Today, researchers speculate that some common virus infections may increase risk of heart disease ...

Multilayered protection

Protecting your health and your heart with an injection in the arm is an easy thing to do.

Fall and winter in Canada is a common time for people to become briefly ill with viruses. We often refer to these illnesses as "colds" or "flus." It is important to realize that the "flu shot" is against influenza, which is a much more severe illness than the "common flu." Influenza is caused by influenza A and B viruses. It is usually associated with a high fever, muscle pain and bad cough, which may last for weeks. It is not as common as the "common flu," but it is much more serious, especially in those who have chronic heart or lung disease, or are elderly. The complications of influenza can include some serious illnesses, such as bronchitis, pneumonia, kidney failure or heart failure.

The flu shot is given every year because the influenza virus is constantly changing. Protection against influenza takes effect about two weeks after receiving the shot.

People of all ages are encouraged to get an annual flu shot and it is best to get one before the influenza season starts. Ask your doctor's office for a flu shot, or contact your public health unit. The influenza season usually runs from December through April.

It is especially important that people with a chest or heart condition as well as everyone over the age of 65 have flu shots each year. Other at-risk groups who should be vaccinated include people with chronic kidney disease and diabetes and those with compromised immune systems such as cancer patients. If you live or work with people with chronic diseases, you can help them by getting yourself vaccinated as well.

Flu shot facts

A flu vaccine uses inactivated or killed influenza viruses to stimulate your immune system to build up antibodies against the live version. It offers good protection against the most virulent viruses responsible for flu present in the world today. It only protects against these particular flu viruses and it will not stop you getting coughs or colds.

A flu shot can't give you flu, and the risk of side effects is tiny. You may experience a local reaction at the injection site consisting of redness and soreness, but this is rare—and there are no symptoms of mild flu, contrary to popular belief.

The shot should not be given to anyone who is allergic to eggs. You shouldn't have a shot if you're already ill.

Fight infection

If inflammation is bad for your arteries, then avoiding infections of all kinds is good for your heart. Here are some quick and easy ways to protect yourself during the cold and flu season.

■ **Wash your hands, often** The number one way to decrease your risk of infection is to wash your hands so you don't carry germs into your body when you eat, rub your eyes or wipe your nose.

Old-fashioned soap works well by loosening germ-laden oils and deposits on the skin so they get swept down the drain when you rinse your hands under running water.

■ **Keep your hands off your face** Try to avoid touching your face with your hands, especially during the cold and flu season, when people around you are bound to be unwell and spreading germs from their hands via doorknobs or escalator rails.

A nasal spray flu vaccine is available in the United States, but not so far in Canada. Unlike the injection, which contains dead influenza viruses, the nasal vaccine is made with weakened live viruses, so is less safe for people with reduced immunity.

You can also get a pneumococcal vaccine to protect against pneumonia—a good idea if you're over 65 or have heart disease. You can have this as a one-time-only immunization (you don't need a booster) at the same time as you have your flu shot.

■ **Clean much-used items** Use a disinfectant spray to clean steering wheels, taps, doorknobs, computer keyboards and telephones. Wash dishes in hot water and let them dry naturally. Keep toothbrushes and towels apart and have several toothbrush holders rather than one communal family rinsing cup.

■ **Eat well and exercise** Eating a healthy diet and getting extra protection with vitamin and mineral supplements can help your body to produce a strong army of disease-fighting cells. Consume fresh fruits and vegetables when possible and always have a good supply of the frozen variety on hand. Getting off the sofa for a daily dose of activity helps to circulate those germ-fighting cells so they can find and destroy invading bacteria and viruses in your bloodstream. Following the 30-Minutes-a-Day Plan will not only help your heart but also boost your immunity.

■ **Soothe nasal membranes** Central heating dries out the protective mucous membranes in your nose and throat, making you more susceptible to infections. If buildings are dry in winter, use non-medicated saline spray several times a day to clean bacteria and other particles from your nose and keep membranes moist.

■ **Stop smoking** Smoke damages the tiny hairs in the nose that filter out bacteria and viruses and also depletes essential immunity-building nutrients. That means smokers are far more susceptible to infections, and usually have infections that are more severe and take longer to heal than non-smokers. (See page 200 for advice on quitting.)

■ **Now wash—and dry—your hands** The number of germs on fingertips doubles after using the toilet. If you are concerned when washing your hands in a public washroom, use a paper towel to turn off the tap. Use another paper towel to dry your hands, then open the door with that paper towel as a

A gum disease vaccine for the heart?

So far, the flu shot is the immunization with the best heart-protection record (particularly for older people) but there may be another vaccine on the way that may lower the odds of heart attacks for certain high-risk individuals. Researchers at Boston University School of Medicine recently found that they can prevent mice from developing *Porphyromonas gingivalis*-accelerated heart disease by immunizing them with a vaccine that protects against periodontal (gum) disease.

As you will learn in the section on Dental plaque (page 212), chronic bacterial infection of the gums—otherwise known as periodontal disease—can increase your risk of having a fatal heart attack. Like other infections, gum disease creates a state of persistent inflammation that may lead to atherosclerosis, or plaque buildup in the arteries. Trials are under way to develop a periodontal vaccine for humans. In the meantime, follow the oral hygiene tips on page 213.

Buy a hygrometer . . .

barrier between you and the handle. In "flu season" this may help to protect you from infectious diseases like cold and flu.

■ **Carry hand cleanser with you** Available in gel or towelette forms, these allow you to clean your hands at any time, even if the nearest water supply is kilometres away. And they work. One study of absenteeism in elementary schools due to infection found schools using gel cleansers had nearly 20 per cent lower absentee rates from infection than those schools using other hand-cleaning methods.

■ **Don't rub your eyes** This is important as the eye provides a perfect entry point for germs and most people rub their eyes or noses or scratch their faces between 20 and 50 times a day. If you must rub, use your knuckle rather than your finger as it is less likely to carry germs.

■ **Keep tissues handy** In October, stock up on tissue boxes and strategically place them around the house, your workplace, your car. Don't let aesthetics put you off. You need tissues widely available so that everyone who has to cough or sneeze or blow their nose will do so in the way least likely to spread germs.

■ **Open your windows in winter** Weather permitting, leave windows just a crack open in the rooms in which you spend the most time. A bit of fresh air helps to clean the air.

■ **Buy a hygrometer** These little gadgets measure humidity. You want your home to measure around 50 per cent. A consistent measure higher than 60 per cent means mould and mildew may start to develop in your walls, fabrics and kitchen; lower than 40 per cent and the dry air makes you more susceptible to germs.

■ **Sit in a sauna once a week** An Austrian study published in 1990 found that volunteers who frequently used a sauna had half the rate of colds during the six-month study period than those who didn't use a sauna at all. It's not clear why this occurred, but sounds like fun!

Dental plaque

It is now apparent that brushing and flossing do more than give you a prettier smile: they can also improve your health. There is increasing evidence that chronic gum disease, as a cause of low-grade inflammation, could be linked to coronary disease. In fact, people with chronic bacterial infections of the gums are nearly twice as likely to have fatal heart attacks as those with healthy gums. In one U.S. study of more than 700 men and women with no history of heart disease, researchers found a direct relationship between missing teeth (an indicator of serious dental disease) and plaque buildup in the arteries. In 1993, another study of 10,000 found that gum disease significantly increased the risk of coronary heart disease.

European researchers treated 94 otherwise healthy patients who had severe gum disease. Before treatment, those with more severe infection had a more than fivefold increase in cardiovascular disease risk.

After treatment of their gum disease, the patients' average risk levels were significantly reduced. Other studies have linked gum disease with increased resting heart rate, abnormal electrocardiograms and poor blood sugar control—all symptoms of, or contributors to, heart disease.

We've intuitively known for centuries that bad teeth signify bad health. It's only recently, though, that we have identified the scientific connection—inflammation. The theory is that bacteria from dental plaque seep into the bloodstream via inflamed gums and produce enzymes that make blood platelets stickier and more likely to clot, contributing to hardening of the arteries.

Brush up on heart health

The good news is that this is a risk factor you can easily control. Here's what to do.

■ **Brush for 2 minutes** Buy a 2-minute bathroom timer (marketed for children) and use it; new electric toothbrushes have a built-in timing mechanism.

Use gentle, circular strokes to brush at a 45-degree angle to your gums. Brush until the timer ends, working on all surfaces of the teeth—front, back and top. Brushing reduces levels of all harmful bacteria in your mouth. Brush twice a day, in the morning and before going to bed—and after lunch and dinner, if possible.

■ **Replace your toothbrush** Most dentists agree that worn-out toothbrushes cannot clean your teeth properly and may actually damage your gums. They advise changing your toothbrush every two to three months

Gum disease symptoms

You can have periodontal disease and not know it, so see your dentist regularly even if your teeth are healthy. Warning signs are:

■ Gums that bleed easily
■ Red, swollen, tender gums
■ Gums that have pulled away from teeth
■ Persistent bad breath or a bad taste in your mouth
■ Permanent teeth that are loose or separating from each other
■ Any change in the way your teeth fit together when you bite
■ Any change in the fit of partial dentures

There is increasing evidence that chronic gum disease, as a cause of low-grade inflammation, could be linked to coronary disease.

because when bristles become splayed, they do not clean properly. Some dentists advocate storing the brush head in hydrogen peroxide.

■ **Floss every day** The Canadian Dental Association estimates that only 30 per cent of Canadians floss daily. To do it properly, you should use about 50 cm (18 in.) of waxed dental floss, wind the majority around your left middle finger and the rest around your right middle finger, leaving a few centimetres in between.

Gently manoeuvre the floss between your teeth and rub it up and down along the sides of each tooth, especially under the gum line. If flossing is difficult, try a floss holder or ask your dentist about interdental devices (tiny brushes) that can make the job easier.

■ **Mouthwashes** Rinsing with an anti-bacterial mouthwash can help to reduce tooth plaque but you should avoid long-term use of alcohol-based mouthwashes; these have been associated with oral cancers (being in contact with the fragile mucosa lining the mouth for longer than the average sip of an alcoholic drink).

■ **Book in advance** Make appointments with the hygienist for cleanings twice a year, or every three months if you have heart disease. Discuss any drugs you take as some, such as high blood pressure pills, can increase your risk of gum disease.

■ **Stimulate saliva** A dry mouth may encourage dental decay. Chewing sugar-free gum will stimulate saliva flow.

■ **Consider antibiotics** People with pre-existing heart conditions, especially valve defects, are at risk of a serious heart infection following dental work. Tell your dentist about your condition and ask your doctor if you need to take antibiotics before dental work.

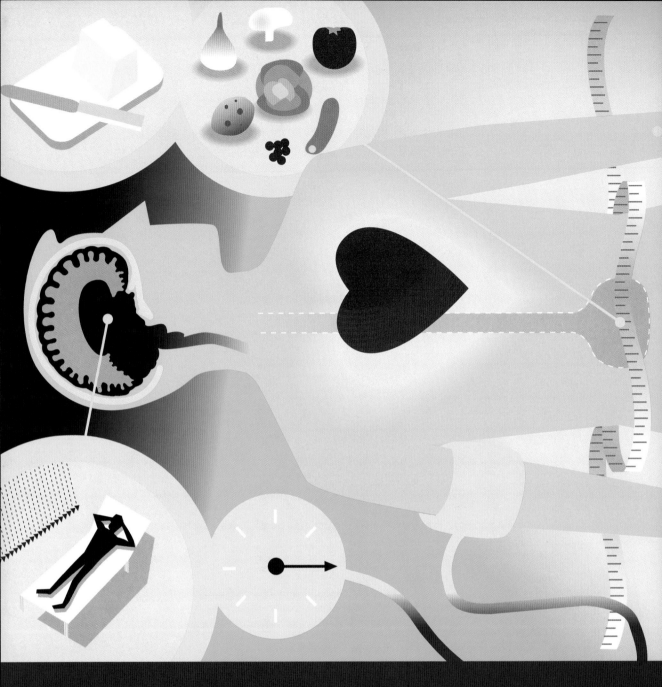

By keeping track of just a few numbers and asking yourself one or two easy questions, you can obtain a surprisingly accurate assessment of the health of your heart.

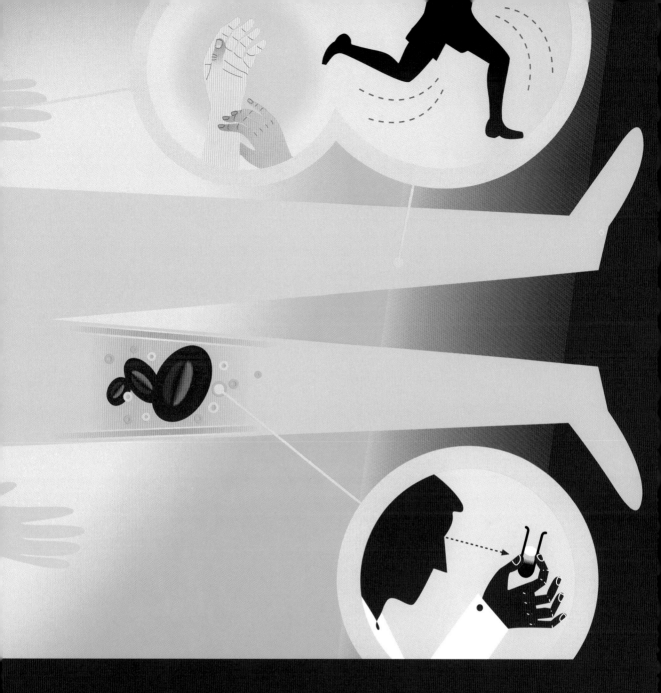

Keeping track

6 numbers that can save your life

How do you keep track of your finances? There are, of course, hundreds of numbers that you could monitor and, if you were a trained expert, you would follow many of them on an almost daily basis. But for most people, financial health boils down to just a handful of reliable numbers: total debt, total assets, monthly income and the rate of return on investments.

The same holds true for your physical health. There are many measurements you could track to the point of obsession and, if you were a doctor, you'd be able to read meanings into the subtle fluctuations that occur from one day to the next.

For most of us, though, our state of health can be revealed by just a few numbers, measured and monitored over time.

Which ones are most relevant?

If you ask a hundred doctors, you may get a hundred different answers. There are no standard guidelines for the best way for individuals to track their own health.

However, if we really do want to take charge of our own heart and health, then each of us needs to know the numbers that best provide a comprehensive report of our physical well-being.

For this book, six measurements have been chosen that will give you a good idea of where you stand in your battle against the seven main heart attackers. These easy-to-obtain figures are important indicators of heart health—and all responsible adults should be aware of theirs.

Three of the numbers you can check quite easily yourself—all you need is a pencil, a tape measure and a watch with a second hand—and the others are standard doctor's office procedures.

Collect these numbers, write them down and keep track of them over time. Together, they will speak volumes about the health of your heart—and your progress on the 30-Minutes-a-Day Plan.

Daily calorie needs

■ **HOW TO CHECK** On this plan, you don't need a calculator and calorie-counting guide to make sure you aren't overdoing it. Instead, the idea is to stick with the plan's wide range of recommended foods in the correct portion sizes. This is an easier, healthier and equally accurate way to judge your energy intake.

■ **HOW OFTEN TO CHECK** For the first two weeks of the plan, check all portions—use the guidelines (page 101) to check meals at home. After that, continue to keep an eye on helpings. One day a week, aim to be very conscious of portion sizes at all meals.

■ **WHY IT'S IMPORTANT** It's easy to overeat, and an extra slice of cheese here, an extra helping of meat there, or a bag of chips "just this once" as a snack all add up. That leads to weight gain, not weight control.

1 DAILY CALORIE NEEDS
Know your food requirements

This is not technically a measurement, but it is a number which, if you pay attention to it, can have a huge influence on your health. As discussed on page 82, few people know exactly how many calories they need, but you can work out your daily calorie needs by multiplying the number of kilograms you weigh by about 28 to 33 (or pounds by 13 to 15), depending on your activity level.

How much food do you actually eat? Many of us snack our way through the day without any real sense of how much we're consuming. In most cases, we eat far more than we need.

In a perfect world, you'd eat just enough to provide fuel for your body. If you were trying to lose weight, you'd eat roughly 500 calories less than your body needs. In reality, though, many of us eat between 100 and 1,000 calories more than we need, every day.

For your health's sake it is vital to discover and understand your daily food needs and whether you're exceeding them. The obvious reason is that overeating leads to weight gain, and becoming overweight is among the worst things you can do for your heart. The slightly less obvious reason is that eating too many calories usually means eating unhealthy foods, which are much higher in calories than natural foods because they usually contain a lot of fat or sugar—or both.

But picky calorie counting is not the best way to achieve your goal of matching your food consumption to your body's energy needs. It is far better to change the type of food you eat. It's almost impossible to consume too many calories if you focus on eating lots of fruits and vegetables. And having a diet rich in produce means you get plenty of vitamins, minerals, antioxidants and other nutrients essential for heart health.

Most women need 2,000 calories a day for good health. Men generally need about 2,550. That roughly equates to 300 to 400 calories for breakfast, 500 to 600 for lunch, 600 to 700 for dinner, and two or three snacks of roughly 100 to 200 calories each.

But your daily calorie need isn't a static number; it can change over time. If you are exercising more, recovering from illness or injury, or going through a period of high stress, your body may need extra fuel. If you've lost weight, the chances are your body requires less fuel than it once did. Then there's metabolism—some of us burn calories more efficiently than others.

The important message is that all adults should be aware of how much food they need to eat each day for optimal health, energy and weight. Calories are the simplest statistical measure—but steak doesn't have its calorie count stamped on it anywhere, and who wants to spend their life looking up everything they eat in a calorie counter and keeping a running total?

The next best way—and the one recommended here—is visual training. This involves learning, for example, what a "small" roll or piece of cake really looks like. For help on judging portion sizes see the guide on page 101.

The calorie-counted meals and snacks described in the 30-Minutes-a-Day Plan should help you with your goal. Simply adjust them to meet your needs.

. . . your daily calorie need isn't a static number; it can change over time.

2 WAIST CIRCUMFERENCE
An efficient way to monitor body fat

Of all the ways to measure whether your weight is affecting the health of your heart, waist size is one of the best. An even more accurate measure is your waist-to-hip ratio (calculated by dividing your waist circumference at its narrowest point by your hip circumference at its widest point): a ratio of more than 0.90 in men or 0.85 in women shows central obesity and may indicate metabolic syndrome.

Remember that fat cells are not just storage vessels for extra calories your body can't burn off. When body fat is packed into your abdomen—in and around your internal organs—the fat cells release inflammatory chemicals and out-of-kilter levels of appetite-controlling proteins. The result is that your risk of heart attack increases as inflammation speeds up atherosclerosis.

In addition, your risk of insulin resistance and metabolic syndrome rise as inflammatory substances interfere with the way muscle and liver cells function. Meanwhile, your natural appetite-suppressing system is disrupted, leading to more overeating and more abdominal fat.

Checking your waistline with a tape measure is the best indicator of how much abdominal fat you have inside. For women, health risk begins to rise with a waist of more than 88 cm (35 in.). For men, risk increases with a measurement of over 102 cm (40 in.).

> Checking your waistline . . . is the best indicator of how much abdominal fat you have inside.

Waist circumference

■ **HOW TO CHECK** Wrap a tape measure around your abdomen, at or near your belly button. Keep it snug but not tight—and don't pull your stomach in: no one else needs to know your measurement.

■ **HOW OFTEN TO CHECK** Every two weeks. A note for women: try not to measure in the week before or during your menstrual period, when water retention may bloat your stomach and give a false measurement.

■ **WHY IT'S IMPORTANT** Regular checks will help you to monitor your progress as abdominal fat melts away on the 30-Minutes-a-Day Plan. It will also inspire you to go back to the program if you slip.

3 LDLs and HDLs Cholesterol counts do count

This section includes two numbers in one category, because it is important to know not just your total cholesterol reading but also your levels of "bad" LDL cholesterol and "good" HDLs. When you see your doctor for blood test results, the lab report may have itemized these two types and perhaps also given a ratio of your total cholesterol to HDLs (TC:HDL). If so, ask for the readings for both forms of cholesterol and the ratio figure and jot them in your diary.

Aim for total cholesterol below 5.2 mmol/l (below 5 mmol/l if you have heart disease or diabetes), and LDL cholesterol levels below 3.5 mmol/l, or below 2 mmol/l if you have a history of heart disease. A healthy HDL level is 1.3 mmol/l or above.

4 BLOOD PRESSURE An indicator of artery health

Blood pressure—the force of blood against the walls of your arteries—rises and falls naturally during the day. When it remains elevated, you have hypertension (high blood pressure) and this carries a higher risk of atherosclerosis, heart disease and stroke.

A reading of 140/90 mm Hg or more is considered high, and if it's between 120/80 and 139/89, you may still be at risk and should be taking steps to prevent the development of hypertension. The movement program and eating plan in this book—high in potassium-rich fruit and vegetables—can help.

LDLs and HDLs

■ **HOW TO CHECK** You will have a blood test after you've fasted for 8 to 12 hours. A doctor's office check is much more reliable than a home cholesterol testing kit, which can't give you those vital LDL and HDL numbers.

■ **HOW OFTEN TO CHECK** If your total cholesterol is consistently higher than 6 to 6.5 mmol/l, your doctor will suggest lifestyle measures and may offer you treatment and recommend regular checkups. Guidelines will be different if you have known heart disease and/or diabetes.

■ **WHY IT'S IMPORTANT** LDL and HDL levels are among the strongest predictors of heart attack risk. Regular checkups will help you to notice trends (are your LDLs steadily rising, your HDLs slowly falling?)—and give you a chance to take steps to correct problems before they occur.

Blood pressure

■ **HOW TO CHECK** Your doctor will check your blood pressure at every visit, but you can also buy a home blood pressure monitor, and studies have shown that people who check their blood pressure at home may keep it under tighter control. But home monitoring should never replace the regular checks by your doctor or nurse—or visit a pharmacy, many of which have free-to-use blood pressure machines.

■ **HOW OFTEN TO CHECK** Ask your doctor how often you should have your blood pressure (BP) measured. You can request a BP check every time you go to the office.

■ **WHY IT'S IMPORTANT** Regular BP checks will help to spot a potential problem early, when lifestyle changes are more likely to resolve high blood pressure.

5 TRIGLYCERIDES
Another type of fat to watch

Triglycerides are made from the fats and carbohydrates you eat, which are converted into a form that can be stored in fat cells. Triglycerides are also released from fat tissue when the body needs extra energy between meals. It's normal to have some triglycerides in your bloodstream, but high levels are linked to coronary artery disease—especially in women.

When you have high triglycerides paired with low HDLs, your risk of insulin resistance and metabolic syndrome may be increased. A normal triglyceride reading is less than 1.7 mmol/l.

Triglycerides

■ **HOW TO CHECK** A triglyceride check is usually done from the same blood sample you give for a fasting cholesterol test.

■ **HOW OFTEN TO CHECK** Your doctor will advise you how often you should have your triglycerides checked.

■ **WHY IT'S IMPORTANT** Regular triglyceride checks are an important early warning system for your heart.

6 MORNING PULSE RATE
Know if your heart is strong

Your pulse is the number of times your heart beats in 1 minute. Regular monitoring of your resting pulse, first thing in the morning, will help you to see if your exercise regimen is strengthening your heart. For example, a normal resting pulse rate is 60 to 90 beats per minute. People who are fit tend to have lower resting pulse rates because their heart muscles are in good shape. But if you don't exercise regularly and your heart rate is lower than the normal range, tell your doctor—it could be a sign of heart disease.

Morning pulse rate

■ **HOW TO CHECK** You'll need a clock or watch with a second hand. The pulse is best measured at the wrist or neck, where an artery runs close to the surface of the skin. To measure the pulse at your wrist, place your index and middle fingers on the underside of the opposite wrist. Press firmly with the flat of your fingers until you feel the pulse. Find a neck pulse either side of your Adam's apple: just press your fingers into the hollows either side of your windpipe. Once you've found your pulse, count the beats for 15 seconds and multiply by four—this will give your pulse rate in beats per minute.

■ **HOW OFTEN TO CHECK** Take your pulse once a month, in the morning before you get out of bed. To check if your exercise program is working, assess your maximum pulse just after exercise and note how long it takes to return to its normal resting rate—the time interval should reduce as you get fitter.

■ **WHY IT'S IMPORTANT** You will know your exercise program is strengthening your heart if your pulse rate gradually falls within the healthy range.

Your health by numbers

Use this book for guidance and enlist your doctor's help to establish your current measurements and set reasonable targets. Then tick off the actions you're willing to take to achieve your goals.

Daily calorie needs

Estimated daily calories: _____

Target daily calories: _____

Calorie surplus: _____

Actions to improve

☐ Eat fewer snacks

☐ Cut back on fatty foods

☐ Eat more vegetables and fruit

☐ Have one meat-free meal each day

Waist circumference

Current waist size: _____

Target waist size: _____

Actions to improve

☐ Cut back on daily calories

☐ Take brisk daily walks

☐ Maintain a stretching program

☐ Maintain a strength-building program

Cholesterol levels

Current total cholesterol: _____

Target total cholesterol: _____

Current HDLs: _____

Target HDLs: _____

Current LDLs: _____

Target LDLs: _____

Actions to improve

☐ Increase daily fibre intake

☐ Eat more fish, olive oil and nuts

☐ Exercise regularly

Blood pressure

Current blood pressure: _____

Target blood pressure: _____

Actions to improve

☐ Cut right back on salt

☐ Eat plenty of potassium-rich fruits and vegetables

☐ Exercise a little more

Triglycerides

Current triglycerides: _____

Target triglycerides: _____

Actions to improve

☐ Replace simple carbohydrates with complex ones

☐ Drink only in moderation

☐ Eat more vegetables every day

☐ Cut down on saturated fats

Morning pulse rate

Current rate: _____

Target rate: _____

Actions to improve

☐ Get heart-pumping exercise regularly

☐ Learn relaxation techniques to lower stress

☐ Get a full night's sleep every night

☐ Lose excess weight

4 numbers to track every day

In this book, you've discovered literally hundreds of new ways to fit naturally nutritious foods, physical activity and relaxation into your day. Each time you choose one of these strategies, you are taking a step toward a healthier lifestyle.

But old habits die hard, and the route is packed with unhealthy temptations. It is so easy to order the large fries, watch a late-night film instead of going to bed at 10 p.m., or buy that huge bacon, lettuce and tomato sandwich and eat the whole thing.

So what is the best way to find out whether you've adopted enough new, healthy habits to make a real difference? That's easy—just use the simple, daily tracking system in this book.

This is how it works: every evening, take a few moments to ask yourself four questions about your day. These four questions distill the key messages and advice of the 30-Minutes-a-Day Plan down to their essence. They won't ever change, so it's easy to remember what they are. Your answers will make it perfectly clear whether you are

staying true to the path toward health, or if your good intentions are not being matched with good actions.

If you find the latter to be the case more often than not, try asking yourself the four questions in the late afternoon instead of the evening. By doing so, you'll give yourself plenty of time to make healthy choices at dinner and during your evening.

The easiest way to travel the road to a long and healthy life involves taking natural, painless steps. A little daily monitoring helps you to do just that. Here are the details.

1 FRUIT AND VEGETABLE CONSUMPTION

If you make just one change because of the 30-Minutes-a-Day Plan, let it be adding fruit and vegetables to every meal you eat. Both lower heart disease by pumping your body full of soluble and insoluble fibre, flooding your bloodstream and cells with artery-protecting antioxidants, and delivering vitamins and minerals that help to control blood pressure and keep arteries flexible.

Fruit and vegetable consumption

■ **ASK YOURSELF** Did I eat at least five portions of fruit and vegetables today?

■ **YOUR GOAL** A total of seven to nine fruit and vegetable servings a day if you can.

■ **TRACKING TRICK** For women: wear nine bangles on the same arm. Each time you have a fruit or vegetable, move one bracelet to the other arm. For men: keep nine paper clips in your pants pocket. Move one to another pocket for each serving of produce you consume.

■ **ADDED BONUS** Aim to put lots of colour on your plate every day—green broccoli, purple grapes, yellow peppers, red tomatoes and orange peaches, for example.

■ **HOW TO CATCH UP** If you've had breakfast and lunch with little or no fruit or vegetables, make up lost ground with an apple, orange or pear in the afternoon, a big salad for dinner, and another fruit snack in the evening.

2 FIBRE CONSUMPTION

Fibre at every meal keeps blood sugar levels steady. This controls cravings, helps you to feel full and stay full longer, and lowers your risk of diabetes and heart disease. But the benefits don't stop there: getting soluble fibre (from oats, rye bread or legumes) drastically cuts cholesterol levels.

High-fibre foods are less processed, too, so you get a complete package of naturally balanced, heart-healthy nutrients at the same time. Whole grains also provide vitamin E and other antioxidants. High-fibre nuts give you monounsaturated fat to preserve "good" HDLs and, if you choose walnuts, omega-3s to keep your heart beating at a steady rate.

Fibre consumption

■ **ASK YOURSELF** Did I have three whole grains plus some nuts and/or beans today?

■ **YOUR GOAL** Two to four servings of whole grains and one or two servings of nuts and/or beans.

■ **TRACKING TRICK** Think 3-2-1. That's three whole grains, two of legumes or vegetables and one serving of nuts.

■ **ADDED BONUS** Make at least one of your fibre-rich grains a soluble-fibre powerhouse such as oatmeal.

■ **HOW TO CATCH UP** If you've eaten a low-fibre breakfast and lunch, then try snacking on nuts during the afternoon and having beans in your main dish at dinner, along with a slice of whole-grain bread. Take a soluble fibre supplement if necessary.

Surprising signs of success

You will soon see that your efforts are paying off. Long before you go back to your doctor for a blood pressure check and a new cholesterol test, the following lifestyle measurements of success will show you that you're on the right track. Expect to begin experiencing these benefits fast—some within a week or two of starting this plan.

■ **More energy** You've got more bounce all day, even during the notorious 3 p.m. slump.

■ **Better sleep** Your slumber is deeper; you wake up feeling more refreshed.

■ **A tighter belt** You can take it in an extra notch or two.

■ **Better-fitting clothes** You look better in your pants or skirts, maybe you can even wear your "skinny" jeans again.

■ **More money in your purse** You've got cash left over from the weekly food budget because you're eating less fast food and buying fewer processed items.

■ **Better moods** Minor irritations don't bother you and you're laughing more. Your outlook is more optimistic.

■ **More strength** It's easier to lift the grocery bags or pick up your children or grandchildren.

■ **Real muscles** Are those biceps you can see in your upper arms? Your muscles are gaining definition. Nice.

3 RELAXATION TIME

Consciously relaxing doesn't mean taking an hour out of your busy day to meditate or have a massage (although if you can do either, you'll feel great). There are dozens of ways to relax without stopping what you're doing.

You can practise mindfulness—being fully aware of what you're doing at any given moment—or take a few minutes to focus on your breathing. You can let go of irritable or impatient thoughts before they double your risk of high blood pressure and heart attack.

And don't underestimate the calming health benefits of having a laugh with your friends, listening to music, walking and playing with your dog, or enjoying nature.

Relaxation time

■ **ASK YOURSELF** Did I give myself at least 15 minutes quiet time to unwind today?

■ **YOUR GOAL** Give yourself that feeling of relaxation every day.

■ **TRACKING TRICK** Think about how you are feeling inside several times a day. You will know if you are tense or agitated.

■ **ADDED BONUS** Once a week, spend at least an hour doing something you really love: bury yourself in a good book, play some sport, disappear into a greenhouse—do whatever gives you pleasure.

■ **HOW TO CATCH UP** In the middle of a stressful day, remind yourself that you'll be far more productive if you give yourself a few minutes to breathe deeply and unwind.

4 MOVEMENT TIME

Physical activity controls weight, burns off abdominal fat, lowers high blood pressure and helps to control rising cholesterol levels. It even soothes inflammation and helps your cells to absorb more blood sugar, cutting the risk of Type 2 diabetes.

On the 30-Minutes-a-Day Plan, you will have discovered dozens of ways to build activity into your daily life—plus a simple plan for strength training to build muscle density and walking to boost cardio-vascular fitness.

Movement time

■ **ASK YOURSELF** Did I get on my feet for fun or exercise today?

■ **YOUR GOAL** Sit for 1 hour less per day. Fit in a brisk, short stroll or two during the day.

■ **TRACKING TRICK** Before lunch and mid-afternoon, ask yourself how long you've been sitting without a break. Then move.

■ **ADDED BONUS** When walking, swing your arms energetically or stride quickly up a hill. March on the spot when on the phone.

■ **HOW TO CATCH UP** At the end of a sedentary day, take the stairs, not the elevator. Stroll around outside for a few minutes before getting into the car. Once home, take the dog for a walk or drag the kids out for a game of "tag." At night, use the television commercial breaks to do the exercises on page 168.

Do I get a day off? The short answer: No

The longer, more compassionate answer: if you are feeling somewhat daunted by your new health regimen and are seeking a "day off" from "being good," then you need to be reminded of the fundamental truth about healthy living. That is, it's not a program that you can go on or come off. It's not a formal diet or rigid exercise regimen, or compulsory stress-relief program, or a weekly visit to the psychiatrist, doctor, nutritionist, gym or personal trainer.

Health is about how you live, each and every moment. It's about sleeping well, and waking up happy, and eating a good breakfast, and enjoying your work, and taking regular breaks, and laughing with friends and family, and having a positive attitude, and enjoying fresh foods, and loving nature, and respecting yourself.

Look at it like this: you are going to sleep, work, eat and have free time each and every day. Health is achieved by going about these activities a little more wisely and healthily, and with a slightly different attitude. As this book stresses, it's the little choices that matter: whole-grain toast instead of white; a walk, not a television show; laughter, not anger. These kinds of minute-to-minute choices are what clean arteries, lower blood pressure, strengthen the heart and make life long and good. If, along the way, you enjoy a little ice cream, an occasional steak or a lazy afternoon, it really doesn't matter, because it's more than balanced by your everyday good choices.

So if you still believe health is achieved by following a program, it's time to break free. A formal program can get you started, teach you healthy choices, help you to break bad habits and form better ones. But in the end, healthy living, done properly, is simply living—but it's a good life.

The reward for healthy living is not merely a
heart at some point in the future. Healthy liv
is like the sun—warming invigorating and un

The 30-Minutes-a-Day
Plan workbook

Putting the healthy heart plan to work

As you have read, the 30-Minutes-a-Day Plan is not a rigid program. Instead, it is a guide—aiming to take no more than 30 minutes each day to integrate the small changes into your life that will help to give you a strong, well-protected heart. But what exactly do you do once you have put this book down?

The following pages aim to answer that question. The book's goal is to make it as easy as possible to embark—and succeed—on the 30-Minutes-a-Day Plan. So here is a short summary of the various components you will find.

■ **The healthy heart starter kit** You've stated your commitment; now it's time to take action. Refer back to the "Getting started" section (page 53), for guidance on your individual priorities. Then turn to this checklist to commit to the specific changes you want to make first, second and third.

■ **My healthy heart contract** Signing an actual contract and, better still, asking a loved one to read and sign it as witness, is a major step forward in your commitment to a healthier heart for life.

Here is one of the most popular yoga routines, which beginners should soon be able to master. Why not give it a try?

■ **The healthy heart daily tracker** This is an easy checklist to fill out each evening to make sure you are making the small, easy changes necessary for heart health. Be sure to make many copies.

■ **The Sun Salutation yoga routine** Here is one of the most popular yoga routines, which beginners should soon be able to master. Why not give it a try?

■ **Bonus strength programs** The Plan's approach to strengthening is to do 5 minutes of focused exercises each day. Here are two weeks of routines, featuring entirely different movements.

■ **Healthy heart recipes** These fresh and delicious tried-and-tested recipes have all been developed as much for flavour as for their health benefits.

■ **Frequently Asked Questions** Doctors treating heart patients are asked many questions. Here are answers to several common ones.

■ **Resources** To enable you to delve more deeply into any of the ideas in this book, we have listed some useful organizations, websites and books.

The healthy heart starter kit

The secret to success with the 30-Minutes-a-Day Plan is slowly and steadily to exchange unhealthy habits and practices with heart-healthy ones. So review the following list of suggested changes, and mark appropriate ones as follows:

I   **Immediate**—I want to start this immediately.
N   **Next**—Once I integrate the first round of changes into my life, I intend to tackle this.
C   **Committed**—This is not an immediate priority, but I will make it happen in the months ahead.
R   **Research**—I want to know more about this before making a commitment and will re-read this book and do a bit of additional research.

EATING

- ☐ Eat a healthier breakfast
- ☐ Eat a healthier lunch
- ☐ Eat a healthier dinner
- ☐ Consume more vegetables with my meals
- ☐ Eat healthier carbohydrates (whole-grain bread, brown rice, sweet potatoes)
- ☐ Eat more fish
- ☐ Eat healthier, less-processed snacks
- ☐ Reduce my intake of sugar
- ☐ Drink more water
- ☐ Drink fewer soft drinks
- ☐ Eat less junk food (chips, candy, ice cream, cookies)
- ☐ Stop eating out of habit, boredom or stress
- ☐ Plan my meals in advance
- ☐ Shop from a shopping list
- ☐ Eat less from fast-food outlets
- ☐ (Other)

MOVING

- ☐ Start each morning with a stretching routine
- ☐ Do 5 minutes of strength exercises a day
- ☐ Take a long, vigorous walk every day
- ☐ Fit in more short walks throughout the day
- ☐ Give yoga a try
- ☐ Agree to stay on my feet longer during the day
- ☐ Resume or take up an active hobby like gardening, rowing or cycling
- ☐ (Other)

LIVING

- ☐ Try to control my temper
- ☐ Work at managing stress more effectively
- ☐ Find ways to laugh more
- ☐ Be more forgiving to myself and others
- ☐ Be more loving to friends and family
- ☐ Reinvigorate my "spirituality" or focus on some unselfish, higher purpose in life
- ☐ Lose a destructive behaviour, such as smoking or excessive drinking
- ☐ Get more sleep each night
- ☐ Change to less toxic cleaning methods
- ☐ Begin a more thorough daily oral health routine that includes flossing
- ☐ Wash hands more often and be more aware of keeping germs at bay
- ☐ Answer the 4 essential health questions each evening (see page 222)
- ☐ (Other)

Which changes do you plan to start immediately? (If you picked more than five, go back over your list and change several to "N," or "next." Overcommitment often leads to failure: start simply—and succeed.)

1 _____
2 _____
3 _____
4 _____
5 _____

What do you need to buy to get started? _____
_____
_____

How will you adjust your routine to get started? _____
_____
_____

How will you reward yourself for successes?

In three days _____
In a week _____
In a month _____

What is your next set of changes?

1 _____
2 _____
3 _____
4 _____
5 _____

How will you make sure you embark on these new changes? (Suggestions include writing them on your calendar, using the start of each month or perhaps the arrival of a monthly magazine as a time for reassessment, asking a loved one to remind you, or using holidays or the seasons to trigger some new goals.)

What are your three-month goals? _____
_____

How will you reward yourself for complete success? _____
_____

How will you reward yourself for partial success? _____
_____

How will you remotivate yourself if only limited success? _____
_____
_____
_____

My healthy heart contract

Date: _____

I acknowledge that:

1 Having a healthy heart and circulatory system is vital to my happiness, health and longevity.

2 A diet of processed foods not only provides poor nourishment for my body and soul but also is not healthy for my heart.

3 Sitting too much can be unhealthy, and a sedentary lifestyle diminishes my heart and well-being.

4 Anger, impatience and constant stress not only reduce my happiness but also cause physical damage to my heart and my body.

Therefore, I vow to myself that I will invest 30 minutes each and every day to eat better, be more active, and improve my mental state, with the goal of not only improving the health of my heart but also increasing my energy levels, reducing my chances of illness, and making it far more likely that I will live a long and happy life.

How I will find 30 minutes each day: _____

_____

Specific changes at which I believe I can best succeed (e.g., eating more fruit, taking lunchtime walks, getting some daily relaxation): _____

_____

How I will monitor my progress: _____

_____

I affirm that:

■ I will maintain reasonable expectations of myself and not let small setbacks get in the way of long-term success.

■ I will review my progress, re-evaluate my strategies, and set new short-term goals every two weeks for the next three months and then every month thereafter.

■ I enter into this contract seriously and will keep it as a reminder of my commitment to my health, happiness, and well-being.

Signature: _____

Witness signature (optional): _____

The healthy heart daily tracker

WHAT I ATE TODAY

Target amounts are in boldface type.

Fruit	1 2 **3 4** 5
Vegetables	1 2 3 **4 5** 6 7
Whole grains	1 2 3 **4 5 6** 7 8
Calcium-rich foods	1 **2 3** 4
Beans	0 **1** 2
Fish	0 **1** 2
Lean poultry or meat	0 1 **2** 3 4
Glasses of water	0 1 2 3 4 5 6 **7 8 9** 10

Were my meals healthy?	Y/N
Were my snacks healthy?	Y/N
Were my food portions correct?	Y/N
Did I eat enough fibre?	Y/N
Did I eat out of habit or compulsion?	Y/N
Did I avoid unhealthy drinks?	Y/N

HOW I MOVED TODAY

Time spent walking _____

Estimated step count _____

Did I limit my television time today?	Y/N
Did I strengthen my muscles today?	Y/N
Did I stretch my body today?	Y/N
Did I do an active hobby today?	Y/N

Energy levels (0 = lifeless; 5 = bursting)

Morning	0 1 2 3 4 5
Afternoon	0 1 2 3 4 5
Evening	0 1 2 3 4 5

HOW I LIVED TODAY

Did I allow myself at least 10 minutes to relax fully?	Y/N
Did I share affection with friends and/or family?	Y/N
Did I laugh heartily at least four times?	Y/N
Was I confident?	Y/N
Was I forgiving?	Y/N

Motivation to be healthy	0 1 2 3 4 5
Positive attitude	0 1 2 3 4 5
Quality of last night's sleep	0 1 2 3 4 5

Health measurements or observations

_____

_____

_____

_____

_____

Notes for tomorrow

_____

_____

_____

_____

_____

_____

_____

_____

_____

The Sun Salutation yoga routine

Having sampled the soothing benefits of yoga by doing the exercises on page 194, you may feel you'd like to know more. There's no better place to start than with the Sun Salutation. A series of 12 graceful, flowing postures, they are regarded as the core of yoga practice.

Each position complements the one before, stretching and strengthening the body in a different way, so that by the time you have finished, you feel flexible and energized from head to toe. (For more on yoga's benefits, see page 192.)

One round of Sun Salutations consists of two sequences, first leading with the right foot (during stepping poses) and the second leading with the left. If you are new to yoga, some of these poses may be too challenging at first, so do the modifications until you feel more comfortable. These modifications are included within the text describing some of the poses. Make sure you read the text before attempting the pose. Also, if you have existing heart problems, these moves may be too strenuous and are not recommended unless approved by your doctor. It is also a good idea to check with your doctor if you have arthritis or other serious medical problems.

How often you practise the Sun Salutations is entirely up to you. Yoga fans sometimes do 12 routines a day, but you can calm stress, increase flexibility and improve your general well-being by doing them as little as once a week.

Remember to breathe evenly and fluidly throughout, inhaling and exhaling as you begin each move. With practice, the 12 steps of the Sun Salutations will flow together as one continuous exercise. Be sure to perform the routine on a comfortably cushioned surface, such as a yoga mat or a carpeted floor.

Step 1 Mountain pose

Stand straight with your feet about hip-width apart and your hands either at your sides or in prayer position in front of your chest. Raise your toes and spread them wide, then place them back on the floor. Your weight should be distributed evenly across the bottom of each foot so you feel grounded, not leaning forward or back. Exhale.

Step 2 Overhead reach

Inhale as you sweep your arms out to the sides and high overhead until your palms are together. Stretch upward, allowing the fullest expansion of your chest, then arch backward and look up at your hands. Hold the position for a few seconds with your body in pose, holding your breath and keeping your eyes focused and your mind silent.

Step 3 Forward fold

Exhale as you gently bend forward from the hips, keeping your palms together, tucking in your head and keeping your back straight and long.
When you've bent as far forward as comfortably possible, grasp the back of your legs (anywhere from the ankles to the thighs), bend your elbows and very gently tuck your chin to your chest and move your upper body toward your legs. Hold for a few breaths.

Step 4 High lunge

Step back with your right foot into a lunge, bending your left knee and keeping it directly over your left ankle (you may need to slide your right foot back farther). Lean forward and press your fingertips or palms into the floor in line with your forward foot. Roll your shoulders back and down and press your chest forward while looking straight ahead.

Relax your hips and let them sink toward the floor while straightening your back leg as much as comfortably possible. Hold for a few breaths.

If it's difficult to reach the floor with your hands in this position, place books on either side of you so you can support your weight with your hands on the books. You may also rest your back leg on the floor if necessary.

Step 5 Plank

Move your left foot back next to your right foot and straighten your body into the plank position. Spread your fingers wide so your middle fingers are pointing forward. Your hands should be on the floor directly beneath your shoulders, and you should look as if you're in a push-up position. Tuck in your tailbone so your legs, hips and torso form a straight line. Push the crown of your head forward, tuck your toes and press your heels back, stretching down the entire length of the back of your body. Hold for a few breaths.

If this is too difficult, perform the move while resting on your knees instead of your toes.

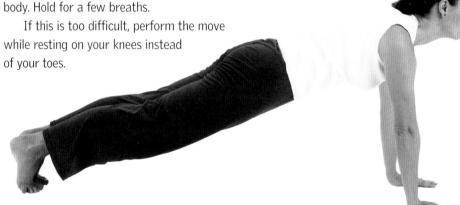

Step 6 Caterpillar

Bend both knees to the floor (if they're not already there), then slowly lower your chin and chest straight down to the floor. Keep your elbows close to your body as you lower your chest between your palms and lift your tailbone toward the ceiling. Hold for a breath.

Step 7 Cobra

Drop your hips to the floor. Raise your head and chest so your torso is supported on your forearms (if you are very flexible, you can extend your arms). Keep your shoulders down and back, pressing your chest forward and reaching toward the ceiling with the crown of your head. Hold for a few breaths.

Step 8 Downward-facing dog

Press your palms into the floor, straighten your arms and legs, and push your hips up so your body forms an inverted V. Let your head and neck hang freely from your shoulders or tuck your chin to your chest, if that's more comfortable. Press your heels toward the floor while pushing your hips toward the ceiling for a full stretch.

To make this position easier, keep your knees bent instead of straightening your legs. You can also place your hands on a low step. Hold for a few breaths.

Step 9 High lunge 2

Step forward with your right foot. Position yourself so your right knee is directly over your right ankle and your left leg is extended behind you. Support your weight by placing your palms or fingertips on the floor in line with your right foot. (Again, if you find it hard to reach the floor, place books under your hands.) Roll your shoulders down and back and press your chest forward, looking straight ahead.

Relax your hips and let them sink toward the floor while straightening your back leg as much as comfortably possible (if flexibility is a problem, keep your back leg resting on the floor). Hold for a few breaths.

Step 10 Forward fold 2

Bring your left foot forward to meet your right. Gently straighten your legs as much as comfortably possible, letting your hands rise off the floor as necessary. Grasp the back of your legs (anywhere from your ankles to your thighs), bend your elbows, and very gently tuck your chin to your chest and move your upper body toward your legs. Hold for a few breaths.

Step 11 Upward sweep

Sweep your arms out to the sides and overhead, stretching them up and back as you expand your chest. Place your palms together and look up toward your hands. Press your feet into the floor and contract your thighs to gently lift your kneecaps upward (without locking your knees). Hold for a few breaths.

Step 12 Mountain return

Sweep your arms out to the sides and down, bringing your palms together in front of your chest. As in Step 1, stand straight with your feet hip-width apart. Raise your toes and spread them wide, then place them back on the floor so your weight is evenly distributed.

Contract your thighs, pulling your kneecaps up and tucking your tailbone so it points straight toward the floor. Lift the crown of your head toward the ceiling, feeling your spine grow long and straight. Drop your shoulders down and back and gently push your chest forward. Hold for a few breaths, then repeat the cycle, this time initiating moves with the other leg.

Frequently asked questions about yoga

Yoga has become established as a popular form of exercise over the past few decades, but some people still equate it with a special religion or something only rubber-jointed people can do. Here are some answers to common questions.

Q What does yoga mean?

A Yoga literally means "union." The practice is designed to unite your mind and body, as well as your spirit, through deep breathing, peaceful meditation and physical poses that both stretch and strengthen the body.

Q Do I need to attend classes?

A No, although yoga classes can be great fun and helpful in providing the motivation to carry on. An instructor can ensure that you are doing the moves correctly. Classes are also a good way to meet like-minded people committed—like you—to improving their health.

Q If I can't touch my toes, can I still do yoga?

A Absolutely. Just as people who are out of shape should walk and lift weights to increase their physical fitness, so people with tight muscles and stiff joints can reap benefits from practising yoga. Just start slowly, modifying the poses as you need to—and never stretch to the point of pain. Within a few weeks, you should see noticeable improvements in your flexibility.

Q Should I see my doctor first?

A It is worth checking with your doctor before taking unaccustomed exercise if you have medical problems, including heart disease, high blood pressure, arthritis or obesity.

Like your mind, your muscles need new
challenges to stay toned and strong.

Bonus strength programs

Imagine doing the same crossword puzzle
every morning over your muesli—day in, day
out. For the first day or two, you might enjoy
speeding up, getting good at it; after three
days or so, your brain would switch off.

Like your mind, your muscles need new
challenges to stay toned and strong. For those
who have made a commitment to increase
their strength, here is a bit of variety—two
more complete, full-body routines.

Like the original routine on page 168
each program gives you two exercises to do
each day (about 5 minutes total), six days
a week. The basic equipment is also the
same: a balance ball, a few dumbbells and,
occasionally, a chair or a step. As before, do
two sets of each exercise, 10 to 12 repetitions
per set, unless instructed otherwise. Note,

however, that some of these exercises feel
awkward at first, particularly those involving
a balance ball.

For best results, you should change your
exercise routine every eight to 12 weeks, so
after a few months, you get out of the
original routine and rotate through these,
then repeat the cycle. Your muscles will stay
stimulated, and so will you.

Caution: It is strongly recommended that
you rehearse the exercises in advance. Also,
consider practising the moves first without
weights, so you can get the hang of doing the
movements correctly, without strain. If you
find that an exercise bothers your lower back,
do not do that exercise.

Monday Back and biceps

Hammer curls

STAND holding a pair of dumbbells by your sides with your palms facing your thighs and your knees slightly bent.
KEEPING your back straight and your elbows tucked close to your sides, slowly curl the weights up toward your collarbone so the end of each weight is near each shoulder. Pause, then lower the weights to the starting position.

Upright rows

STAND with your feet shoulder-width apart, holding the dumbbells in front of you with your arms extended and your palms facing your thighs. Keep your shoulders back and down.
KEEPING the weights close to your body, slowly pull the dumbbells straight up along your body until they reach collarbone height. Your elbows should be above the weights, pointing outward. Do not let your shoulders lift. Pause, then return to the starting position.

Chest press

LIE back on your balance ball so it supports your torso from your neck to your mid-back, with your knees bent and your feet flat on the floor. Hold the dumbbells over your chest with your arms extended and your palms facing your feet so the weights are end to end.
BEND your arms and slowly lower the weights toward your chest until your upper arms are parallel to the floor. Pause, then contract your chest muscles and push the weights back up to the starting position.

Overhead extension

GRASP the end of a dumbbell with both hands and sit on your balance ball or the edge of a chair. Lift the weight over your head and hold it with your elbows close to your ears. Remember to pull in your stomach.
KEEPING your shoulders down and your elbows close to your head, lower the weight behind your head until your forearms are just past parallel to the floor. Pause, and then return to the starting position.

243

THE 30-MINUTES-A-DAY PLAN WORKBOOK

Wednesday Legs and core

244

Step and extend

STAND about a foot away from a flight of stairs with your feet hip-width apart, with your hand on the wall or railing for support. Keeping your upper body straight, step forward with your left foot, placing it on the centre of the second step.

PRESS into your left foot and extend your left leg to lift your body. As you step up, extend your right leg slightly behind you. Pause and reverse the motion, stepping back down to the floor while keeping your left foot planted. Finish a set with your left foot, then repeat with the other foot.

Balance ball rolls

KNEEL on a mat or carpeted floor with your balance ball in front of you. Clasp your hands together and place your hands, wrists and forearms on the ball. Lift your feet and shins off the floor and balance on your knees, leaning slightly into the ball.

PRESS into the ball with your hands and forearms and roll the ball forward, pivoting on your knees until your body is extended at about a 45-degree angle from the floor (you'll feel your abdominal muscles "engage" to hold this position and stabilize your spine). Pause, then contract your abs to pull your body back to the starting position.

Thursday Back and biceps

Concentration curls

SIT on your balance ball or the edge of a chair with your legs bent and your feet flat on the floor about shoulder-width apart. Hold a weight in your right hand. Bend slightly from the hips (keeping your back straight) and extend your right arm toward the floor, resting the elbow against the inside of your thigh. Place your left hand on your left leg for support.
SLOWLY bend your right elbow, curling the weight toward your right shoulder. Pause at the top of the lift, then slowly lower back to the starting position. Complete a set with your right arm, then repeat with the left.

Bird dog

KNEEL on your hands and knees on a carpeted floor or mat. Keep your back straight and your head and neck in line with your back.
EXTEND your left leg and then your right arm, bringing them in line with your back or slightly higher than your torso, if possible. Your fingers and toes should be pointed. Pause, squeezing your gluteal (buttocks) and back muscles to maintain balance. Return to the starting position, then repeat on the opposite side. Alternate for a full set on each side.

Friday
Chest and triceps

Alternating punches

LIE back on your balance ball so it supports your torso from your neck to your mid-back, with your knees bent and your feet flat on the floor. With your right hand, hold a dumbbell over your chest with your arm extended and your palm facing your feet so the weight is positioned horizontally. With your left hand, hold a dumbbell beside your chest, also horizontally but at right angles to the other weight (that is, parallel to your torso).

SLOWLY lower the weight in your right hand, rotating your wrist as you come toward your body so the weight ends up beside your chest. Immediately press the left weight up, rotating your wrist so your arm is extended with the dumbbell horizontal. Pause, then lower the weight back to the starting position. Alternate for a full set on each side.

French curl

LIE on the floor with a supportive pillow beneath your head, shoulders and upper back. Bend your knees 90 degrees and place your feet flat on the floor. Hold a pair of dumbbells straight above your body and angled slightly back so that your hands are above your head with the palms facing each other.

KEEPING the rest of your body still, slowly bend your elbows and lower the weights behind your head. Pause, then straighten your elbows and return to the starting position.

Bonus program ONE
Saturday Legs and core

Side lunge

STAND straight. Move your feet farther than shoulder-width apart into a straddle stance. **BEND** your right knee and shift your weight to the right, lowering your buttocks toward the floor as far as you can. Keep your right knee in line with your toes. Then push back up to the starting position. Repeat on the other side. Alternate for a full set with each leg.

Shoulder roll

LIE face up on your balance ball in a "bridge position," with your upper back against the ball, your hips lifted in line with your back, your knees bent at 90 degrees and your feet flat on the floor. Extend your arms over your chest and clasp your hands together.

EXHALE and lower your hands to the right as far as comfortably possible. Your left shoulder, torso and maybe even your buttock will rise as your right hip lowers. Pause, then return to the starting position. Repeat on the opposite side. If you are afraid of losing your balance, brace your toes against a wall to prevent rolling too far as you perform this move.

Monday Back and biceps

Criss-cross curls

STAND holding a pair of dumbbells at your sides, with your palms facing your thighs and your knees slightly bent. **KEEPING** your back straight and your elbows tucked close to your sides, slowly bend your right elbow and curl the weight up and across your body so your right hand is below your left shoulder with the palm facing your body. Pause, then return to the starting position. Repeat with the other arm. Alternate for a full set with each arm.

Chest lift

LIE face down on the floor with your hands under your chin, your palms down and your elbows pointed to the sides.
WITH hips pressed to the floor, lift your head, chest and arms a little way off the floor. Pause, then lower. Try tightening your buttocks as you do this. Stop if you develop back pain.

Bonus program TWO

Tuesday Chest and triceps

Wall push and clap

PLACE your hands against a wall or a high tabletop. Move your feet back so your body is angled about 45 degrees from the floor. It should form a straight line from your heels to your head.

BEND your arms and lower yourself until your elbows are bent at 90 degrees. Don't let your back arch. Push up as hard as you can, clap your hands once, and return to the starting position before immediately dropping into another repetition. Keep your core tight throughout.

One-arm overhead extension

GRASP a dumbbell with your right hand and hold it overhead. Bend your arm and lower the weight behind your head so your elbow points toward the ceiling.

SLOWLY extend your arm again, stopping before you lock your elbow into a perfectly straight position. Pause, then lower again. Repeat for a full set and swap sides.

249

THE 30-MINUTES-A-DAY PLAN WORKBOOK

Wednesday
Legs and core

Split squat

STAND in front of a stable chair, facing away from it. Lift your right leg behind you and rest the top of your foot on the seat of the chair. Keep your arms at your sides.

SLOWLY bend your left leg until your left thigh is nearly parallel to the floor. As you bend your leg, lift your arms straight in front of you until parallel to the ground. Pause, then return to the starting position. Do not let your back arch. Complete a set, then swap legs. For a more intense leg workout, hold dumbbells in your hands and keep them at your sides as you bend.

Balance ball drops

LIE face up on the floor, arms by your sides. Grasp the balance ball between your feet and ankles and raise your legs toward the ceiling.

KEEPING your torso stable and your legs extended, slowly lower the ball toward the floor to 45 degrees (don't arch your back). Pause, then return to the starting position. To make the move more challenging, put your hands behind your head, lift your head and shoulders off the floor and perform the move from that position. Your abdominals should be tight throughout this exercise and you must not let your back lift off the floor. Caution: If this exercise bothers your back, don't do it.

Thursday Back and biceps

Butterfly curls

STAND with your knees slightly bent, holding a pair of dumbbells by your sides with your arms turned so your palms face out as much as comfortably possible.
KEEPING your back straight and your elbows tucked close to your sides, slowly curl the weights up toward the outside of your shoulders. Pause, then return to the starting position.

Superman

LIE face down with your legs straight behind you, toes pointed and arms straight ahead. Hold your head straight in line with your spine and lifted off the floor at a comfortable level.
SLOWLY raise your right arm and your left leg at the same time until both are a little way off the floor. Hold, then slowly return to the starting position. Repeat with the left arm and leg. Alternate arms and legs throughout the exercise until you have completed half a set on each side. Stop if you get any back pain doing this exercise.

Bonus program TWO

Friday Chest and triceps

Pullovers

LIE face up on the floor with your knees bent and your feet flat. Grasp a dumbbell around the stem with both hands and hold it above your chest so the weight is parallel to your body.

KEEPING your elbows straight, lower your arms down and back over your head as far as comfortably possible (don't arch your back). Pause, then return to the starting position.

Bent-over kickbacks

PLACE your right knee and right hand on the seat of a chair so your back is parallel to the floor. Grasp a dumbbell with your left hand, keeping your elbow at your side so your forearm is perpendicular to the floor.

EXTEND your left arm backward until the forearm is parallel to the floor. Pause, then return to the starting position. Complete a full set, then change sides.

Saturday Legs and core

Sumo squat

STAND with your feet slightly wider than shoulder-width apart, with your toes pointing to the sides. Place your hands on your hips (you can hold dumbbells at hip level to make the move harder). Squat down toward the floor a little way.

LIFT your heels and balance on the balls of your feet, deepening the squat until your thighs are nearly parallel to the floor. Pause, then lower your heels and rise to the starting position.

THE 30-MINUTES-A-DAY PLAN WORKBOOK

Lean back

SIT on the floor, back straight and legs out in front. Bend your knees, putting your feet flat on the floor. Extend your arms in front of you at chest height with the palms facing down.

LEAN back so you are balancing on your tailbone and your feet are off the floor. Your abs should be working to stop you from falling backward. Pause, then return to the starting position. Keep your chin tucked in while performing this exercise.

Healthy heart recipes

... the criteria for dishes that we consider truly heart healthy ... are the ones we've used to develop the recipes in the pages ahead.

There are many cookbooks that claim to offer recipes that are "healthy" but never bother to define the term. In fairness, that's partly because there is no formal definition of a healthy recipe, and one doctor's opinion may differ from another's.

The following are the criteria for dishes that we consider truly heart healthy; they are the ones we've used to develop the recipes in the pages ahead.

These recipes:
- Use a minimal number of processed foods
- Feature mostly fresh ingredients, particularly vegetables or fruits
- Use whole, unrefined carbohydrates
- Use a minimal amount of refined sugar
- Have no added salt
- Are low in saturated fat
- For main courses, have less than 600 calories per serving
- Use proven heart-healthy ingredients, such as salmon, olive oil, whole-wheat flour, rolled oats, beans, broccoli and garlic.

You may find a few exceptions. For example, our delicious goat cheese salad has a few more calories and a little more fat than many of the other dishes. But goat cheese is also full of protein and calcium and is actually lower in fat than many other cheeses.

Similarly, French apple cake has a "few" more calories than other desserts but it is packed with healthy ingredients—and apples are, of course, one of the "superfoods" listed on page 103.

Most people don't eat meals that are anywhere close to these healthy standards. Don't despair. Take one small step at a time. Start by reducing portion sizes, then add a few more fruits and vegetables. Next, work to break your butter habit. With time and practice, you'll discover that you're naturally choosing the healthy alternative—and that your weight is dropping and your health improving.

Meanwhile, try out the recipes here. Each one has a full nutritional analysis so you can see precisely what you are eating and incorporate the dish into your healthy eating plan. But health is not by any means the sole criterion. Just as importantly, these are all recipes that everyone can enjoy.

On the menu

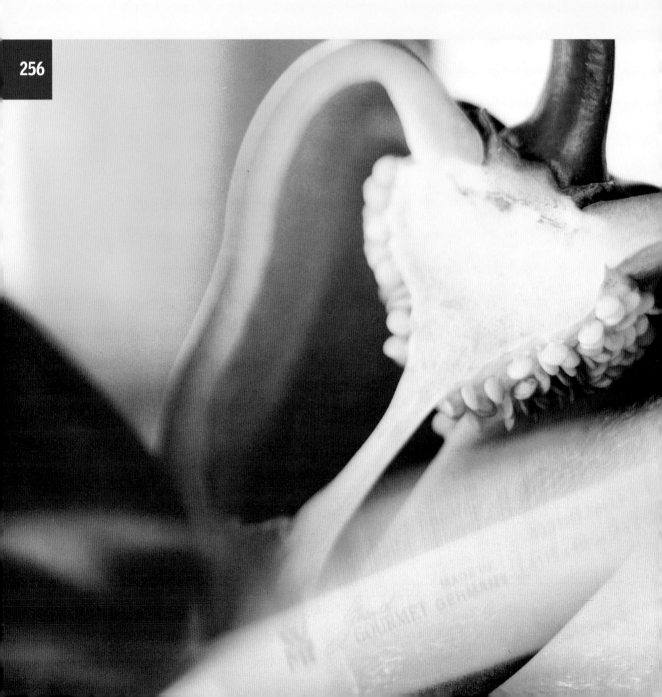

Breakfasts

Snacks & starters

Soups

Fish & seafood

Poultry

Beef, lamb & pork

Vegetarian

Side dishes

Desserts

Breakfasts

♥ Stirring in fruit adds vitamin C
nuts and seeds add vitamin E

Dried fruit compote

■ Serves 4

■ Preparation time 10 minutes plus cooling time

■ Cooking time 25–30 minutes

1¼ cups orange juice
4 tablespoons clear honey
1 teaspoon finely grated orange zest
1 teaspoon finely grated lemon zest
1 tablespoon lemon juice
pinch of ground cloves
pinch of grated nutmeg
225 g (8 oz) mixed dried fruit, such as prunes,
    apricots, apples and peaches
⅓ cup currants or raisins

1 In a medium saucepan, combine the orange juice, honey, orange and lemon zests, lemon juice, cloves and nutmeg. Bring to a boil over moderate heat, then reduce the heat and simmer for 5 minutes.

2 Add the dried fruit and currants to the pan. Bring back to a boil, then reduce the heat, cover and simmer for 15–20 minutes or until the fruit is very soft.

3 Transfer to a serving bowl and allow the fruit to cool to room temperature in the syrup.

PER SERVING calories 223, saturated fat 0 g, total fat 0.4 g, sodium 28 mg, cholesterol 0 mg, protein 2.5 g, carbohydrate 58 g, fibre 4.5 g.

Crunchy toasted cereal with fruit and nuts

- ■ Serves 10
- ■ Preparation time 30 minutes
- ■ Cooking time 50–55 minutes

4 tablespoons clear honey
4 tablespoons apple juice
4 cups rolled oats
1 cup bran flakes or additional rolled oats
¾ cup wheat germ
⅓ cup flaked almonds
2 dessert apples, or 60 g (2¼ oz) dried apples
⅔ cup raisins
⅓ cup sunflower seeds

1 Preheat the oven to 325°F (160°C). In a saucepan, combine the honey with the apple juice. Heat, stirring, until almost boiling. Remove from the heat and allow to cool.

2 Mix together the oats, bran flakes, wheat germ and almonds on a baking tray. Pour over the honey mixture and toss until the grains and nuts are all coated. Spread out in an even layer.

3 Place the tray in the oven and bake, stirring occasionally, for 30 minutes or until toasted and golden brown. Remove from the oven and allow to cool, stirring occasionally.

4 Reduce the oven temperature to 250°F (120°C). If using dessert apples, halve and core them, then thinly slice. Arrange the slices on two baking trays in a single layer.

5 Place in the oven to dry for 15–20 minutes, turning the slices once. Allow to cool slightly, then chop the apples coarsely. (If using dried apples, chop them coarsely.)

6 Combine the toasted grain mixture with the chopped apples, raisins and sunflower seeds. Store the cereal in an airtight container in the fridge for up to 1 month. Serve with 2% milk or plain low-fat yogourt.

PER SERVING calories 306, saturated fat 0.7 g, total fat 10 g, sodium 19 mg, cholesterol 0 mg, protein 10 g, carbohydrate 46 g, fibre 5 g.

Strawberry bran waffles

- Makes 10 waffles
- Preparation time 15 minutes
- Cooking time 15 minutes

1 cup whole-wheat flour
1 cup bran flakes
1 teaspoon baking powder
1 cup 2% milk
½ cup low-fat sour cream
1 teaspoon clear honey, plus more to serve
2 egg whites
2 cups strawberries, sliced

1 Heat your waffle iron according to the manufacturer's instructions. In a large bowl, combine the flour, bran flakes and baking powder.

2 Make a well in the centre of the dry ingredients and add the milk, sour cream and honey. Mix together to make a batter.

3 Whisk the egg whites until stiff peaks form, then fold into the batter until just blended.

4 Pour enough batter into the centre of the waffle maker to cover two-thirds of the grid. Close the lid and bake for about 4 minutes or until the lid will lift up easily. Remove the waffle with a fork and keep hot while baking the remainder.

5 Serve the waffles hot with the sliced strawberries and honey to taste.

PER WAFFLE calories 87, saturated fat 1.5 g, total fat 2.5 g, sodium 91 mg, cholesterol 1 mg, protein 4 g, carbohydrate 13 g, fibre 2 g.

♥ Using egg whites, low-fat dairy products and just enough ham for taste reduces the fat content.

Ham and cheese frittata

■ Serves 4

■ Preparation time 15 minutes

■ Cooking time 25–30 minutes

4 tablespoons 2% milk
¼ cup low-fat sour cream
4 whole eggs
4 egg whites
2 tablespoons freshly grated Parmesan cheese
good pinch of freshly ground black pepper
1 tablespoon olive oil
2 onions, coarsely chopped
175 g (6 oz) lean ham, coarsely chopped
100 g (3½ oz) reduced-fat mozzarella
    cheese, grated

1 In a mixing bowl, combine the milk with the sour cream until blended. Add the whole eggs and then the egg whites, one at a time, whisking well after each addition. Stir in the Parmesan cheese and pepper.

2 In a 25 cm (10 in.) non-stick frying pan, heat the oil over moderate heat. Add the onions and cook, stirring, for 7–9 minutes or until soft and golden brown. Add the ham to the pan and cook, stirring, for a few more minutes.

3 Spread the ham and onion mixture evenly in the pan. Reduce the heat to low. Pour the egg and milk mixture into the pan and sprinkle over the mozzarella cheese.

4 Cover and cook for 15–20 minutes or until the frittata is set and puffed. Transfer to a serving plate, cut into wedges and serve.

PER SERVING calories 300, saturated fat 6 g, total fat 18 g, sodium 741 mg, cholesterol 271 mg, protein 28 g, carbohydrate 6 g, fibre 0.7 g.

Muffin pizzas

- Serves 6
- Preparation time 20 minutes
- Cooking time 35 minutes

6 English muffins
225 g (8 oz) mild Italian sausages, sliced
1 large onion, coarsely chopped
1 red or green pepper, coarsely chopped
2 garlic cloves, finely chopped
225 ml tomato sauce
2 teaspoons dried rosemary, crumbled
100 g (3½ oz) reduced-fat mozzarella cheese,
    grated

1 Preheat the oven to 375°F (190°C). Slice the muffins in half and arrange them, cut side up, in a single layer on a baking tray. Bake for 8–10 minutes or until lightly browned.

2 Heat a non-stick frying pan and add the sliced sausages. Cook, stirring, for 6 minutes or until the fat is rendered. Using a slotted spoon, transfer the sausage slices to a plate. Drain off most of the fat from the pan.

3 Add the onion, red or green pepper and garlic to the pan and cook for about 5 minutes. Stir in the tomato sauce and rosemary. Return the sausage slices to the pan and simmer, stirring occasionally, for 3–4 minutes.

4 Spoon a little of the sausage mixture onto each muffin half and top with the mozzarella. Bake for 4–5 minutes. Serve hot.

PER SERVING calories 358, saturated fat 5 g, total fat 16 g, sodium 742 mg, cholesterol 17 mg, protein 15 g, carbohydrate 40 g, fibre 2 g.

♥ Tomatoes—used here in a salsa—contribute the heart-healthy phytochemical lycopene.

Turkey bites with tomato and fruit salsa

■ Serves 6

■ Preparation time 15 minutes

■ Cooking time 30 minutes

900 g (2 lb) turkey breast (in one piece)
3 egg whites
1 cup fresh breadcrumbs
½ teaspoon finely chopped garlic
½ teaspoon ground celery seeds
½ teaspoon paprika
¼ teaspoon hot chili powder
¼ teaspoon freshly ground black pepper
⅓ cup all-purpose flour
2 tablespoons olive oil
2 large tomatoes, diced
1 mango, diced, or 2 peaches, skinned and diced

1 Preheat the oven to 350°F (180°C). Pull off the skin from the turkey breast and remove the meat from the bone. Cut the breast across into 2.5 cm (1 in.) slices. Cut the slices into 2.5 cm (1 in.) strips.

2 Lightly whisk the egg whites together in a shallow dish until just foamy. In another shallow dish, combine the bread crumbs with the garlic, celery seeds, paprika, chili powder and half of the pepper, then spread out evenly.

3 Dredge the turkey strips very lightly with flour, then dip into the egg whites to cover completely. Finally, coat with the seasoned breadcrumbs. Place on a paper towel.

4 In a large non-stick frying pan, heat 1½ teaspoons of the oil over moderate heat. Add one-quarter of the turkey strips and cook for 2–3 minutes or until browned on all sides. Transfer to a large baking tray.

5 Brown the remainder of the strips, in three batches, using the rest of the oil. Then bake the turkey for about 15 minutes or until tender and cooked through.

6 Meanwhile, make the salsa. In a bowl, combine the diced tomatoes, mango and remaining pepper. Serve with the turkey bites.

PER SERVING calories 275, saturated fat 1 g, total fat 5 g, sodium 198 mg, cholesterol 85 mg, protein 41 g, carbohydrate 17 g, fibre 1.5 g.

Cheese and pepper soufflés

- Serves 4

- Preparation time 30 minutes

- Cooking time 25 minutes

4 green or red peppers
1 tablespoon butter
2 tablespoons all-purpose flour
¾ cup 2% milk
1 egg yolk
good pinch of freshly ground black pepper
115 g (4 oz) reduced-fat Cheddar cheese, grated
4 green onions, finely chopped
4 egg whites
2 tablespoons freshly grated Parmesan cheese

1 Preheat the oven to 400°F (200°C). Cut the tops off the peppers and reserve. Remove the core and seeds from inside the peppers. Cut a thin slice from the base of each pepper so it will stand upright.

2 Bring a saucepan of water to a boil. Add the peppers and their tops, cover and simmer for 3 minutes or until barely tender. Drain and place upright in a baking dish.

3 Melt the butter in another saucepan. Add the flour and cook, stirring, for 1–2 minutes. Remove from the heat and stir in the milk. Return to the heat and simmer until thickened.

4 Cool slightly, then stir in the egg yolk, pepper and cheese. Mix in the green onions.

5 Whisk the egg whites until stiff peaks form, then carefully fold into the cheese sauce.

6 Divide the filling among the peppers and sprinkle with the Parmesan. Bake for 25 minutes or until the filling is puffed and golden. Put the tops on the peppers and serve.

PER SERVING calories 262, saturated fat 7 g, total fat 13 g, sodium 361 mg, cholesterol 80 mg, protein 19 g, carbohydrate 18 g, fibre 3 g.

Tomato and basil scones

■ Makes 22 scones

■ Preparation time 20 minutes

■ Cooking time 12 minutes

2 cups all-purpose flour
$\frac{1}{3}$ cup whole-wheat flour
2 tablespoons wheat germ
4 teaspoons baking powder
good pinch of freshly ground black pepper
1 plum tomato, seeded and finely chopped
2 tablespoons chopped fresh basil
2 teaspoons tomato paste
250 g plain low-fat yogourt or
    $\frac{3}{4}$ cup buttermilk
2% milk to glaze

1 Preheat the oven to 450°F (230°C). In a large bowl, mix together the plain flour, whole-wheat flour, wheat germ, baking powder and pepper.

2 In a smaller bowl, mix the tomato, basil and tomato paste with the yogourt. Add to the flour mixture. Mix with a fork to make a soft dough that leaves the sides of the bowl.

3 Turn the dough out onto a lightly floured surface and knead lightly four to six times. Roll out to 1 cm ($\frac{1}{2}$ in.) thickness. Cut out rounds using a floured 5 cm (2 in.) cutter, using a firm downward action without twisting the cutter.

4 Gather the dough trimmings and press them together, without kneading, then roll out and cut more rounds.

5 Arrange the rounds, 2.5 cm (1 in.) apart, on a lightly greased baking tray. Brush the tops of the scones with 2% milk, then bake for 10–12 minutes or until golden. Serve warm.

PER SCONE calories 55, saturated fat 0.1 g, total fat 0.4 g, sodium 95 mg, cholesterol 0.1 mg, protein 2.2 g, carbohydrate 11 g, fibre 0.8 g.

Soups

♥ Shrimp are a source of selenium, which helps to protect the cardiovascular system.

Hot and sour shrimp soup

■ Serves 8

■ Preparation time 15 minutes

■ Cooking time 25 minutes

6 cups homemade fish stock
1 tablespoon finely chopped lemongrass, or
    ½ teaspoon finely grated lime zest
1 garlic clove, finely chopped
1 fresh red or green chili pepper, finely chopped
225 g (8 oz) button mushrooms, sliced
115 g (4 oz) raw shrimp, peeled and deveined
2 tablespoons rice vinegar or white wine
    vinegar
1 tablespoon reduced-sodium soy sauce
1 tablespoon cornstarch
2 green onions, thinly sliced

1 Combine the fish stock, lemongrass, garlic and chili pepper in a saucepan. Bring to a simmer. Partly cover and cook for about 5 minutes.

2 Stir in the mushrooms and shrimp. Simmer, partly covered, for a further 3 minutes or until the mushrooms are soft and the shrimp have turned pink.

3 In a small bowl, combine the vinegar and soy sauce with the cornstarch until smooth. Stir this mixture into the simmering soup, then bring back to a boil. Remove from the heat, stir in the green onions and serve.

PER SERVING calories 35, saturated fat 0 g, total fat 0.4 g, sodium 163 mg, cholesterol 28 mg, protein 4 g, carbohydrate 4 g, fibre 1 g.

Gazpacho

■ Serves 6

■ Preparation time 20 minutes plus chilling time

3 slices French bread
1 large red or green pepper, coarsely chopped
1 red onion, coarsely chopped
½ cucumber, peeled, seeded and sliced
4 plum tomatoes, cored and quartered
¼ cup fresh basil or parsley leaves
1 garlic clove, finely chopped
2 tablespoons olive oil
2 tablespoons red or white wine vinegar
3 cups tomato juice
good pinch of freshly ground black pepper

1 Remove the crusts from the bread and tear the bread into pieces. Place in a bowl and cover with water. Soak for at least 5 minutes.

2 Drain some of the water from the bowl, then, with your hands, squeeze out most of the remaining water from the bread. Reserve the soaked bread.

3 Place the red or green pepper, red onion and cucumber in a food processor and process until very finely chopped. Pour the mixture into a large bowl.

4 Add the tomatoes and basil to the food processor and process until very finely chopped but not totally puréed. Add to the pepper mixture in the bowl.

5 Add the garlic, oil, wine vinegar, soaked bread and tomato juice to the food processor and process until blended. Stir into the vegetable mixture until thoroughly combined.

6 Add the black pepper. Cover the bowl and chill the soup for at least 1 hour before serving.

PER SERVING calories 112, saturated fat 0.6 g, total fat 4 g, sodium 371 mg, cholesterol 0 mg, protein 3 g, carbohydrate 16 g, fibre 2 g.

♥ To keep this soup healthily low in calories and fat, it is thickened with puréed vegetables.

New England clam chowder

- Serves 8
- Preparation time 25 minutes
- Cooking time 50 minutes

12 fresh clams, scrubbed, or 2 cans (147 g each)
    baby clams, drained and rinsed
6 cups homemade fish stock
25 g (1 oz) lean salt pork or reduced-sodium
    bacon, coarsely chopped
2 large onions, coarsely chopped
450 g (1 lb) potatoes, peeled and diced
2 cups 2% milk
good pinch of freshly ground black pepper
2 tablespoons chopped fresh parsley

1 Put the clams and 4 tablespoons of the fish stock in a large saucepan. Cover, bring to a boil and steam for about 5 minutes or until the shells open. Remove the clams with a slotted spoon; strain and reserve the stock. When cool enough to handle, remove the clams from their shells and chop them coarsely.

2 Cook the salt pork or bacon in the saucepan over moderate heat for 3 minutes or until crisp. With a slotted spoon, remove the pork and discard. If using bacon, reserve to garnish.

3 Add the onions to the pan together with 4 tablespoons of the stock. Sauté for about 5 minutes or until soft but not browned.

4 Stir in the potatoes, remaining fish stock and reserved clam stock. Bring to a boil. Simmer, partly covered, for about 10 minutes or until the potatoes are very tender.

5 Remove from the heat. Purée 2 ladlefuls of the vegetables in a blender or food processor until smooth. Add the purée to the soup and return to the heat.

6 Stir in the milk and the chopped clams. Simmer for about 5 minutes. Add the pepper and parsley and serve, garnished with the bacon, if used.

PER SERVING calories 104, saturated fat 0.8 g, total fat 2 g, sodium 298 mg, cholesterol 11 mg, protein 6 g, carbohydrate 16 g, fibre 2 g.

Cream of leek and potato soup

■ Serves 8

■ Preparation time 15 minutes

■ Cooking time 45 minutes

1 tablespoon olive oil
225 g (8 oz) leeks, white part only, thickly sliced
1 large onion, coarsely chopped
6 cups homemade or canned low-sodium
    chicken or vegetable stock
450 g (1 lb) potatoes, peeled and diced
good pinch of freshly ground white pepper
⅓ cup low-fat sour cream
snipped fresh chives to garnish (optional)

1 In a large saucepan, heat the oil over moderate heat. Stir in the leeks and onion with ¾ cup of the stock. Cover and cook, stirring frequently, for about 10 minutes or until soft but not browned.

2 Add the potatoes to the saucepan and stir to coat with the leek and onion mixture.

3 Pour in half of the remaining stock and bring to a boil. Partly cover, then simmer for 15–20 minutes or until potatoes are very soft.

4 Remove from the heat. Using a ladle, transfer the contents of the pan to a blender or food processor and purée until very smooth.

5 Pour the remaining stock into the pan. Add the vegetable purée and bring the soup to a simmer, stirring constantly. Season with the white pepper.

6 Remove from the heat and stir in the sour cream. Ladle into soup bowls and garnish with the chives, if using.

♥ Leeks give this soup a delicious fresh flavour and also add fibre.

PER SERVING calories 111, saturated fat 2.5 g, total fat 5.5 g, sodium 94 mg, cholesterol 10.5 mg, protein 2.5 g, carbohydrate 13 g, fibre 2 g.

♥ Chicken is an excellent source of protein and without its skin is also low in fat.

Chicken, rice and spinach soup

■ Serves 8

■ Preparation time 10 minutes

■ Cooking time 30 minutes

¾ cup long-grain white rice
8 cups homemade or canned low-sodium
    chicken stock
225 g (8 oz) skinned and boned chicken breasts,
    cut into 5 mm (¼ in.) slices
350 g (12 oz) fresh spinach leaves
1 tablespoon lemon juice
good pinch of freshly ground black pepper

1 Place the rice in a sieve and rinse under cold running water until the water runs clear.

2 Place the rice in a large saucepan with the chicken stock and bring to a boil. Simmer for about 10 minutes.

3 Add the sliced chicken to the pan and simmer, partly covered, for a further 5 minutes. Stir in the spinach and continue simmering for another 5 minutes or until the rice is tender and the chicken and spinach are cooked.

4 Season with the lemon juice and pepper, then serve hot.

PER SERVING calories 120, saturated fat 0.1 g, total fat 1 g, sodium 204 mg, cholesterol 20 mg, protein 10 g, carbohydrate 18 g, fibre 2.5 g.

Fish & seafood

Poached salmon steaks with horseradish and chive sauce

■ Serves 4

■ Preparation time 10 minutes

■ Cooking time 30 minutes

2 cups 2% milk
1½ cups water
2 tablespoons lemon juice
1 small onion, thinly sliced
1 celery stalk with leaves, coarsely chopped
1 carrot, coarsely chopped
4 black peppercorns
4 salmon steaks, about 115 g (4 oz) each
1 tablespoon bottled grated horseradish
½ cup low-fat sour cream
½ cup reduced-fat mayonnaise
2 tablespoons chopped fresh chives
freshly ground black pepper

1 Pour the milk into a large non-stick frying pan and add the water, lemon juice, onion, celery, carrot and peppercorns. Bring to a boil over medium heat, then cover and simmer for about 10 minutes.

2 Add the salmon steaks to the pan and bring the liquid back to a boil. Reduce the heat, cover and poach the fish for about 10 minutes or until the flesh flakes easily when tested with a fork.

3 Meanwhile, combine the horseradish, sour cream, mayonnaise, chives and pepper to taste in a bowl. Stir until evenly mixed.

4 Using a large slotted spatula, transfer the salmon steaks to a platter lined with a paper towel. Allow to drain. Discard the poaching liquid.

5 Transfer the salmon steaks to serving plates and spoon over the horseradish and chive sauce. Serve hot.

PER SERVING calories 404, saturated fat 7 g, total fat 27 g, sodium 382 mg, cholesterol 70 mg, protein 29 g, carbohydrate 11 g, fibre 1 g.

Broiled citrus trout

- Serves 4
- Preparation time 15 minutes plus marinating time
- Cooking time 20 minutes

1 lemon, thinly sliced
1 lime, thinly sliced
1 small red onion, sliced
4 tablespoons chopped fresh parsley
½ cup orange juice
2 teaspoons olive oil
2 garlic cloves, finely chopped
¼ teaspoon dry mustard
¼ teaspoon dried rosemary, crumbled
good pinch of freshly ground black pepper
4 rainbow trout, about 225 g (8 oz) each, cleaned
vegetable oil cooking spray

1 Place the lemon, lime and onion slices in a shallow dish large enough to hold the fish in one layer. Add the parsley, orange juice, oil, garlic, mustard, rosemary and pepper, and stir until well mixed.

2 Add the fish to the dish and turn the fish to cover with the mixture. Cover the dish and leave to marinate in the fridge for about 1 hour.

3 Preheat the broiler. Cover the rack in the grill pan with foil and perforate it. Coat the foil with vegetable oil spray. (Do not use the spray near the hot broiler.)

4 Using a slotted spatula, transfer the fish to the foil-covered grill rack. Strain the marinade into a small saucepan; reserve the lemon, lime and onion slices. Warm the marinade over low heat.

5 Broil the fish, about 13 cm (5 in.) below the heat, for 6–8 minutes, brushing frequently with the marinade.

6 Carefully turn the fish over and brush with the marinade. Arrange the lemon, lime and onion slices in an even layer on top of the fish, then return to the broiler and cook for a further 6–8 minutes. Serve hot.

PER SERVING calories 265, saturated fat 0.4 g, total fat 10 g, sodium 116 mg, cholesterol trace, protein 39 g, carbohydrate 4 g, fibre 0 g.

♥ Fish fillets, baked on a bed of fresh vegetables, make an easy and nutritious one-dish dinner.

Fish baked on a bed of broccoli, sweet corn and red pepper

■ Serves 4

■ Preparation time 15 minutes

■ Cooking time 50 minutes

4 firm white fish fillets, 115–175 g (4–6 oz) each, fresh or frozen and thawed
2 tablespoons fat-free vinaigrette
1 tablespoon fine dried bread crumbs
1 tablespoon freshly grated Parmesan cheese
¼ teaspoon paprika
1 tablespoon olive oil
1 cup broccoli florets
1 cup frozen sweet corn kernels, thawed
1 red pepper, cut into thin strips
1 small red onion, thinly sliced
2 tablespoons chopped fresh parsley
1 tablespoon chopped fresh basil, or 1 teaspoon dried basil
good pinch of freshly ground black pepper

1 Place the fillets in a shallow dish and brush with the vinaigrette. Cover and refrigerate.

2 In a small bowl, combine the bread crumbs with the Parmesan cheese and paprika.

3 Preheat the oven to 425°F (220°C). Brush four individual ovenproof dishes, or a 33 x 23 x 5 cm (13 x 9 x 2 in.) ovenproof dish with oil.

4 In a large bowl, mix together the broccoli, sweet corn, red pepper, onion, parsley, basil and black pepper. Divide the vegetable mixture evenly among the dishes. Cover with foil and bake for 35–40 minutes or until the vegetables are just tender.

5 Uncover the dishes and top the vegetables with the fish fillets. Cover again and bake for 8–10 minutes or until the fish is just cooked and still moist in the thickest part.

6 Uncover the dishes and sprinkle with the bread crumb mixture. Bake, uncovered, for a further 2–3 minutes or until the topping is golden. Serve immediately.

PER SERVING calories 223, saturated fat 1.5 g, total fat 6 g, sodium 171 mg, cholesterol 56 mg, protein 27 g, carbohydrate 15 g, fibre 3 g.

Poultry

♥ The white breast meat of turkey is exceptionally low in fat and cholesterol.

Roast turkey breast with garlic sauce

■ Serves 10

■ Preparation time 20 minutes

■ Cooking time 2 hours

1 turkey breast, bone-in, about 2.25 kg (5 lb)
3 tablespoons olive oil
¼ teaspoon freshly ground black pepper
15 garlic cloves, unpeeled, lightly crushed to
    break the skins
1½ cups homemade or canned low-sodium
    chicken stock
2 teaspoons lemon juice

1 Preheat the oven to 350°F (180°C). Cut off any fat from the turkey breast, then place it, skin side up, in a shallow roasting pan. Brush the oil all over the breast and sprinkle with half of the pepper. Cover loosely with foil and roast for about 45 minutes.

2 Remove the foil and scatter the garlic cloves around the turkey, coating them with the pan juices. Roast, uncovered, for a further 1¼ hours or until a thermometer inserted into the thickest part of the breast reads 170°F (75°C).

3 Remove the skin, then transfer the turkey to a platter. Cover it with foil and keep warm. Spoon off all the fat from the roasting pan, leaving the pan juices. With a spoon, squeeze the garlic cloves from their skins into the pan.

4 Place the roasting pan over medium heat. Stir in one-third of the stock and heat until bubbling. Transfer the mixture to a blender or food processor and purée until smooth. Return to the roasting pan and bring to a boil over medium heat. Stir in the remaining stock and pepper and the lemon juice. Simmer for about 3 minutes. Slice the turkey breast and serve with the garlic sauce.

PER SERVING calories 216, saturated fat 1 g, total fat 5 g, sodium 105 mg, cholesterol 99 mg, protein 42 g, carbohydrate 1 g, fibre 0.2 g.

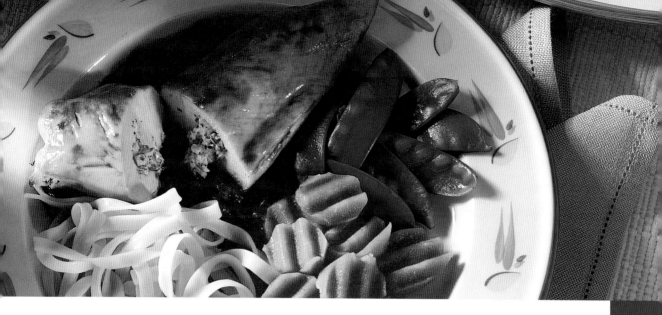

Herb-stuffed chicken breasts

■ Serves 4

■ Preparation time 15–20 minutes

■ Cooking time 25 minutes

85 g (3 oz) goat cheese, at room temperature
1 garlic clove, finely chopped
2 tablespoons finely chopped fresh parsley
1 tablespoon finely chopped fresh mint, or
  ¾ teaspoon dried mint
good pinch of freshly ground black pepper
4 chicken breasts (skinless and boneless),
  about 675 g (1½ lb) in total
1 tablespoon olive oil
450 ml marinara or other tomato
  pasta sauce (optional)

1 Preheat the oven to 350°F (180°C). To make the stuffing, mix the goat cheese with the garlic, parsley, mint and pepper in a medium bowl.

2 Cut off any fat from the chicken breasts. Remove the long fillet strip from the underside of each one and reserve for another use.

3 With a sharp knife, cut a deep horizontal slit, about 5 cm (2 in.) long, in each chicken fillet, starting at the rounded end. Take care not to cut through the sides of the fillets.

4 Using a teaspoon, insert about a quarter of the stuffing into the slit in each fillet so that it fills the pocket completely but does not spill out of the opening.

5 Fasten the opening with a wooden skewer, weaving the stick through the edges of the chicken a few times.

6 Place the fillets on a rack in a roasting pan and brush with a little of the oil. Roast for 20 minutes or until the chicken is cooked through. Meanwhile, preheat the broiler.

7 Brush the fillets with the remaining oil, then broil for about 5 minutes. Serve with warmed marinara or tomato sauce, if desired.

PER SERVING calories 245, saturated fat 3 g, total fat 8 g, sodium 104 mg, cholesterol 118 mg, protein 42 g, carbohydrate 1 g, fibre 0.5 g.

Chicken and vegetable stir-fry

- Serves 4
- Preparation time 20 minutes
- Cooking time 12 minutes

2 chicken breasts (skinless and boneless),
    about 350 g (12 oz) in total
2 teaspoons cornstarch
½ cup chicken stock
2 tablespoons reduced-sodium soya sauce
1½ tablespoons sunflower oil
2 garlic cloves, finely chopped
1 tablespoon finely chopped fresh ginger
2 red or green peppers, thinly sliced
2 carrots, thinly sliced
2 celery stalks, thinly sliced
2 cups button mushrooms, sliced
good pinch of freshly ground black pepper

1 Dry the chicken breasts with a paper towel and cut off any fat. Cut each fillet across at an angle into very thin slices.

2 In a small bowl, mix together the cornstarch, stock and soya sauce. Set aside.

3 Heat the oil in a wok or non-stick frying pan over high heat until a piece of pepper sizzles when added to the oil. Add the garlic and ginger and stir-fry for 1–2 minutes or until lightly browned and fragrant.

4 Add the chicken slices to the wok and stir-fry for 3–4 minutes or until browned and cooked through. Using a slotted spoon, transfer the chicken to a bowl.

5 Allow the oil in the wok to reheat, then add the sliced vegetables and mushrooms. Stir-fry for about 4 minutes or until softened and lightly browned.

6 Return the chicken and its juices to the wok and stir in the cornstarch mixture. Cook, stirring, until the liquid comes to a boil and thickens slightly. Season with the pepper, then serve.

PER SERVING calories 192, saturated fat 1 g, total fat 5.5 g, sodium 275 mg, cholesterol 61 mg, protein 23 g, carbohydrate 13 g, fibre 3 g.

New-style chicken salad

- ■ Serves 4
- ■ Preparation time 25 minutes plus marinating time
- ■ Cooking time 10–15 minutes

4 chicken breasts (skinless and boneless),
    about 675 g (1½ lb) in total
2 red, yellow or green peppers, sliced
1 large red onion, thickly sliced
2 zucchini, thickly sliced
¾ cup cherry tomatoes, halved
4 tablespoons olive oil
2 tablespoons lemon juice
1 teaspoon finely grated lemon zest
2 teaspoons dried basil
good pinch of freshly ground black pepper
4 handfuls of mixed salad leaves

1 Cut each chicken breast into 4 slices. Place in a shallow dish. Combine the peppers, onion, zucchini and cherry tomatoes in another shallow dish.

2 In a small bowl, mix together the oil, lemon juice and zest, basil and pepper. Spoon half of this mixture over the chicken slices and the remainder over the vegetables. Toss to coat. Cover both dishes with plastic wrap and leave to marinate in the fridge for at least 2 hours.

3 Preheat the broiler. Remove the chicken from the marinade and spread out in the broiler pan. Discard the marinade. Grill the chicken for 6–8 minutes or until cooked through, turning once. Transfer the chicken to a plate, cover and keep warm.

4 Drain the vegetables and place in the broiler pan. Broil until browned and softened, turning once and brushing twice with the marinade. Serve the broiled chicken and vegetables on a bed of salad leaves.

PER SERVING calories 330, saturated fat 2 g, total fat 13 g, sodium 112 mg, cholesterol 118 mg, protein 43 g, carbohydrate 9 g, fibre 3 g.

Beef, lamb & pork

♥ A change in proportions is the secret here. Roast a generous serving of vegetables alongside a smaller piece of meat to create a nutritionally balanced meal.

Herb-roasted beef

■ Serves 6

■ Preparation time 15 minutes

■ Cooking time 1 hour 40 minutes

1 lean boned beef rib roast about 900 g (2 lb), rolled and tied
good pinch of freshly ground black pepper
1 cup fresh herbs, such as parsley, basil, sage, rosemary, thyme and chives, or 1½ tablespoons dried mixed herbs
2 tablespoons Dijon mustard
1 tablespoon olive oil
3 large onions, cut into eighths
6 small zucchini, cut into thirds
1 cauliflower, cut into florets

1 Preheat the oven to 350°F (180°C). With a sharp knife, trim all the fat from the beef. Season with the pepper.

2 Place the fresh herbs in a food processor with the Dijon mustard and process to chop very finely, scraping down the sides of the bowl occasionally. Transfer to a small bowl. (If using dried herbs, just mix with the mustard.)

3 Spoon the herb mixture onto the beef and spread it evenly to cover all sides. Put the oil in a large roasting pan and add the beef. Roast for 30 minutes.

4 Arrange the onions, zucchini and cauliflower florets in the pan around the roast. Toss the vegetables to coat them thoroughly with the pan juices.

5 Roast for a further 1 hour or until a thermometer inserted in the centre of the meat reads 160°F (70°C) for medium. Turn the vegetables occasionally so that they cook evenly.

6 Remove from the oven. With a slotted spoon, transfer the vegetables to a serving dish and keep them warm. Place the roast on a cutting board, cover and leave to rest for 5 minutes. Slice the beef and serve with the vegetables.

PER SERVING calories 300, saturated fat 4.5 g, total fat 12 g, sodium 227 mg, cholesterol 90 mg, protein 37 g, carbohydrate 9 g, fibre 3 g.

Barbecued steak and vegetables

■ Serves 4

■ Preparation time 20 minutes plus marinating time

■ Cooking time 20 minutes

3 tablespoons olive oil

3 tablespoons red wine vinegar

2 tablespoons Dijon mustard

2 garlic cloves, finely chopped

1 teaspoon each dried basil and oregano

good pinch of chili flakes

good pinch of freshly ground black pepper

4 lean round steaks, about 115 g (4 oz) each,
    trimmed of all fat

2 red or green peppers, cut lengthwise into
    2.5 cm (1 in.) strips

3 zucchini, each cut lengthwise into 4 strips

2 red or yellow onions, cut across into
    1 cm (½ in.) slices

1 To make the marinade, mix together the oil, vinegar, mustard, garlic, basil, oregano, chili flakes and pepper in a small bowl.

2 Place the steaks in a dish just large enough to hold them in one layer and pour the marinade over them. Turn the steaks in the marinade to coat both sides. Cover and leave to marinate in the fridge for at least 2 hours.

3 Remove the steaks from the refrigerator and allow to come to room temperature. Pour off the marinade into a small bowl. Prepare the barbecue, setting the grill 10–13 cm (4–5 in.) above the heat, or preheat the broiler.

4 Place the steaks on the barbecue, or under the broiler, and cook for about 6 minutes on each side for medium, or to taste. Meanwhile, using a small brush, coat the vegetable pieces with the reserved marinade.

5 Transfer the steaks to a platter, cover with foil and keep warm. Add the vegetables to the barbecue or broiler and cook until browned and softened, turning once and brushing twice with the remaining marinade. Serve the vegetables with the steaks.

PER SERVING calories 275, saturated fat 3 g, total fat 14 g, sodium 74 mg, cholesterol 67 mg, protein 28 g, carbohydrate 10 g, fibre 2.5 g.

♥ Spinach supplies potassium, which helps to lower blood pressure and is a great source of many of the antioxidants that may protect against heart disease, such as vitamins C, E and beta carotene.

Leg of lamb stuffed with spinach

■ Serves 8

■ Preparation time 20 minutes

■ Cooking time 1½–2 hours

1 leg of lamb, about 1.6 kg (3½ lb),
    boned and butterflied
good pinch of freshly ground black pepper
2 packages frozen chopped spinach, about
    300 g each, thawed and drained
1 teaspoon olive oil
1 shallot or small onion, finely chopped
2 garlic cloves, finely chopped
115 g (4 oz) feta or ricotta cheese

1 Preheat the oven to 375°F (190°C). Trim all the fat from the lamb, then open it out flat and pat dry with a paper towel. Season the inside with the pepper.

2 Press the spinach in a sieve with a wooden spoon to squeeze out any remaining liquid. Place the spinach in a bowl.

3 In a small non-stick frying pan, heat the oil over medium heat. Add the shallot, or onion, and garlic and sauté for 3–4 minutes or until softened and lightly browned. Add to the spinach.

4 Spread the spinach mixture over the butterflied lamb and crumble the cheese on top. Roll up the butterflied lamb and, with kitchen string, tie at regular intervals.

5 Place the stuffed lamb, seam side down, on a rack in a roasting pan. Roast for 1½–2 hours for medium (an instant-read thermometer inserted into the meat should read 160°F (70°C), or 1¾–2¼ hours for well done. The internal temperature should read 170°F (75°C).

6 Remove the lamb from the oven and allow to rest for about 10 minutes before slicing.

PER SERVING calories 306, saturated fat 8 g, total fat 17 g, sodium 420 mg, cholesterol 126 mg, protein 36 g, carbohydrate 2 g, fibre 1.5 g.

Mediterranean lamb stew

■ Serves 6

■ Preparation time 20 minutes

■ Cooking time 2 hours 40 minutes

675 g (1½ lb) boned lean shoulder of lamb
1½ tablespoons olive oil
2 large onions, sliced
2 garlic cloves, finely chopped
1 tablespoon all-purpose flour
2 teaspoons chopped fresh rosemary, or
    1 teaspoon dried rosemary
1–2 cups beef stock
1½ cups tomato juice
1 can (540 ml) chickpeas, drained and rinsed
2 zucchini, cubed
1½ cups cherry tomatoes, halved
good pinch of freshly ground black pepper
2 teaspoons chopped fresh basil, or
    1 teaspoon dried basil

1 Using a sharp knife, trim all the fat and cartilage from the lamb, then cut the meat into 2.5 cm (1 in.) cubes.

2 In a flameproof casserole, heat 1 tablespoon of the oil over medium heat. Add the onions and garlic and sauté for about 10 minutes or until well browned. With a slotted spoon transfer to a plate.

3 Heat the remaining oil in the casserole over medium-high heat. Add the lamb and sauté, stirring, for about 3 minutes or until well browned on all sides. Sprinkle the flour and rosemary over the meat and cook for a further 1½ minutes or until the flour is absorbed.

4 Return the onions to the casserole together with 1 cup stock and the tomato juice. Bring to a boil, then cover and simmer gently for 1 hour. Stir in the chickpeas. Cook, covered, for a further 1–1¼ hours or until the lamb is almost tender.

5 Stir in zucchini, tomatoes, pepper and basil. Add more stock if the stew is becoming too thick. Cook for about 15 minutes longer or until the lamb is very tender when pierced with a fork. Serve hot.

PER SERVING calories 330, saturated fat 6 g, total fat 17 g, sodium 370 mg, cholesterol 85 mg, protein 28 g, carbohydrate 17 g, fibre 4 g.

♥ Fresh, lean pork is a good source of high-quality protein, B vitamins and zinc.

Grilled pork in barbecue sauce

■ Serves 4

■ Preparation time 10 minutes

■ Cooking time 20 minutes

450 g (1 lb) lean pork tenderloin, cut
    across into 8 thin slices
good pinch of freshly ground black pepper
1 can (540 ml) chopped tomatoes
⅓ cup unsweetened apple juice
2 tablespoons dark brown sugar
1 tablespoon cider vinegar
¼ teaspoon Tabasco sauce

1 With a sharp knife, trim any fat from the pork slices. Place the slices, two at a time, between sheets of parchment paper and lightly pound with a rolling pin. Season with the pepper.

2 To make the barbecue sauce, combine the tomatoes and their juices with the apple juice, sugar, vinegar and Tabasco sauce in a saucepan. Bring to a boil over medium heat, then simmer gently for about 10 minutes or until rich and thick. Keep hot.

3 Heat a ridged cast-iron grill pan until very hot and a drop of water sprinkled on the pan evaporates immediately. Add the pork slices and grill for about 2 minutes on each side or until cooked through.

4 Transfer the pork steaks to a platter and pour the barbecue sauce over them. Serve hot.

PER SERVING calories 188, saturated fat 1.5 g, total fat 5 g, sodium 120 mg, cholesterol 71 mg, protein 25 g, carbohydrate 12.5 g, fibre 1 g.

Pork loin stuffed with winter fruits

- Serves 6
- Preparation time 20 minutes
- Cooking time 1½ hours

¾ cup chicken stock
1 cup pitted prunes, coarsely chopped
1 cup dried apricots, coarsely chopped
1 boneless pork loin, about 900 g (2 lb)
good pinch of freshly ground black pepper
1 garlic clove, finely chopped
1 teaspoon dried thyme
2 tablespoons Madeira or port wine (optional)
2 tablespoons dark molasses

1 In a small saucepan, bring the stock to a boil over medium heat. Remove from the heat and stir in the prunes and apricots. Leave to soak for at least 15 minutes or until very soft.

2 Meanwhile, preheat the oven to 325°F (160°C). Trim all the fat from the pork loin, then open it out and pat dry with a paper towel. Season the inside with pepper.

3 Drain the soaked fruit, reserving the liquid in the saucepan. Place the fruit along one of the long sides of the pork loin. Scatter the chopped garlic and thyme over the fruit.

4 Fold the long edge of meat over the fruit and roll up the loin. With kitchen string, tie at regular intervals to seal in the stuffing.

5 Place the loin, seam side down, on a rack in a roasting pan. Roast for about 30 minutes. Meanwhile, add the Madeira or port wine, if using, and molasses to the reserved soaking liquid and bring to a boil to make the glaze.

6 Brush the glaze evenly over the pork loin. Roast for a further 1 hour or until tender and an instant-read thermometer inserted into the meat reads 170°F (75°C). Brush with the glaze every 10 minutes during the hour of cooking.

PER SERVING calories 280, saturated fat 2 g, total fat 6 g, sodium 135 mg, cholesterol 95 mg, protein 34 g, carbohydrate 21 g, fibre 3 g.

Mediterranean lentils with mushrooms

■ Serves 8

■ Preparation time 20 minutes plus marinating time

■ Cooking time 30 minutes

4 tablespoons olive oil
finely grated zest and juice of 1 lemon
1 teaspoon dried thyme
1 teaspoon dried oregano
good pinch of freshly ground black pepper
450 g (1 lb) cremini mushrooms, halved
2 cups brown, red or green lentils
1 can (540 ml) chopped tomatoes
½ cup vegetable stock
⅓ cup pitted black olives, sliced

1 To make the marinade, combine the oil, lemon zest and juice, thyme, oregano and pepper in a large bowl.

2 Add the mushrooms to the marinade and toss to coat well. Leave to marinate at room temperature for about 1 hour.

3 Meanwhile, rinse the lentils in a sieve under cold running water. Transfer into a saucepan and cover with water. Bring to a boil, then partly cover the pan and simmer for 15–20 minutes or until the lentils are almost tender. Drain well.

4 Heat a large non-stick frying pan over medium heat. Add the mushrooms with the marinade and sauté, stirring constantly, until softened and browned.

5 Add the lentils, tomatoes with their juices, stock and olives. Stir to mix. Bring to a boil, then simmer, partly covered, for 10–15 minutes or until the lentils and mushrooms are very tender. Serve hot or warm.

PER SERVING calories 217, saturated fat 1 g, total fat 8 g, sodium 123 mg, cholesterol 0 mg, protein 13 g, carbohydrate 25 g, fibre 5 g.

Vegetable and three cheese lasagna

- ■ Serves 6
- ■ Preparation time 35 minutes
- ■ Cooking time 1 hour 40 minutes

2 tablespoons olive oil
2 large onions, coarsely chopped
2 garlic cloves, finely chopped
2 cans (540 ml) chopped tomatoes
2 tablespoons tomato paste
½ teaspoon dried oregano
½ teaspoon dried basil
3 zucchini, diced
2 large carrots, diced
2 celery stalks, diced
9 lasagna noodles
475 g ricotta cheese
1 egg white
2 tablespoons finely chopped fresh parsley
85 g (3 oz) reduced-fat mozzarella cheese, sliced
2 tablespoons freshly grated Parmesan cheese

1 In a saucepan, heat 1 tablespoon of the oil over moderate heat. Sauté the onions and garlic for about 5 minutes until soft. Add the tomatoes with their juices, the tomato paste and herbs. Simmer, stirring occasionally, for 15 minutes until thickened.

2 Meanwhile, in a non-stick frying pan, heat the remaining oil over medium heat and sauté the zucchini, carrots and celery, stirring frequently, for 7 minutes or until slightly soft.

3 Bring a large pan of water to a boil. Add the lasagna noodles and cook according to package instructions. Drain. In a small bowl, combine the ricotta, egg white and parsley.

4 Preheat the oven to 350°F (180°C). Spread a quarter of the tomato sauce over the bottom of a 33 x 23 x 5 cm (13 x 9 x 2 in.) baking dish. Arrange a third of the noodles over it in an even layer. Spread half the ricotta mixture over the pasta and scatter half the vegetables on top.

5 Repeat the layers, then add another layer of sauce and the last of the noodles. Spread the remaining sauce on top and scatter over the mozzarella and Parmesan. Bake for about 45 minutes or until browned around the edges.

PER SERVING calories 370, saturated fat 7 g, total fat 15 g, sodium 475 mg, cholesterol 40 mg, protein 19 g, carbohydrate 40 g, fibre 4 g.

Spicy beans

- Serves 6

- Preparation time 12 minutes plus soaking time

- Cooking time 1½–2 hours

200 g (7 oz) dried pinto beans
2 tablespoons olive oil
3 large onions, coarsely chopped
2 large carrots, coarsely chopped
2 tablespoons mild chili powder
1¾ cups vegetable stock
1¾ cups cold water
dash of Tabasco sauce
good pinch of freshly ground black pepper

1 Place the beans in a large bowl and cover generously with cold water. Cover the bowl with a plate and leave to soak for at least 8 hours or overnight. Drain the beans.

2 In a large flameproof casserole or heavy saucepan, heat the oil over medium heat. Add the onions, carrots and chili powder and sauté, stirring, for about 5 minutes or until the vegetables are slightly softened.

3 Stir in the stock and cold water and bring to a boil. Add the beans. Bring back to a boil and boil for 10 minutes.

4 Partly cover the pan and simmer, stirring occasionally, for 1–1½ hours or until the beans are tender when tested with a fork and most of the liquid has been absorbed.

5 If there is a lot of liquid, remove the lid, raise the heat slightly and boil, stirring occasionally, for 5–10 minutes.

6 Remove from the heat and stir in the Tabasco sauce and pepper. Serve hot.

PER SERVING calories 162, saturated fat 0.6 g, total fat 4.5 g, sodium 54 mg, cholesterol 0 mg, protein 9 g, carbohydrate 23 g, fibre 7 g.

♥ Goat cheese is a good source of protein and calcium, but has a lower fat content than many traditional cheeses.

Warm goat cheese salad

- Serves 4
- Preparation time 7 minutes plus marinating time
- Cooking time 4–6 minutes

4 tablespoons olive oil
3 tablespoons white wine vinegar
1 garlic clove, finely chopped
2 tablespoons chopped fresh herbs, such as
    parsley or chives
good pinch of freshly ground black pepper
dash of Tabasco sauce
1 log of goat cheese, about 225 g (8 oz)
1 baguette
4 handfuls of salad leaves

1 In a large bowl, combine the oil, vinegar, garlic, herbs, pepper and Tabasco sauce. Cut the cheese across into 12 slices. Add to the bowl and toss to coat with the marinade. Cover and leave to marinate for at least 1 hour.

2 Preheat the broiler. Cut the baguette into twelve 2 cm ($^3/_4$ in.) slices and place on the broiler rack. Toast on one side for 2–3 minutes.

3 Drain the cheese, reserving the marinade. Turn the toast over and place a slice of cheese on top of each. Broil for a further 1–2 minutes.

4 Make a bed of salad leaves on each plate. Place the cheese-topped toast on the leaves and spoon over the reserved marinade.

Healthy heart recipes MAIN COURSES

PER SERVING calories 546, saturated fat 12 g, total fat 27 g, sodium 955 mg, cholesterol 52 mg, protein 21 g, carbohydrate 57 g, fibre 3 g.

Black-eyed pea casserole

- Serves 8

- Preparation time 15–20 minutes plus soaking time

- Cooking time 1 hour 10 minutes

150 g (5½ oz) dried black-eyed peas
2 tablespoons olive oil
2 large onions, coarsely chopped
2 large carrots, coarsely chopped
4 celery stalks, coarsely chopped
2 garlic cloves, finely chopped
4 cups water
3 cups homemade or canned low-sodium
    vegetable stock
225 g (8 oz) potatoes, peeled and cubed
225 g (8 oz) turnips, peeled and cubed
½ teaspoon dried thyme
½ teaspoon dried rosemary
good pinch of freshly ground black pepper

1 Place the peas in a large bowl and cover generously with cold water. Cover the bowl with a plate and leave to soak for at least 8 hours or overnight. Drain the peas.

2 Heat the oil in a flameproof casserole or heavy saucepan and sauté the onions, carrots, celery and garlic for 5–8 minutes.

3 Add the water and stock together with the peas, potatoes, turnips and herbs. Bring to a boil and boil for 10 minutes.

4 Partly cover the casserole and simmer for 45 minutes or until the peas are tender. Uncover, season with the pepper and simmer for a further 10 minutes. Serve hot.

PER SERVING calories 104, saturated fat 0.5 g, total fat 3.5 g, sodium 74 mg, cholesterol 0 mg, protein 6 g, carbohydrate 22 g, fibre 4.5 g.

Side dishes

♥ This slightly chewy grain is rich in soluble fibre, which can help to lower "bad" LDL cholesterol.

Nutty lemon barley

- Serves 8
- Preparation time 10 minutes
- Cooking time 55–60 minutes

2 tablespoons olive oil
2 onions, finely chopped
3 celery stalks, finely chopped
200 g (7 oz) pearl barley, rinsed
1⅓ cups homemade or canned low-sodium
    vegetable stock
1 teaspoon finely grated lemon zest
½ teaspoon dried oregano
good pinch of freshly ground black pepper
2 tablespoons sunflower seeds or pine nuts
1 tablespoon lemon juice
⅓ cup raisins
2 tablespoons chopped fresh parsley

1 In a wide, heavy saucepan, heat the oil over medium heat. Add the onions and celery and sauté, stirring, for about 7 minutes or until softened and lightly browned.

2 Stir in the barley until well coated with the oil. Pour in the stock and add the lemon zest, oregano and pepper.

3 Bring the stock to a boil, then reduce the heat, cover the pan and simmer, stirring occasionally, for about 40 minutes or until the barley is nearly cooked and almost all of the liquid has been absorbed.

4 Meanwhile, toast the sunflower seeds in a dry non-stick frying pan over medium heat, stirring frequently or shaking the pan, until they are golden brown. Remove from the heat and transfer to a plate.

5 Stir the lemon juice and raisins into the barley mixture. Cover the pan again, remove from the heat and leave to stand undisturbed for about 5 minutes.

6 Gently stir the toasted sunflower seeds and parsley into the barley. Serve hot.

PER SERVING calories 165, saturated fat 0.5 g, total fat 5 g, sodium 47 mg, cholesterol 0 mg, protein 3.5 g, carbohydrate 28 g, fibre 1 g.

Chickpea ratatouille

- Serves 4
- Preparation time 20 minutes
- Cooking time 55–60 minutes

3 tablespoons olive oil
2 large onions, coarsely chopped
2 garlic cloves, finely chopped
2 red, green or yellow peppers, diced
4 zucchini, sliced
1 large eggplant, diced
1 can (540 ml) chopped tomatoes
1 can (540 ml) chickpeas, drained and rinsed
1 teaspoon dried oregano
1 teaspoon dried basil
1 teaspoon dried thyme
good pinch of freshly ground black pepper
2 tablespoons chopped fresh parsley

1 In a flameproof casserole or heavy saucepan, heat 2 tablespoons of the oil over medium heat. Add the onions and garlic and sauté, stirring, for about 7 minutes or until softened and golden.

2 Add the diced peppers and sauté, stirring, for about 7 minutes or until lightly browned. Using a slotted spoon, transfer the vegetable mixture to a bowl.

3 Add the zucchini to the casserole and sauté, stirring frequently, for about 7 minutes or until softened. Transfer to the bowl with the onions and peppers.

4 Heat the remaining oil in the casserole. Add the eggplant and sauté, stirring constantly, for about 6 minutes or until slightly softened.

5 Return all the sautéed vegetables to the casserole and add the tomatoes with their juices, the chickpeas, dried herbs and pepper. Stir to combine.

6 Cover and simmer gently for 25–30 minutes or until the vegetables are tender. Stir in the parsley. Serve hot or at room temperature.

PER SERVING calories 257, saturated fat 2 g, total fat 12 g, sodium 212 mg, cholesterol 0 mg, protein 10 g, carbohydrate 29 g, fibre 8 g.

♥ Cauliflower provides vitamin C and fibre, and may also help to protect against cancer.

Cauliflower provençale

- Serves 4
- Preparation time 20 minutes
- Cooking time 15 minutes

1 cauliflower
1 red pepper, diced
2 tomatoes, coarsely chopped
⅓ cup homemade or canned low-sodium
    vegetable stock
¼ cup pitted black olives, sliced
good pinch of freshly ground black pepper

1 Cut off the leaves and stalk from the cauliflower, then break or cut the florets from the core. Arrange the florets in the top of a steamer over boiling water, cover and steam for 9–10 minutes or until almost tender.

2 Meanwhile, in a saucepan combine the red pepper, tomatoes and stock. Bring to a boil over medium heat, then cover and cook, stirring occasionally, for about 3 minutes or until the pepper is almost tender.

3 Add the cauliflower and olives to the tomato sauce and toss to coat. Cover again and cook, stirring occasionally, for a further 2–3 minutes or until the cauliflower is tender. Season with the black pepper and serve.

Healthy heart recipes SIDE DISHES

PER SERVING calories 70, saturated fat 0.5 g, total fat 2.5 g, sodium 112 mg, cholesterol 0 mg, protein 4.5 g, carbohydrate 7 g, fibre 3 g.

♥ With these delicious oven fries, you get all the nutritional benefits of potato—vitamin C and potassium—with little of the fat of regular fries.

Oven fries

■ Serves 4

■ Preparation time 15 minutes

■ Cooking time 30–35 minutes

900 g (2 lb) large baking potatoes or sweet
    potatoes, scrubbed but unpeeled
2 teaspoons olive oil
good pinch of freshly ground black pepper

1 Preheat the oven to 450°F (230°C). Place two baking trays in the oven to heat.

2 Cut the potatoes lengthwise into 1 cm (½ in.) slices, then cut the slices lengthwise into 1 cm (½ in.) strips. In a large bowl, combine the oil and pepper. Add the potatoes and toss well so that they are evenly coated.

3 Spread out the potatoes in a single layer on the hot baking trays. Return to the oven and bake, turning once, for 30–35 minutes or until browned, crisp and cooked through.

PER SERVING calories 182, saturated fat 0.2 g, total fat 1.9 g, sodium 16 mg, cholesterol 0 mg, protein 5 g, carbohydrate 38 g, fibre 3 g.

Couscous with summer vegetables

- Serves 8
- Preparation time 12 minutes
- Cooking time 20–25 minutes

2 tablespoons olive oil
3 celery stalks, diced
3 carrots, diced
2 zucchini, preferably 1 green and 1 yellow,
    sliced
¼ cup fresh basil, shredded, or 1 tablespoon
    dried basil
good pinch of freshly ground black pepper
Tabasco sauce to taste
1½ cups couscous
2 cups homemade or canned low-sodium
vegetable or chicken stock

1 In a large saucepan, heat the oil, add the celery and carrots and sauté, stirring, for about 7 minutes or until softened but not browned.

2 Add the zucchini and cook, stirring, for a further 2–4 minutes or until slightly softened.

3 Add the basil with the pepper and a few dashes of Tabasco sauce and toss to mix.

4 Add the couscous to the saucepan and gently mix with a wooden spoon to coat the couscous grains well.

5 Pour the stock into the saucepan and gently stir. Bring the stock to a boil, then cover the saucepan and remove from the heat.

6 Allow the couscous to stand for about 5 minutes or until the grains are tender and all the liquid has been absorbed. With a fork, lightly fluff up the couscous to separate the grains, then serve hot.

PER SERVING calories 126, saturated fat 0.5 g, total fat 3 g, sodium 45 mg, cholesterol 0 mg, protein 3 g, carbohydrate 22 g, fibre 1.5 g.

♥ This salad is high in protein, thanks to the yogourt and pasta. Increase the vitamin content by adding lots of crunchy fresh vegetables.

Macaroni primavera

■ Serves 4

■ Preparation time 15 minutes

■ Cooking time 20 minutes

1 cup small broccoli florets
½ cup frozen peas
2 carrots, cut into matchsticks
225 g (8 oz) elbow macaroni
375 g (13 oz) plain low-fat yogourt
6 tablespoons reduced-fat mayonnaise
1½ teaspoons Dijon mustard
3 tablespoons red wine vinegar
good pinch of freshly ground black pepper
2 celery stalks, coarsely chopped
1 red onion, coarsely chopped
2 tablespoons chopped fresh parsley, chives or
    basil

1 Bring a large saucepan of water to a boil. Fill a bowl with ice water. Add the broccoli to the pan and simmer for 1–2 minutes or until tender but still crisp. Using a slotted spoon, transfer the florets to the ice water.

2 Return the pan to a boil and add the peas. Simmer for about 2 minutes, then transfer to the ice water.

3 Return the pan to the boil again and add the carrots. Simmer for 3–4 minutes or until tender but still crisp. Add to the ice water.

4 Bring the pan back to a boil. Add the pasta and cook according to the package instructions. Drain in a colander and rinse under cold running water.

5 To make the dressing, put the yogourt, mayonnaise, mustard, wine vinegar and pepper in a bowl and stir until thoroughly blended.

6 Drain the vegetables and toss with the pasta and dressing. Add the celery and onion. Sprinkle over the herbs and mix well. Serve at room temperature or chilled.

PER SERVING calories 361, saturated fat 2 g, total fat 9 g, sodium 290 mg, cholesterol 6 mg, protein 14 g, carbohydrate 60 g, fibre 5 g.

Desserts

Cantaloupe with raspberry sauce

■ Serves 4

■ Preparation time 20 minutes

350 g (12 oz) frozen raspberries
1 teaspoon lemon juice
2 tablespoons clear honey
1 large, ripe cantaloupe
fresh mint leaves to garnish

1 Reserve a few raspberries for garnish and keep them frozen. Put the remaining raspberries in a food processor or blender and purée until smooth. Press the purée through a medium-mesh sieve.

2 Add the lemon juice and honey to the raspberry purée and stir to mix well. Set aside.

3 Cut the cantaloupe into quarters and remove the seeds and fibres. Peel the quarters. Using a sharp knife, slice each quarter lengthwise without cutting completely through. Open out each quarter into a fan shape.

4 Spread one-quarter of the raspberry purée on the centre of four serving plates. Place a cantaloupe fan on each plate and decorate with fresh mint leaves and the reserved raspberries.

PER SERVING calories 173, saturated fat 0 g, total fat 0.5 g, sodium 20 mg, cholesterol 0 mg, protein 2.5 g, carbohydrate 42 g, fibre 5 g.

Walnut and raisin pudding

- Serves 4
- Preparation time 12 minutes
- Cooking time 30–35 minutes

½ cup orange juice
1 egg yolk
1 teaspoon clear honey
1 teaspoon vanilla extract
⅔ cup cooked rice
¼ cup raisins
¼ cup walnuts, chopped and toasted
3 egg whites
vegetable oil cooking spray or vegetable oil

1 Preheat the oven to 325°F (160°C). In a large mixing bowl, mix the orange juice with the egg yolk, honey and vanilla extract.

2 Stir in the cooked rice, raisins and toasted walnuts. In another bowl, whisk the egg whites until soft peaks form, then carefully fold into the rice mixture with a large metal spoon.

3 Pour into four ramekins that have been lightly coated with vegetable oil spray or lightly greased with vegetable oil.

4 Place the ramekins in a baking pan. Carefully add boiling water to the pan to a depth of 2.5 cm (1 in.). Bake for 30–35 minutes or until the puddings are just set. Serve hot.

PER SERVING calories 167, saturated fat 1 g, total fat 8.5 g, sodium 58 mg, cholesterol 50 mg, protein 5 g, carbohydrate 19 g, fibre 0.5 g.

♥ Puddings need eggs to rise, but here you can limit the yolks—which contain fat and cholesterol—and use more protein-rich egg whites.

French apple cake

■ Serves 8

■ Preparation time 30 minutes

■ Cooking time 40–50 minutes

2 tablespoons butter plus 1 teaspoon for the pan
1 tablespoon clear honey
1 tablespoon light brown sugar
4 apples, peeled, cored and cut into 8 wedges
1/3 cup currants or raisins
3 cups all-purpose flour
1 teaspoon baking powder
1 teaspoon baking soda
1 teaspoon each ground ginger and cinnamon
3 egg whites
1 egg yolk
1/2 cup concentrated apple juice
4 tablespoons sunflower oil
4 tablespoons clear honey
1 teaspoon vanilla extract
250 g plain low-fat yogourt

1 Preheat the oven to 350°F (180°C). Lightly grease a 23 cm (9 in.) cake tin with 1 teaspoon of the butter.

2 In a large non-stick frying pan, melt the rest of the butter over medium heat. Stir in the honey and brown sugar and cook until the sugar has dissolved. Add the apples and cook, stirring frequently, for about 10 minutes or until just tender. Spoon the apples into the cake pan and sprinkle the dried fruit on top.

3 In a medium bowl, combine the flour, baking powder, baking soda and spices. In another bowl, using an electric mixer or whisk, beat the egg whites until soft peaks form. Gently stir in the egg yolk, concentrated apple juice, oil, honey and vanilla extract.

4 Gently fold in about one-third of the flour mixture, followed by one-third of the yogourt. Repeat until all the flour and yogourt are incorporated. Pour the mixture over the apples. Bake for 40–50 minutes or until well risen.

5 Cool in the pan for 10 minutes, then turn out upside down onto a serving plate. Take care when turning out because the cake will be very juicy. Serve warm or cold.

PER SERVING calories 320, saturated fat 3 g, total fat 10 g, sodium 300 mg, cholesterol 34 mg, protein 7 g, carbohydrate 54 g, fibre 2 g.

Apricot and pear compote

- Serves 4
- Preparation time 5 minutes plus cooling time
- Cooking time 15 minutes

1⅓ cups orange juice
finely grated zest and juice of 1 lemon
2 tablespoons clear honey
2 teaspoons vanilla extract
1 whole clove
8 fresh apricots, halved
2 firm but ripe pears, quartered
2 tablespoons raisins

1 In a saucepan, combine the orange juice, lemon zest and juice, honey, vanilla extract and clove. Bring to a boil, then reduce the heat and simmer for 5 minutes.

2 Add the apricots and pears and bring back to a boil. Reduce the heat, cover and simmer for 5–8 minutes or until the fruit is just tender.

3 Add the raisins, then remove the pan from the heat. Leave the fruit to cool to room temperature in the syrup. Remove the clove before serving.

♥ Fruit and fruit juices are among the best food sources of potassium, which helps to lower blood pressure.

PER SERVING calories 127, saturated fat 0 g, total fat 0.3 g, sodium 17 mg, cholesterol 0 mg, protein 1.5 g, carbohydrate 31 g, fibre 3 g.

♥ Walnuts are high in unsaturated fats. Recent studies suggest that eating walnuts regularly may help to protect against heart attacks.

Lemon and walnut frozen yogourt

■ Serves 6

■ Preparation time 20 minutes plus freezing time

■ Cooking time 2 minutes

¾ cup 2% milk
1 envelope (7 g) powdered gelatin
½ cup caster (superfine) sugar
250 g plain low-fat yogourt
4 tablespoons lemon juice
finely grated zest of 1 lemon
½ cup walnuts, coarsely chopped

1 Put the milk in a saucepan, sprinkle over the gelatin and let stand for 1 minute. Stir in the sugar and set over low-medium heat. Warm, stirring, for about 2 minutes or until the gelatin and sugar have dissolved.

2 Remove from the heat and allow to cool until thickened, stirring occasionally. Then transfer the mixture to a large bowl and whisk in the yogourt, lemon juice and lemon zest. Stir in the walnuts.

3 Freeze the mixture in an ice cream machine, following the manufacturer's instructions. If you do not have a machine, pour the mixture into a freezerproof container and freeze for 1 hour or until set around the edges. Beat the mixture until smooth, then return to the freezer. Freeze for a further 30 minutes, then beat again. Repeat the freezing and beating several times more until the frozen yogourt has a smooth consistency, then leave it to freeze for at least 1 hour before serving.

PER SERVING calories 170, saturated fat 1 g, total fat 7 g, sodium 46 mg, cholesterol 2.4 mg, protein 5 g, carbohydrate 23 g, fibre 0.3 g.

You must look after
self but you should
k after the health
your loved ones.

Frequently asked questions

Doctors get many questions—millions of them. But while the words used to ask the questions may be different, the underlying concerns don't change very much from person to person or from year to year. With this in mind, we decided to provide answers to 11 of the most common questions people ask regarding heart health. We hope they will be a useful extra resource as you put the 30-Minutes plan into action.

Q I hate all those good-for-you foods. What should I do?

A What makes unhealthy food so tasty—and unhealthy—is excessive salt, sugar or fat. For example, when you eat a potato chip or tempting fries, it's not the potato that delights your taste buds, it's the oil and salt. The good news: over time, you can train yourself to be less attached to these flavours. When you do, you'll discover that "good for you" foods can taste far more wonderful than salty or sugary junk foods.

Start by making the easiest, smallest changes. Do you have coffee and a Danish pastry to start the day? Make one change, such as adding a glass of antioxidant-rich orange juice or replacing the Danish pastry with a fruity, bran muffin. Similarly, make one healthy swap at lunch—substitute mustard for the rich mayonnaise on your sandwich or add an apple to the meal, for example. Then do the same at dinner. Your goal is to make small, acceptable adjustments to your diet and stick with them. When they become second nature, add a few more. Along the way, reduce the salt, butter and sugary drinks you consume. In time, your taste buds will become less reliant on salty, sugary, fatty flavours and more satisfied with fresher, healthier foods.

Q I cook for the whole family, and they refuse to change what they're eating. How can I stay on track?

A Parents often give in to family demands but when it comes to health, that's a big mistake. You must look after yourself but you should also look after the health of your loved ones. Remember that the seeds of heart disease are sown in childhood.

So don't let family pressures defeat you. Introduce your healthy favourites little by little and gradually reduce the amount of salt or sugar you add. Eat small main course portions yourself and have a salad on the side if no one else wants vegetables.

Another strategy: swap ingredients. Replace some or all of the butter in recipes with canola or olive oil; use low-fat cheese (and less of it); sneak more vegetables into casseroles, soups and sauces; and cook lower-fat cuts of meat. From time to time, offer delicious strawberries and peaches for dessert or make a fresh fruit salad, topped with yogourt rather than cream. Your family will begin to eat more healthily without even realizing it.

Q What if I've eaten unhealthy foods all my life? Is the damage done?

A One of the greatest rewards of healthy eating is an immediate upgrade in your body's health. Research shows that eating a healthy diet can help reduce "bad" cholesterol, lower blood pressure and improve overall heart health. The bottom line: it's never too late to reap the benefits of a heart-healthy eating plan.

Q I hate seafood. I love beef. That's not going to change—ever. Am I doomed?

A Not at all. A healthy, 100 g (3½ oz) portion of lean beef is good for you because it's packed with vitamins B_6 and B_{12}, both of which help control levels of homocysteine, a substance linked to heart risk. And beef today has significantly less artery-clogging saturated fat than in the past. Just be sure to look for lean cuts.

But you are missing out on the heart benefits provided by the omega-3 fatty acids found in fish, so try omega-3 eggs or omega-3 dairy products, choose walnuts when you're snacking on nuts and try a sprinkle of ground flaxseed (another source of omega-3s) on your cereal.

Q Whenever I try to eat healthily, I end up throwing away lots of uneaten vegetables and fruits that have gone bad. Any suggestions?

A Yes, that can be a problem. It's easy to stock up on lots of delicious fruits and vegetables, then run out of time or opportunities to eat them before they rot. And that seems such a waste of money. Try these four solutions.

1 Calculate your vegetable and fruit needs for the week and shop for just that amount. That may sound obvious but many shoppers tend to buy what looks good at the grocery store that particular day, without a specific use in mind. That inevitably leads to overshopping (or, for those without a vegetable habit, undershopping).

2 Try making fresh fruits and vegetables more user-friendly. Take an apple and a bag of baby carrots to work, cut up that cantaloupe and keep it in the fridge in a covered container, and put cut-up raw vegetables on the table before dinner.

3 Make soup each weekend with whatever vegetables haven't been used during the week. Throw in a can of beans, lots of vegetables, plenty of herbs and, if appropriate, leftovers from the week, and you'll have an improvised minestrone soup that will feed you and the family all weekend.

4 Keep a stock of frozen vegetables and frozen or canned fruit in unsweetened juice that will last much longer.

Q **My doctor believes that medicine is the best treatment for my high blood pressure. I would like to try some alternative ways to treat my high blood pressure. What should I do?**

A Look at the alternative versus conventional healing issue from a new perspective that your doctor will easily appreciate: the best approach is healthy living plus conventional therapies (if you need it). That means a balanced diet and exercise. If your blood pressure (or cholesterol, triglycerides or blood sugar) stays above normal despite lifestyle changes, you must consult a doctor and be happy that medical science can treat you. The two approaches work together, not in opposition.

If your blood pressure is very high, your doctor may not feel comfortable suggesting that you stop your medicines to give lifestyle changes a try. That makes sense as sudden rises in blood pressure can be dangerous. Ask the doctor how the two of you can work together to monitor your blood pressure while you make changes, so you can see if your drug doses can be lowered. This may mean more frequent trips to the doctor's office or buying and learning to use a home blood pressure monitor. Good luck.

Q **Ever since I found out that I have high cholesterol, I've felt really scared. It sounds silly but I'm walking around worried that I could have a heart attack at any moment. What should I do?**

A First, understand that many people with high cholesterol never have heart attacks, principally because high cholesterol is only one of many risk factors. If you only have one risk factor, you are at less risk than someone who has others, such as high blood pressure. The best way to manage your fears is with facts. The most important thing is to make sure that your cholesterol is properly assessed and do your utmost to reduce all other risk factors. This, in itself, will help you to reduce your overall risk.

Then, discuss the pros and cons of taking a cholesterol-lowering drug. Also discuss creating treatment goals. Having specific, numerical health targets to work toward can also help to make heart health a less intimidating, more achievable goal. Finally, ask your doctor how often your cholesterol needs to be rechecked to be sure it's dropping into a healthy range and staying there.

Even if you're taking cholesterol-lowering medication, create a healthy diet and exercise program for yourself, using this book as your basis. Some of your fears will dissipate when you start living more healthily, and more will go away as you start to experience the benefits of greater energy, fewer colds, better sleep and lower weight.

Q I detest exercise. How can I motivate myself to get moving?

A If you're like most exercise haters, what you detest is probably what you remember from a school gym class or the last health club you visited—the sweaty clothes, awkward moves and overall embarrassment. The "exercise" recommended in the 30-Minutes-A-Day Plan, which is the same exercise that can cut your heart disease risk in half, doesn't involve tube socks, sweatbands, or jumping up and down. You don't even have to change out of your normal work or casual clothes. Simply go out the door and walk around your building or neighbourhood. No huffing, puffing or discomfort is required. Enjoy your walks as a chance to catch some fresh air and grab a mental pick-me-up. When you stop thinking of exercise as suffering and punishment, you'll soon find yourself enjoying the chance to stretch your legs and get your blood circulating better, which is all exercise really is.

Q My life is so hectic, I don't feel that I can handle any more responsibility. How can I change my eating, exercise and lifestyle habits without adding even more stress?

A Slow down and take it one small step at a time. The beauty of this plan is that it's designed to reduce the stress in your life. If you feel overwhelmed, simply go to the "Getting Started" section on page 53 and find out which part of your life is most in need of a tune-up. Then wait until those new habits become second nature before tackling the next batch. Every little change you make reduces your risk, so you don't have to adopt all of the advice in this book overnight to have a healthier heart. You will be surprised, though, at how easily these tips fit into your routine and become a normal way of life.

Q I smoke. Is it worth making any other changes if I can't quit?

A Absolutely. Smoking is a major risk factor for heart disease. In fact, it's the biggest, but there are eight other lifestyle factors—including stress, obesity, sedentary living and eating too few fruits and vegetables—that have been linked to heart disease and that you can do something about right now even if you can't eliminate tobacco use immediately. What's more, once you start making healthy lifestyle changes, such as eating fresh foods and walking in the fresh air, you'll probably find it easier to leave cigarettes behind.

Q If I already have heart disease, won't exercise raise my risk for a heart attack?

A It's true that if you're at high risk of having a heart attack, you should talk to your doctor before engaging in any vigorous exercise. You should also avoid strenuous activity and lifting heavy weights (it's especially risky to hold your breath during weightlifting or other exertion). But simply walking round the block and doing some stretches will help to strengthen your heart, so your risk will decrease. If you feel nervous about exercise, by all means talk to your doctor, who can help you to find the level of physical activity that's right for you.

Resources

You can help yourself by getting more information on the dangers of heart disease, how to quit smoking and how to eat a healthier and well balanced diet. Information is available to better your heart health. Here is a selection of organizations, websites and books that can help you toward a heart-healthy life.

Organizations

Canadian Cancer Society
www.cancer.ca
National Office
10 Alcorn Avenue, Suite 200
Toronto, ON M4V 3B1
Telephone: (416) 961-7223
Fax: (416) 961-4189
Email: ccs@cancer.ca

Canadian Cardiovascular Society
www.ccs.ca
222 Queen Street, Suite 1403
Ottawa, ON K1P 5V9
Telephone: 1-877-569-3407
(613) 569-3407
Fax: (613) 569-6574

Canadian Dental Association
www.cda-adc.ca
1815 Alta Vista Drive
Ottawa, ON K1G 3Y6
Telephone: (613) 523-1770
Email: reception@cda-adc.ca

Canadian Diabetes Association
www.diabetes.ca
National Life Building
1400-522 University Avenue
Toronto, ON M5G 2R5
Telephone: 1-800 BANTING (226-8464)
Email: info@diabetes.ca

Canadian Medical Association (CMA)
www.cma.ca
1867 Alta Vista Drive
Ottawa, ON K1G 3Y6
Telephone: 888-267-9703
Fax: (613) 236-8864
Email: cmamsc@cma.ca

Canadian MedicAlert® Foundation
www.medicalert.ca
2005 Sheppard Avenue East, Suite 800
Toronto, ON M2J 5B4
Telephone: (416) 696-0267

Canadian Task Force on Preventive Health Care
www.ctfphc.org
Department of Family Medicine
The University of Western Ontario
Clinical Skills Building, 2nd Floor
London, ON N6A 5C1
Telephone: (519) 850-2511
Fax: (519) 850-2522

Canada's Association for the 50Plus (CARP)
www.carp.ca
National Head Office
27 Queen Street East, Suite 1304
Toronto, ON M5C 2M6
Telephone: (416) 363-8748
Fax: (416) 363-8747
Email: carp@50plus.com

The College of Family Physicians
of Canada
www.cfpc.ca
2630 Skymark Avenue
Mississauga, ON L4W 5A4
Telephone: 1-800-387-6197
Fax: (905) 629-0893

Dieticians of Canada
www.dieticians.ca
480 University Avenue, Suite 604
Toronto, ON M5G 1V2
Telephone: (416) 596-0857
Fax: (416) 596-0603

Health Canada
www.hc-sc.gc.ca
Tunney's Pasture
Ottawa, ON K1A 0K9
Telephone: 1-866-225-0709
Fax: (613) 941-5366

Heart and Stroke Foundation
of Canada
www.heartandstroke.ca
222 Queen Street, Suite 1402
Ottawa, ON K1P 5V9
Telephone: (613) 569-4361
Fax: (613) 569-3278

University of Ottawa Heart Institute
www.ottawaheart.ca
Heart Health Education Centre
40 Ruskin Street
Ottawa, ON K1Y 4W7
Telephone: (613) 761-5000
Fax: (613) 761-5323

Other Resources

Alcoholics Anonymous
www.alcoholics-anonymous.org

Canada's Food Guide to Healthy Eating
www.hc-sc.gc.ca/fn-an/food-guide-aliment/fg_rainbow-arc_en_ciel_ga_e.html

Canadian Health Network
www.canadian-health-network.ca

The Canadian Women's Health Network
www.cwhn.ca

HealthyEating.net
www.healthyeating.net

Quit Smoking
www.hc-sc.gc.ca/hl-vs/tobac-tabac/quit-cesser/index_e.html

Books

Heartsmart: the Best of Heartsmart Cooking (endorsed by the Heart and Stroke Foundation of Canada)
Bonnie Stern (Random House Canada, 2006)

The Harvard Medical School Guide to Lowering Your Cholesterol
Mason Freeman (Harvard Medical School, 2005)

The New Lighthearted Cookbook: Recipes for Healthy Heart Cooking (endorsed by the Heart and Stroke Foundation of Canada)
Anne Lindsay (Key Porter, 2003)

Index

Picture credits

© RD indicates images that are the copyright of The Reader's Digest Association Ltd.

**Additional Reader's Digest
Project Staff**

U.S. Contributing Editor
Marianne Wait

U.K. Contributing Editor
Rachel Warren Chadd

Illustrator
Andrew Baker

Researcher
Angelika Romacker

Picture Researcher
Rosie Taylor

Indexers
Hilary Bird
Robert Ronald

Art Director
Nick Clark